A Common Man's View on Political Dishonesty: Political Leaders Who Set The Worst Example

Dave Garland

This work is dedicated to the Common Man in the United States of America. Never forget that at the end of the day it is you who have the final say. We elect our political leaders, they represent We The People.

This work is also dedicated to my friends, who helped me through this process, whether they knew it or not.

Table of Contents

I. Introduction

Throughout the course of human history, mankind has always been forced to deal with politics. Whether we like it or not, it has become a part of our everyday lives. During this time, mankind has been faced with both good and bad political leaders. We can trace the roots of leadership back to the first civilization at Mesopotamia, the land between the rivers. We can trace the idea of Code of Laws back to King Hammurabi, and the Magna Carta written in 1215 AD. During this time, the types of leaders we had were quite different. Students of history will likely remember hearing stories of Alexander The Great's astonishing conquests and Nero Caesar's twisted pastimes, all while debating whether Napoleon Bonaparte was a French hero or a general sent straight from Hell. The amount of debate put into what makes a good leader or a bad leader has fascinated historians and political scientists for centuries, and will likely continue to do so, including in this text.

For our purposes, we will be looking at current political leaders. Because this is a shorter text, the list of cases has been narrowed down to three Democrats and three Republicans. The Democrats were listed first because they are currently the party in power, starting with President Barack Obama, former Secretary of State Hillary Clinton and New York Governor Andrew Cuomo. On the Republican side we have Speaker of the House John Boehner, Senate Minority/Majority Leader Mitch McConnell, and Senator John McCain. There are particular reasons why each of them is on the list. However, this is not a full list. There are plenty of other current American political leaders that could be on this list, but are not due to constraints of space and time.

The reasons these particular six are on this list are not individualistic, but comparative. President Obama, Secretary Clinton, Speaker Boehner and Majority Leader McConnell each hold key positions in their party. For President Obama it is self-explanatory, Secretary Clinton is considered to be the frontrunner for the Democrats in 2016 in the race for the Presidency, Speaker Boehner is the Speaker of the House, technically the highest positioned Republican in politics, and Majority Leader McConnell, being the Senate Majority Leader holds a similar position. Governor Andrew Cuomo and Senator John McCain are added to the list as other elements of the party who have shown similar traits to those above. Their roles will be explained further on.

Not only were these six picked for their positions in their respective parties, but they were also picked due to the dishonesty, abrasiveness and sometimes even rudeness they have shown towards other leaders and their constituents. A Gallup poll from September 5-8 in 2013 shows the trust that people have towards government. While 51% of respondents have either a great deal of trust or a fair amount of trust for the Executive branch, only 34% have a great deal of trust or a fair amount of trust for the Legislative branch[1].

This doesn't seem too bad at first, some of the party line responses you would expect. However, when the question is phrased differently, so is the response. When respondents were asked how much of the time do you think you can trust government in Washington to do what is right, the numbers show that in 2010 around 81% responded only some of the time or never. That is a significant jump from the 51% who trusted the Executive branch and 34% who trusted the Legislative branch in 2013.

The main point of this work is to focus not only on the dishonesty these politicians show every day, but to take it a step further and look at not only the lies but the behind the scenes actions that these men and women partake in. Many questions will be posed, many current pieces of legislation will be questioned, and many who read this will likely be frustrated by things said by these elected officials. Unfortunately, there are not many concrete answers to the questions or a concrete way to push for more honesty in politics.

Although in this piece we do not have any examples, there are some examples where dishonest politicians have paid the price for their actions towards their constituents. The most popular, most historic and the most recent that comes to mind is the recent Congressional election in Virginia in which House Majority Leader Eric Cantor, the number 2 in the House, lost to Dave Brat, a conservative college professor in the Republican Primary. This is a case we hope to highlight in future works as a positive example of what can happen when citizens are fed up with their dishonest elected officials.

It is also important to note that only two of these individuals are not up for re-election. Those individuals are Barack Obama and John Boehner. However, their roles are still important to this work.

It is important to note before we analyze each figure that this is for informational purposes only. We do not mean to denigrate or degrade the office that any of these leaders have held in the past, currently hold or may hold in the future. The goal is to simply get the word out that everyday citizens see many politicians as dishonest. They look for a way to do something about it, but they feel they can't. It is our hope to empower these everyday citizens by pointing out the actions of each politician, noting their next election, and providing a starting point for everyone to do their own research on a particular topic.

We hope you are informed and enjoy the following sections!

II. Barack Obama

"After a century of striving, after a year of debate, after a historic vote, healthcare reform is no longer an unmet promise, it is the law of the land." President Barack Obama, March 23, 2010

There is no question that when Barack Obama was taking the oath of office on January 20, 2009 many people felt that there was a great amount of hope and change on the way. President Obama, the 47 year old Democrat from Illinois, campaigned on many grand promises, including ending the wars in Iraq and Afghanistan and reforming the broken healthcare system. Many Americans, Democrats and Republicans, were happy to see change in the White House. Many were frustrated by the policies from the Bush administration, especially the two long wars in Iraq and Afghanistan. Obama campaigned with a very positive message of changing the current system, attempting to show Americans that things could be better. There are many debates today over whether or not President Obama did make things better. There is no current definitive answer, but there are many questions that have been left unanswered that may not be answered until after President Obama's term in office ends.

To understand the motives of the man in office we must first look at the past and what motivated the man to take office in the first place. While there are many different theories floating around as to what Barack Obama may or may not have done before he became

President or where he was born, I will not address these theories. They are for the time being, simply theories, and it would be unfair to judge a man on unfounded theories.

Early Years

Barack Hussein Obama was born on August 4, 1961 in Honolulu, Hawaii. Obama's mother, Ann Dunham, was from Wichita, Kansas, and his father, Barack Obama Sr. was from Nyanza Province, Kenya. Barack Obama barely saw his father, as his parents divorced when Barack was quite young. Following the divorce, Obama's mother married another man, Lolo Soetoro, who was from Jakarta, Indonesia. The new family moved to Jakarta for a bit of Barack's childhood, but Barack came back to Hawaii to live with his grandparents at the age of 10.

After graduating from High School, Barack Obama went to Occidental College in Los Angeles for approximately two years, and then transferred to Columbia University in New York. Obama graduated in 1983 with a degree in political science. In 1985 Obama began his career as a community organizer in the South Side of Chicago for low income residents. In 1988, Obama started his law education at Harvard law school. In 1991, Obama would graduate magna cum laude from Harvard.

After law school, Obama returned to Chicago to the law firm Miner, Barnhill and Galland to practice as a civil rights attorney. During this same time, Obama worked at the University of Chicago law school, where he would work from 1992 to 2004. Also in 1992, Barack would marry Michelle Robinson, another attorney from Chicago.

Barack Obama first entered Illinois politics in 1996 when he ran for a seat in the Illinois State Senate and won. Obama had been known from his advocacy work across Chicago and the autobiography he wrote in 1995, *Dreams From My Father: A Story of Race and Inheritance.* During his time in the State Senate, Obama focused on healthcare reform, ethics reform and education programs for the poor.

Although this is little known to many, Obama ran for a US House of Representatives seat in 2000 where he was unable to win the Democratic primary. However, this did not deter Obama from continuing his career in politics and attempting to keep pushing higher up. In 2004, Obama launched his campaign for US Senate in Illinois. Obama quickly found quite a bit of praise from fellow Democrats, and was invited to give the keynote address for Senator John Kerry at the 2004 Democratic National Convention. This address helped Obama quite significantly, and he was noted as a key up and coming Democrat. In the general election for US Senate, Obama easily defeated the Republican candidate, Alan Keyes, 70 percent to 27 percent. This was surely a key moment in a bright future for a young politician[4,11].

Senate Career

Barack Obama's time as a Senator was relatively short, as he was inaugurated in January of 2005, but then was out in January of 2009 when he took the oath of office to be the 44th President of the United States. Senator Obama's main achievements came in bills attempting to reduce the number of weapons of mass destruction in Europe, Russia and the former Soviet states. Specifically, Obama co-sponsored a bill with Republican Senator Richard Lugar called the Lugar-Obama initiative. This had the goal of reducing the number of biological, chemical, nuclear and conventional weapons in the former Soviet states. Senator Obama also worked with Oklahoma Republican Tom Coburn to create the Coburn-Obama Transparency Act which created the website USAspending.gov. This website details all of the organizations where all federal funds go. The site gives a breakdown of how the organization received the funds and why.

Presidential Campaign

Senator Barack Obama started his 2008 Presidential campaign on February 10, 2007 in Springfield, Illinois. By then Senator Obama had written his second book, *The Audacity of Hope*, which gave him a significant following across the country(This has actually now become a common practice for many candidates today, we have seen Hillary Clinton and Andrew Cuomo already have books released in early 2015). Despite the decent following Obama had amassed over the years, he still faced an uphill battle in defeating New York Senator Hillary Clinton and former Vice Presidential candidate John Edwards for the Democratic nomination. However, Senator Obama was able to make a name for himself with his outstanding public speaking skills and the ability to connect with everyday people.

Many in the country were shocked on January 3, 2008 when Senator Obama defeated both Senator Clinton and Senator John Edwards by 8 percent each in the Iowa Primary. This proved to many in the country that this young Senator from Illinois was a true contender for the top leadership position in the country. Although Clinton won the New Hampshire primary a few days later, Obama closed January by winning the South Carolina primary by a significant margin of 55 to 27 percent. Although Iowa was a significant showing for Obama, this can be seen as a sign that the momentum for the Obama campaign would continue for quite some time.

Although it was quite obviously not the primary focus of the campaign, many found it captivating that the Democratic Party had a chance to make history during this election. The two frontrunners in the race were Senator Barack Obama, an African-American and Senator Hillary Clinton, a woman. Senator Obama was aware of this and used the momentum to show he could make history. Starting in South Carolina, African-American voters started to show up significantly for Obama in the polls. The idea of the first African-American President was a positive step for Americans, and would continue to give Senator Obama momentum throughout the entire election.

Senator Obama would make it through the rest of the primaries with relative ease. On August 28, 2008, Senator Obama accepted the nomination for President for the Democratic Party. He would now go on to face Arizona Senator John McCain, the Republican nominee for President. Senator Obama decided just before he officially became the nominee to select Delaware Senator Joe Biden as his running mate. McCain responded by choosing Alaska Governor Sarah Palin to be his running mate. This gave McCain the first initial bump in the polls as he took the initial lead. However, it was clear after each debate that it was McCain who was facing the uphill battle. During the campaign, Senator Obama promised tax cuts for 95% of Americans, healthcare for all and to end the wars in Iraq and Afghanistan among all things. This also helped to increase his popularity, especially against John McCain, a man some consider to be a war hawk.

On November 4, 2008, Senator Barack Obama defeated Senator John McCain 53 percent to 46 percent in the popular vote and 365 to 173 by Electoral College votes. Obama was able to win the traditionally blue states, and then some of the swings states including Florida, Ohio, Virginia and North Carolina. Obama was also able to win the youth vote by a significant margin, showing his promise of "hope and change" resonated well with first time voters. Many saw this as a historic occasion, and it certainly was. However, no one knew exactly what to expect out of the young Democrats first term at the highest office in the nation[5,6,7].

The Presidency

Guantanamo Bay

To be fair, when Barack Obama was inaugurated President of the United States in January of 2009; he inherited quite a few issues. President Obama faced a financial crisis that hit its worst point in September of the year before, was still dealing with two wars in the Middle East, Iraq and Afghanistan, and faced heavy pressure to enact the changes he promised during his campaign. President Obama's first task was the creation of a new healthcare law, which would eventually be called the Affordable Care Act, or Obamacare. However, President Obama's first executive orders as President pertained to the actions at Guantanamo Bay, the military detention facility in Cuba that had garnered quite a negative reputation during the Bush years. Obama had campaigned that he would close Guantanamo Bay during his time in office, but to this day, has failed to follow through.

President Obama's criticisms of Guantanamo Bay came during the 2008 election in which Obama questioned what was really going on at Guantanamo Bay and whether it was legal or not. In an address to both the Senate and the House of Representatives on February 24, 2009, President Obama had this to say about the closure:

"To overcome extremism, we must also be vigilant in upholding the values our troops defend – because there is no force in the world more powerful than the example of America. That is why I have ordered the closing of the detention center at Guantanamo Bay, and will seek swift and certain justice for captured terrorists – because living our values doesn't make us weaker, it makes us safer and it makes us stronger."[12]

To this day, President Obama and Congress have made no progress in the closure of Guantanamo Bay together. Prisoners have been transferred to other countries, and incoming prisoners are held in federal facilities across the nation, but at this time there are still many detainees in Guantanamo Bay. Some would say the President tried, and Congress failed, but to most others, it appears he simply doesn't care. Many are starting to wonder if the closure of Guantanamo Bay on the grounds of human rights was just another dig at George W. Bush for reelection or a dream that escaped the ambitious leader once he was elected.

President Obama himself seems to be making progress on closing Guantanamo Bay, but is not really working with Congress to do so. All of the bipartisan opposition seems to be doing nothing, and it seems the closing of Guantanamo Bay has been a campaign promise to get elected that really wasn't thought out that much. It will be interesting to see if the President actually manages to close Guantanamo without the help of Congress, who are still adamantly opposed. This is discussed again under the "Executive Orders" section.

Healthcare

"No matter how we reform health care, I intend to keep this promise: If you like your doctor, you'll be able to keep your doctor; if you like your health care plan, you'll be able to keep your health care plan." Green Bay, Wisconsin, June 11, 2009.

That was only one of many times that we heard that line. The Affordable Care Act was on its way, but it would not affect current healthcare plans. This was before the bill's passage in 2010, before the Supreme Court, before the 2012 election, before the shutdown, and of course, before the infamous reading of *Green Eggs and Ham* on the Senate floor. If there is one thing to praise President Barack Obama for, it was his consistency on passing healthcare reform. To this day, "if you like your plan, you can keep your plan" is still repeated by Democrats across the country. So promises were made, but what actually happened in the process of the passing of the bill, the judicial review that followed, and the actual implementation is all subject to strict scrutiny and debate even five years later.

President Obama's signature healthcare plan is officially known as the Patient Protection and Affordable Care Act, but is more commonly noted as the Affordable Care Act or Obamacare[8]. The bill was formally signed into law on March 23, 2010 by President Obama after clearing key hurdles in the House and the Senate. Since its creation, Obamacare was plagued with political biases. The vote in the House of Representatives for Obamacare was 219-212, with the 219 being in favor. Not one single Republican member of the House voted for Obamacare, and 34 Democrats joined the Republicans to vote against the bill. In the Senate, the vote was 60-39, with one Republican Senator not voting. Besides the one Republican who did not vote, all Republicans voted against the bill, and all Democrats and the two independents voted for the bill. Legal opposition to the bill started almost immediately, as Republicans began only a few days after the bill's passage to propose legislation to repeal Obamacare. So far, all efforts have failed, even the famous effort by Republican Senators Mike Lee of Utah and Ted Cruz of Texas in 2013.

The Individual Mandate- Tax or Penalty?

The first major controversy that came up in reference to the Affordable Care Act was the legality of the individual mandate. This mandate requires that all Americans have some form of healthcare, or face a penalty. To put it into perspective, someone without health insurance who does not sign up for Obamacare could face a monthly fine until they do sign up. In 2010, twenty six states, several individuals and the National Federation of Independent Business took up a suit challenging the legality of the individual mandate and the Medicaid expansion, arguing that Congress didn't have the power to penalize American citizens who did not wish to get the healthcare plan. The Court of Appeals for the Eleventh Circuit upheld the Medicaid expansion, but struck down the individual mandate, claiming Congress didn't have the power to exercise a penalty over the American people.

The Obama administration spent quite a bit of time trying to convince the American public that the individual mandate was not a tax. In 2009, President Obama told ABCs George Stephanopoulos "to say that you've gotta take responsibility to get health insurance is absolutely not a tax increase."[13] This was the continued line that the administration would argue even throughout the court proceedings. "It's not a tax increase."

In June of 2012, Supreme Court Chief Justice John Roberts disagreed with the Obama administrations narrative. The Supreme Court, led by Roberts, upheld the individual mandate, classifying it as a tax, and claiming that Congress does have the power to regulate taxation. Chief Justice Roberts summed up the courts answer by stating:

"Such an analysis suggests that the shared responsibility payment may for constitutional purposes be considered a tax. The payment is not so high that there is really no choice but to buy health insurance; the payment is not limited to willful violations, as penalties for unlawful acts often are; and the payment is collected solely by the IRS through the normal means of taxation. Cf. Bailey v. Drexel Furniture Co., 259 U. S. 20 –37. None of this is to say that payment is not intended to induce the purchase of health insurance. But the mandate need not be read to declare that failing to do so is unlawful. Neither the Affordable Care Act nor any other law attaches negative legal consequences to not buying health insurance, beyond requiring a payment to the IRS. And Congress's choice of language—stating that individuals "shall" obtain insurance or pay a "penalty"—does not require reading §5000A as punishing unlawful conduct. It may also be read as imposing a tax on those who go without insurance. See New York v. United States, 505 U. S. 144 – 174. Pp. 35–40."[14, 15, 16]

Thus, the aggravation grew. The mandate that "wasn't a tax" became a "tax."

Botching The Rollout

This example isn't as clear cut as the others, but it still fits into the narrative that the Obama administration has been ill-prepared over the years. The first chance for open enrollment was October 1, 2013, in the midst of the infamous government shutdown. This was eventually delayed by the shutdown, which occurred that very same day due to efforts in the House and the Senate to block the funding of Obamacare through appropriations into the next fiscal year. The man most associated with the shutdown was Texas Senator Ted Cruz (keep that in mind, that becomes key in a few paragraphs).

Many blew the shutting down of the government completely out of proportion, acting as if certain programs being shut down for a short amount of time were a disaster. Although some were, such as the cutting of pay to members of the military, most of the effects were not as bad as many had made it out to believe. It was disgraceful that members of Congress were still being paid, although many of them donated their salaries to charities or refused to be paid until the shutdown was over. This was started by the ones accused of starting the shutdown itself, including Senators Cruz and Lee and Congressman Louie Gohmert of Texas.

So why did Senator Cruz make such a big fuss about the impending impact of Obamacare? And was it justified? Cruz infamously took the Senate floor in an effort to "defund Obamacare," an effort started by Senator Mike Lee of Utah the month before. Senator Lee's opposition to Obamacare is rooted with the fundamental principles of the Constitution. Last year, Senator Lee had this to say to the founder of TheBlaze, Glenn Beck:

"Laws are supposed to be made by Congress, not by a court…and not [by] the president, who has now amended Obamacare twice. Once in saying, individuals have to comply with the law during their first year but employers don't. Then in saying, we aren't even going to require people to prove their income."[18]

Senator Cruz's 21 hour speech on the Senate floor was also key opposition to Obamacare, but it in turn caused most of the blame of the government shutdown to fall on Senator Cruz. The points Cruz raised during the speech were good ones, and they were quite valid, but unfortunately went unaddressed most of the time. Senator Cruz noted most of Congress didn't actually read the original Obamacare bill when it was passed; noting former Speaker of the House Nancy Pelosi's infamous saying of "passing the bill to see what's in it."

Senator Cruz also noted how many in Congress are not listening to their constituents, and that most of the American people are opposed to Obamacare and its implementation. Cruz also went onto note the thousands of pages of regulations that have been added due to the 2400 page bill that is Obamacare. One could spend an entire book analyzing both Senator Lee and Senator Cruz's words from those days, but for our purposes, it is the response from the administration that is key in this aspect.

Both Senators Lee and Cruz would constantly go onto say clearly that they did not wish to shut down or defund the government, only Obamacare due to serious questions of its legality. However, on October 1, 2013, the government shutdown did occur. Of course when the shutdown occurred, the fingers were pointed directly at "Republicans," mainly Senator Cruz and anyone who stood with him on the Senate floor during that 21 hour span.[19, 20, 21]

The day that the shutdown started, President Obama came out speaking out against the shutdown, his first words were these:

"Good morning, everybody. At midnight last night, for the first time in 17 years, Republicans in Congress chose to shut down the federal government. Let me be more specific: One faction, of one party, in one house of Congress, in one branch of government, shut down major parts of the government -- all because they didn't like one law."[22]

Although President Obama would avoid saying the names directly, everyone knew he was addressing Senators Lee and Cruz in particular. President Obama also called on Speaker Boehner repeatedly to sit down with him to restore the government. In the end, Boehner and Senate Minority Leader Mitch McConnell would throw Senators Cruz and Lee under the bus, and agree to end the government shutdown, with nothing in return but a pass from the administration. (Thus part of the reason why Speaker Boehner and Senate Majority Leader McConnell are on the Republican side of this dishonesty list).[23,24]

So by October 20, 2013, the government shutdown was over, and it was time to get back to business on Obamacare, making sure people were able to sign up to get covered under Obamacare before 2014. Sounds like a smooth process from there, right? Not exactly. After all, that time was spent blaming the conservatives and Republicans for the government shut down and delaying Obamacare, the Obama administration would run into yet another problem when they faced technical issues with the website, *Healthcare.gov.* Shortly after the shutdown ended, the government attempted to launch *Healthcare.gov,* the website where people could sign up for Obamacare. However, the Democrats faced an uphill battle when technical issues delayed the rollout yet again.

While the issues have been fixed for now, initial estimates are that the website first cost the administration $118 million, while the technical issues required another $56 million in repairs. The technical issues would continue for quite some time, but now seem to be under control. Perhaps the Obama administration should have listened to those like Senator Cruz and Senator Lee who suggested that the country was not yet ready for rollout of the controversial health care law, only time will tell if the initial problems will turn out to be a success, right now however, it does not look promising.[25,26]

The Truth- Jonathan Gruber Tells All

It really doesn't help the case of an already unpopular law when one of its architects publically makes comments about how the law was passed. This is exactly what happened with the Affordable Care Act only a few years after its passage. The controversy surrounded an economist with the Massachusetts Institute of Technology, Jonathan Gruber, who helped to create the Affordable Care Act, along with Massachusetts's healthcare plan when Mitt Romney was Governor. Between 2010 and 2013, Gruber had been caught on video making comments about the Affordable Care Act, how it was written, and how it was presented to the American public.

It wasn't the fact that Gruber made comments that had him heavily criticized in public; it was the nature of the comments. One video had Gruber reportedly saying that the Affordable Care Act was passed due to the stupidity of the voter, and that people truly don't know what was in the bill. In another video Gruber claimed that the Affordable Care Act would actually impact more plans than originally stated, and that most people would feel the impact in the coming years.

Several of these videos have been taken down to avoid embarrassment from the places in which Gruber was filmed making these comments. This however did not prevent Congress from questioning Gruber extensively on the comments made. In December of 2014, Gruber testified to the House Oversight and Reform Committee at the time headed by Representative Darrell

Issa. At the hearing, Gruber admitted to South Carolina Congressman Trey Gowdy that he knew very little about politics and that he was making the comments to sound smart around other intellectual minds. The exchange between Gruber and Gowdy is one worth watching if you haven't yet, and cannot be explained in words.

Of course you can't blame the words of one man on the President or the President's staff, but when similar allegations had already been widespread and someone puts a face and name to the comments, it is hard to ignore. Many have asked why Gruber had to testify in front of Congress for his comments. Its freedom of speech isn't it? However, when an unpopular law is passed and someone later claims they did so deceivingly questions must be asked. Many have wondered from the start if the President and his staff were being completely upfront about the Affordable Care Act, and now a man who actually worked on it is making claims that contradict those of the Presidents. No matter which side of the aisle this was, it would be wrong for Congress to not inquire into the comments made and why they were actually made.

It will be interesting to see where the Gruber testimony leads, as many Republicans are still skeptical of the Affordable Care Act and how effective it actually is. This is an issue that will remain controversial for quite some time, and will always be a significant mark on President Obama's record, whether it turns out to be good or bad for him.

I.R.S. - What Else Must I Say?

The IRS, or Internal Revenue Service, is undoubtedly the most despised bureaucracy in the nation. No one is happy come April when they must file their taxes, and no one is happy when they see part of their paycheck went to the federal government. So is it possible to make the most despised agency in the federal government even more despised? Absolutely, and it has happened under the Obama administration.

To be fair, there were rumors that the IRS was used as a weapon under the Nixon administration in the 1970's. However, we should have learned from the past. Unfortunately, we did not. Therefore it was of little surprise to many conservatives between 2009 and 2013 when reports began to pop up across the country of unfair treatment of Tea Party or conservative groups by the IRS. The groups were reportedly singled out to either be given a hard time or simply ignored all along. Many requests for tax exempt status were apparently ignored in several offices across the country. An investigation was started in 2010 to figure out whether the claims had validity or not.

It appears at this point that not many are actually disputing that something was done wrong by the IRS; the biggest question is who actually was involved. At the forefront of the investigation is the head of the IRS Exempt Organizations division, Lois Lerner. Lerner has testified in front of Congress, but has "plead the Fifth" asserting that any answers may incriminate her, and that without evidence Congress could not force her to speak on the acts committed. However, through their own investigation, Congressional officials and watchdog groups have found out most of what happened, just not exactly who was involved. It will be interesting to see how the new Congress handles the investigation, but here is what is known so far about the targeting:

Certain groups that have filed for this special tax exempt status have been undoubtedly scrutinized heavily during President Obama's administration. A recent report indicated that there was specific targeting against many Tea Party/conservative groups and even a few Progressive liberal groups.[27]

Reports have even come back that a few Democratic congressional leaders, notably Maryland Representative Elijah Cummings and New Hampshire Senator Jeanne Shaheen, were involved in the targeting of certain groups, both have denied these claims and have been reelected since the claims first came out.[28]

The status that the plot targeted was that of "nonprofit 501(c)(4) groups." This means organizations that are not paying their employees from the money that they get. Quite a few of these groups actually turned out to be Christian groups who wanted the status for charitable reasons. This status would have allowed the organizations to go on without having to pay certain taxes because those working for the organization are not benefiting from the money that comes in.

Groups targeted were those who included the words "Tea Party", "Patriots", "9/12 Project", "Progressive", "occupy", and "Israel", just to name a few. It should be noted that some would explain that the Tea Party and Progressives are the "extreme" in each party, and that could be the reasoning for the targeting. Though it still wouldn't be an excuse.

Several individuals have also claimed that they have been targeted by the IRS for more strict supervision as well.

The targeting took place in a few different ways. One way was that groups that filed for 501(c)(4) status were ignored and their requests pushed aside for a significant amount of time. Another way the targeting took place was scrutinizing the groups more than they should have been. Extra questions were asked about their incomes, their employees and their affiliations, which should not have made a difference after the original applications were already processed.

Although some elected Democrats have been tied to the targeting, and there are significant whispers that the IRS, Treasury Department and the Justice Department all coordinating in some way, nothing has directly linked President Obama to this scandal. In

May of 2013, Steven Miller, the head of the IRS resigned due to the scandal, and he has been the highest up official to resign or be connected to the scandal at all. The investigation is still ongoing.[29, 30, 31]

The Issues

There have been multiple separate investigations into the IRS scandal on both sides. Members of Congress and the Media have come out on both sides to condemn what has happened, but have not gone as far as to suggest what should actually be done. Some preliminary investigations have concluded that there was no "criminal" wrongdoing in the targeting. That makes it difficult to actually go somewhere with the aftermath of the scandal.

However, suspicion has risen in the case for many reasons. The most significant focuses around Lois Lerner herself. Quite a few times since Lerner first testified in front of Congress about the targeting scandal she has been asked to produce her emails to show what happened during certain time periods. The IRS claimed that two years of Lerner's emails, between 2009 and 2011 specifically, had been lost due to a "computer crash." Republicans have reacted in different ways to this, all of them voicing clear frustration. The Chairman of the House Ways and Means Committee Dave Camp, a Republican from Michigan, had this to say about the incident:

"The fact that I am just learning about this, over a year into the investigation, is completely unacceptable and now calls into question the credibility of the IRS's response to Congressional inquiries… Just a short time ago, Commissioner [John] Koskinen promised to produce all Lerner documents. It appears now that was an empty promise."[27]

The investigation has been plagued with issues like this, officials testifying in front of Congress unable to come up with the answers to questions being asked or provide the documents that

Congress has been looking for. Another example was when Lois Lerner eventually testified in front of Congress. It took some time, but she eventually agreed. However, when most of the questions were asked, especially those that may have been incriminating, Ms. Lerner pleaded the fifth, meaning she invoked her Fifth Amendment right to not have to incriminate herself. This just showed that Lerner was hiding something, whether it was a blatant attempt to target these organizations or a grave mistake she made that could put her into a great deal of trouble.

In November and December of 2014 some of Lerner's missing emails have turned up thanks to several watchdog groups across the country. It has not yet been made clear exactly what is on the emails, as the House Oversight and Government Reform committee is likely still looking through these emails.

In December of 2014 the House Oversight and Government Reform committee led by Republican Congressman Darrell Issa released a report on its findings up until that point of the IRS scandal. Although the investigation was not complete, the report was significant because it was the last one by Issa, who was not selected to be the chair of the Oversight Committee in the next Congress. Democrats were pleased to note that the report did not link the IRS targeting to the White House or any other government organization besides the IRS. One headline even described Issa as the "chief witch hunter" in the investigation.

However, the report is still significant in a few different ways. The first is that the investigation is still ongoing, and because of that we still don't know all the answers and nothing is certain. The other point that the report made is that while currently nothing links the IRS scandal to the White House, President Obama and members of his administration could have done more to stop the scandal, and they did not. Issa noted that the President promised a full and thorough investigation with the full support of the government, and Congress has felt that is not what has happened.

This brings us to the point of why the IRS scandal falls on this list. Although the President may not have been directly involved, once he heard about this happening he should have launched a full investigation himself or fully cooperated with Congress. It wouldn't have mattered if this was President Bush or President Obama, the targeting of groups based on their political beliefs is wrong and should not be tolerated. As President of the United States, President Obama also should have been more aware of what is going on in his administration. The targeting continued even after rumors came out, for one it never should have started, but beyond that it should have been shut down as soon as it became public.[29,30,31]

Race Relations

Steve Inskeep, NPR: "Is the United States more racially divided than it was when you took office six years ago, Mr. President?"
President Obama: "No, I actually think that it's probably in its day-to-day interactions less racially divided. But I actually think that the issue has surfaced in a way that probably is healthy."

Interview released on December 29, 2014.[32]

As much as we don't want to touch on this topic, we feel it is quite necessary in this instance. Many figured when Barack Obama was elected President of the United States in 2008 that it was a sign that race relations were clearly improving in the country. We had finally gotten past the days where African Americans could not hold certain jobs, including elected offices. Days of discriminating at restaurants or the polls were finally over, it had become a time where someone's race, ethnicity, or religion would not play a major negative factor in their day to day lives. Many thought those conversations were now over, that kind of equality was now common sense.

Or so we all thought.

2014 has seen a great deal of the conversation of race come back up, as the President alluded to in his answer to Steve Inskeep from NPR. The truth is we have seen both sides of racism emerge in 2014, and that has only made things worse. Of course we still have people who think that it is okay to be biased against a certain race such as African Americans, which will never change. Thankfully that is a small minority now, and if we keep asserting that what they're saying is wrong, that minority will continue to shrink. Will it ever completely disappear? Of course not, there are still people who think that what Adolf Hitler and the Nazis stood for was right (of course we do not find too many differences between modern Neo-Nazis and racists). That is one of the negatives of human thinking; there will always be those with disgusting and disparaging thoughts that will never change.

However, the other side we have seen is those who are taking advantage of racism for political gains. Right away we will emphasize that we do not believe it was President Obama's intention to use race for political gain when he got into office, once the issues came up, he dealt with it the way he felt he should, but it was not his initial intent to use these issues for political gain. Others, however, have used race for political gain. The first two names that come to mind are Reverend Al Sharpton and Reverend Jesse Jackson, with Sharpton being the most infamous and currently relevant of the two. Two other names that have caused tension recently are New York City Mayor Bill de Blasio and Attorney General Eric Holder. Another example of race being used for political gain can be found in the Mississippi Republican Primary from 2014, in which incumbent Senator Thad Cochran held off a challenge from state Senator Chris McDaniel by "using the race card." Emphasis on the roles of Holder, de Blasio and Cochran are subject for further debate in another section.

We do not believe that President Obama or Attorney General Holder have in anyway intended to incite race issues. That is not what happened, that is not their intent. However, it has been their reaction to the issues that has caused race issues to actually become worse, and not better. To understand their reactions, we must first look at the past of these men and some of the incidents that have arisen while they have been in office.

After Barack Obama graduated law school, he worked as a civil rights attorney in Chicago. During his time in the Illinois Senate, Obama worked on several bills involving civil rights and issues of race, including a few regarding racial profiling by law enforcement. This shows that he has devoted some of his career to dealing with civil rights issues, so we should not be surprised to see him addressing some of these as President of the United States, we would be surprised if he did not as a matter of fact.

Attorney General Eric Holder on the other hand had been a little quieter before he was appointed Attorney General. Holder was not involved in private practices too much, as he worked for the US Justice Department office soon after he graduated from Colombia Law School. During Holder's time as Attorney General however the Justice Department focused on attempting to end voting ID laws in states such as Texas, Arizona and Alabama. Some of those fights are still ongoing today, with the Justice Department claiming those laws are racist and only hurt minorities in the states.[33]

There have been three cases in particular in the past few years, two in 2014 alone that have brought race issues back into the spotlight recently. The first one was the Trayvon Martin shooting in February of 2012. In this case, 17 year old African American Trayvon Martin was shot in an altercation with a 28 year old Hispanic man named George Zimmerman. Zimmerman claimed he stopped Martin to question him about several break ins in the area and Martin attacked Zimmerman. Zimmerman was armed, and the struggling resulted in the two fighting for the gun, in which Zimmerman fired first. In July of 2013, Zimmerman was acquitted of second degree murder and manslaughter, sparking a national outrage.

From the start, many claimed that the whole incident was about race. Al Sharpton and others like him publically stated that Zimmerman had racially profiled Martin, and that is what led to the altercation. They stated multiple times that if Zimmerman had just left Martin alone, there would not have been an altercation and Martin would still be alive. However, while everything was unfolding, a story came out from an anonymous source stating that a few years earlier when an African American man had been beaten by the local police, Zimmerman was one of the first to reach out to the African American community and speak out. This severely put into question of whether Zimmerman had racist intentions or not.

Remarks from President Obama and Attorney General Holder did not exactly help the situation either. On July 19, 2013, a week after the verdict, President Obama had this to say about the case:

"You know, when Trayvon Martin was first shot I said that this could have been my son. Another way of saying that is Trayvon Martin could have been me 35 years ago. And when you think about why, in the African American community at least, there's a lot of pain around what happened here, I think it's important to recognize that the African American community is looking at this issue through a set of experiences and a history that doesn't go away."[34]

Also adding to the tension, Attorney General Eric Holder announced after the decision that the Justice Department had opened a civil rights investigation into the case. They were looking at the death of Trayvon Martin along with Florida's "Stand Your Ground" laws, which is what Zimmerman used in his defense. As of right now, no civil rights charges were filed against Zimmerman from the Justice Department.[35]

After the decision came out we also saw a great deal of protests and demonstrations around the country. There were even some cases in which people responded through crimes, breaking into stores and looting because they felt that the decision in the case was wrong. Only a few days after the verdict came out, stories of crimes committed by those wanting "revenge" started to appear. In Milwaukee a man was beaten on the street, and witnesses recall the assailants saying "this is for Trayvon Martin." At the end of July, a man was robbed in Washington by several males who told him that "this is for Trayvon." These are only a few examples unfortunately.[36,37]

We are in no way attempting to place the blame on President Obama or Attorney General Holder for the aftermath of these issues, but there are different things they could have done. We ask two questions in this particular issue. The first, why did Attorney General Holder feel the need to open a civil rights investigation? Florida had already committed to looking into the "Stand Your Ground" laws, the federal government had no need to intervene. And second, couldn't President Obama have used more healing words? If the President had left it at it could have been his son, alright that's one point. A teen caught out, possibly doing something he shouldn't have, and got into trouble. Once the President added in the point about the African American community, the issue changed to race, which is where men like Sharpton would pick up and run with the point, twisting the words of the President and anyone else who then wishes to speak on the issue to make their own political gain.

Unfortunately, 2014 saw two more cases that have sparked national outrage, and have caused tensions to rise. The first was the Michael Brown case in August and the Eric Garner case in July. Both of them involved law enforcement, which added to already heightened tensions, and only led the way for an increase in incendiary rhetoric, intentional or not.

Although the Eric Garner case happened first, the Michael Brown case was the one that caught the most media attention, and had the decision that came down first. In August of 2014, 18 year old Michael Brown was walking down a street in Ferguson, Missouri when he was stopped by Ferguson police officer Darren Wilson. Brown and an accomplice had been walking in the middle of the street, and Officer Wilson directed them to move to the sidewalk as they were blocking traffic. No one knows exactly what was said, but Brown approached the car, and a fight ensued and Officer Wilson ended up shooting Brown, killing him.

Before many of the details of the case came out, people were out on the streets not only protesting and demonstrating, but rioting. The shooting was on August 9, and by August 10 the violent protests started. People began looting stores in Ferguson and even damaging and burning some of them. The protests continued for a little over a week until Missouri Governor Jay Nixon announced that Ferguson was in a state of emergency and that the National Guard would be deployed to calm the violence. By then, thousands of dollars of damage had already been done, many were wounded and the entire country was captivated by the events transpiring in the middle of the country.

Protests would continue across the country for a few months, even though the investigation was ongoing. About a week after the shooting, the police department released the name of the officer involved in the shooting, along with surveillance video of what appeared to be Michael Brown and his accomplice committing a strong armed robbery down the street only a short time before they were stopped. During this time the county prosecutor's office was presenting evidence to the Grand Jury. This process was to determine whether or not to press charges against Officer Wilson, not to determine innocent or guilt. Some evidence was leaked during the process, but not all of it or enough for the public to make an opinion of the case. Many protestors claimed that there would be rioting if Officer Wilson was not charged, and others actually threatened Wilson and other police officers for the same reason.

On November 24, the Grand Jury decision not to indict Officer Wilson was announced. The response by the protestors was abhorrent. Violence resumed in the area, and by the end of the night 12 buildings were burned down, over 100 shots were fired and 61 people were arrested for crimes such as looting, burglary and arson across the city of Ferguson. People in other parts of the country also called for protests and violence against police officers. Within the next few weeks, the protests, violence and threats of more violence would continue. Some of these threats even prompted Darren Wilson to resign from the Ferguson Police Department, as people threatened to attack other officers if Wilson still worked for the department.

However, many of these same protestors ignored a lot of the facts in the case. We will not go into details about the case, but there are a few things in particular that the St. Louis County Prosecutor said that we want to highlight. The most significant was that many of the witnesses changed their stories, multiple times. This is exactly what St. Louis County Prosecutor Robert McCulloch said on November 24 about that issue:

"Several witnesses adjusted their stories in their subsequent statements. But some even admitted they did not witness the event at all but merely repeated what they heard in the neighborhood or assumed. Fortunately for the integrity of our investigation, almost all of initial witness interviews, including those of opposite Wilson were recorded."[38,39,40,41]

The point is people spun the situation to suit their agendas, as we saw when Al Sharpton came onto the scene with this situation.

Sharpton was right in Ferguson when the first mention of race came up, and kept pushing his agenda and stating that law enforcement in the United States is racist. Sharpton and those like him don't care about the facts, they only care about themselves and how they look.

The Eric Garner case was somewhat similar to that of the Michael Brown case, but with a little different type of controversy. On July 17, Eric Garner was accused of selling cigarettes on the streets of Staten Island, New York. Officers approached Garner and told him to stop, Garner claimed he was not selling these cigarettes, and began to argue with the officers. The officer at the head of the controversy, Officer Daniel Pantaleo, went to restrain Garner, and Garner pulled away. It was debated as to what happened next, but multiple officers ended up restraining Garner, who was significantly bigger than the officers. Garner ended up on the ground as the officers were putting the handcuffs on. Critics then claim Officer Pantaleo put Garner into a chokehold, which is against NYPD policy, but not illegal. Others claimed it was a headlock and not a chokehold. Unfortunately, once Garner was restrained, he stopped breathing and was dead within an hour.[42]

Critics and protestors claimed that it was the chokehold that prevented Garner from breathing and subsequently caused his death, but others claim it was the older man's poor health. Garner was 43 years old and 350 pounds. The medical examiner noted the chokehold as the cause of death, but also noted that asthma and heart disease were also contributing factors.[42]

Just as in the Michael Brown case, Reverend Al Sharpton again stuck his neck out and attempted to get involved in the situation. However, this time Sharpton was met with more rejection, as several members of Garner's family claimed they did not want Sharpton around, and several claimed the issue wasn't about race, which many were trying to claim it was from the start.

On December 3, the decision came down from the Grand Jury, no indictment on Officer Pantaleo. Again protestors were furious, and demonstrations were frequent around the country, especially in New York City. Due to the fact that the timings of the Grand Jury decisions were so close together, it is easier to discuss this case and the Michael Brown case together, especially in reference to reactions. Protestors across the country claimed the deaths of Brown and Garner were due to the racism and overreactions of police, but the facts do not necessarily support those claims. Unfortunately over the next few weeks we would see the consequences of such claims rise in some of the most horrific ways.

On December 20, 2014 New York Police Department officers Wenjian Liu and Rafael Ramos were shot and killed in their patrol car on the streets of New York City by a man who claimed on Instragram that he was going to kill police officers for the deaths of Michael Brown and Eric Garner. Even before this happened, protestors were chanting that they wanted "dead cops," and several arrests were made for threatening police officers in the days leading up and the days after. Also that night in Florida another police officer, Charles Kondek, was murdered by a gunman with unknown intent. Since then, we have also seen attacks on law enforcement in Los Angeles and Florida, just to name a few.[43, 44]

While again it is important to emphasize that President Obama and Attorney General Holder were not responsible for these deaths, things could have been done differently as leaders to show more support for law enforcement. After the decisions came out in Ferguson and New York City, Attorney General Holder announced he was considering a civil rights investigation in both cases. One was not opened in Ferguson, but the investigation has been opened in New York City for the Garner case. Due to the backlash he faced with the Trayvon Martin comments, President Obama has not said as much with these two cases. The President has called for calm and restraint and for the protests to be nonviolent. However, after both decisions came out, President Obama has stated that it is important to have the discussions we are having, and at one point even stated these types of discussions were "personal" for him.[45]

This is where we get to the point of where this fits into our overall topic. The President is not being dishonest in this instance, but instead here we should be looking at the examples set. Several elected officials besides President Obama have gone out and made public statements that have not helped the situation at all, including New York City Mayor Bill de Blasio. Many in the country feel that these elected officials have turned on them, and that they do not truly represent their beliefs. When President Obama was first elected in 2008 many hoped the issues of race would no longer be issues anymore and that we could all move on. However, people today are sick of hearing about it, and they actually feel things are worse than they were before.

President Obama and Attorney General Holder should be condemning the violent protests and the harsh rhetoric, but unfortunately they have only done so partially. They should speak out fully against those advocating for violence, and those claiming that America is still racist. It doesn't look good for you when the number one race baiter in the country becomes your "civil rights aide." It is not necessarily President Obama's words that make him dishonest in this case, but his actions. The truth is, President Obama is not setting the example for healing that many would like to see. He is only partially there, and to fully set the stage to heal, he should be condemning the violent protestors and condemning those like Sharpton who try to claim these situations are all about racism. The President should also be standing with law enforcement, showing them he has their back and will support them as they enforce the laws. Law enforcement officers are in danger every time they put on the uniform and go into work, and they should know the leaders who are supposed to represent them have their backs. Hopefully we will see this change in the coming months.

Executive Orders

"I taught constitutional law for ten years. I take the Constitution very seriously. The biggest problems that were facing right now have to do with George Bush trying to bring more and more power into the executive branch and not go through Congress at all, and that's what I intend to reverse when I'm President of the United States of America."

Candidate Barack Obama, Town hall event in Lancaster, PA 2008.[46]

Campaigning at its finest. This is not something new; this is not something that only candidate Obama has done, pretty much all candidates have done it. We could list instances of every single official in this book doing the same thing, but we'll wait until we actually get to their chapters. However, President Obama has the most examples, as he is the President of the United States. However, the first rule of executive orders is that we must look past the numbers, and look at what each of the orders actually does. Looking at the numbers makes you believe certain Presidents have expanded executive powers more than all others. But you need to look at what exactly the orders did to understand who really expanded executive powers.

President Obama hasn't exactly been shy about this point either. During the 2014 State of the Union address, the President boldly stated:

"America does not stand still, and neither will I, so wherever and whenever I can take steps without legislation to expand opportunity for more American families, that's what I'm gonna do."[47, 48]

President Obama faced heavy backlash on both sides for this comment, especially from Republicans in Congress who felt they were simply being ignored. If you watch the video clip of when the President says that, you can also notice Speaker John Boehner's reaction when this is said. Boehner was clearly frustrated to hear this said right in front of the entire Congress, but has done little to stop it. Many stood up in the following weeks to speak out against this rhetoric from the President, but not too much has been done to stop it.

So we go back to the point of it's not how many, but what. President Obama has been heavily criticized over this point as well. During President Obama's time in office, many have criticized the media, especially NBC, for being blindly pro-Obama and pro-Democrat (with the counter being that Fox is pro-Republican). However, even NBC's popular show "Saturday Night Live" could not defend the President from his executive order in November of 2014. They aired a skit that was a parody of the famous "Schoolhouse Rock."[49]

The skit shows a bill explaining the legislative process to a young student, and then the President appears. The President pushes the bill down the Capital Hill steps and then introduces an "executive order." The executive order introduces himself by stating "I'm an executive order and I pretty much just happen." When stating what he can do, the executive order states "I'll create a national park, or a new holiday." The President responds by stating "or grant legal status to five million undocumented immigrants." The executive order is amazed, and replies "go big or go home." At the end of the skit, the young student watching all of this states "I think want to go into the private sector," representing Americans clear frustration with the way government works today.

Although it was just a satirical skit, the portrayal was fairly accurate. Of course the President isn't pushing bills down the steps of Capital Hill or replacing all bills with executive orders, but the argument could be made that President Obama has overstepped on this recent action. The action in particular that this skit was referring to was President Obama's announcement that due to Congress' inability to do anything on immigration reform, he was going to issue an executive order granting legal status to undocumented immigrants who have been in the United States for a certain period of time. This is exactly what the President said on November 20:

"Now here's the thing: We expect people who live in this country to play by the rules. We expect that those who cut the line will not be unfairly rewarded. So we're going to offer the following deal: If you've been in America for more than five years; if you have children who are American citizens or legal residents; if you register, pass a criminal background check, and you're willing to pay your fair share of taxes — you'll be able to apply to stay in this country temporarily without fear of deportation. You can come out of the shadows and get right with the law. That's what this deal is."[50]

President Obama stated earlier in that very same speech that he had the legal authority as President for this type of action, and that former Presidents had done the same thing. He also blamed House Republicans for blocking a bill that the Senate had passed with 68 votes, showing bipartisan support. The President would continue to say this isn't amnesty, but that the current way things were being handled was the real example of amnesty.

Numbers put forth by the Migration Policy Institute and the Washington Post state that this will affect around 4 million undocumented immigrants today, with the possibility for that number growing in the future. Critics claimed that both Presidents Ronald Reagan and George HW Bush issued similar executive actions during their time, but here are a few differences. President Reagan's action affected far less workers, and Bush's just a few more. Neither adds up to the 4 million President Obama's does. You could of course argue times were different and there were less immigrants in the country at that time, but in response to that you could state maybe there was a different reason to let them in, and the rhetoric was different, neither Bush nor Reagan was stating they were doing it because the House wouldn't. The other is that Obama campaigned on stopping these types of orders, not continuing them, but that is what he has done.[51, 52, 53,]

However, here is another truth with the claims of Reagan and Bush's executive orders. They didn't happen. The actions that the media keep talking about come from a law Congress passed in 1986, the Simpson-Mazzoli act. Once Congress passed the act, Reagan signed it into law. There was no executive order; and there were not threats from Reagan that he would do it alone. They worked together to pass that act, it was not a singular action.[54, 55]

As of January 1, 2015, the immigration order has not been an executive order. No one knows what exactly happened, but it is currently not the rule of law in the country. The President laid out the plan in November, and claimed it would happen, but nothing ever did. So why is there all the rhetoric then? Why did the President state he would work without Congress, then actually do nothing? We do not have the answers to these questions, but there are other acts that the President has taken that also make us question what the overreach of power has looked like so far.

However, it is more in the face of the people when one campaigns on not doing it then decides he needs to anyway. Of course some executive orders are necessary; we wouldn't expect Congress to vote on establishing a new committee within the White House (as many of the initial executive orders are when a President is first elected). Other orders necessary involve simply continuing former orders that are set to expire on a yearly basis, again something that could be very simple that doesn't affect the function of government or the everyday lives of citizens too much.

Recent acts have shown us that for an act from the President to be considered an overreach of power it doesn't just have to be an executive order. In 2014 President Obama faced heavy backlash over several actions taken, specifically in reference to releasing prisoners from Guantanamo Bay, without consulting Congress. Earlier we mentioned that the President had promised to close Guantanamo Bay, but in his first five years failed to follow through on that promise. He seems to now be taking matters into his own hands, releasing prisoners in the middle of the night to other countries. To be fair, he isn't simply "letting them go" as some may suggest. Those who are released from Guantanamo Bay are sent to other countries to be watched by foreign governments. They simply are no longer the responsibility of the US government or on US soil.

The first big case of this that we saw was in June of 2014 when President Obama authorized the release of five prisoners from Guantanamo Bay with associations to the Taliban in order to secure the release of an Army Sergeant, Bowe Bergdahl. Bergdahl had been captured by the Taliban in Afghanistan in June of 2009, and hadn't been seen in public since. The Army is still investigating exactly how Bergdahl disappeared, as there are many unanswered questions. Lawmakers were quick to place blame on the President for this action, claiming he did not give them the required 30 days' notice before releasing the prisoners from Guantanamo Bay.[56]

Most lawmakers and Americans are not necessarily upset about what we got out of the deal, we got back an American soldier, and many were pleased with that, but many were upset that five members of the Taliban were released back to the Middle East, and that Congress was not directly consulted. Leaders in both the House and the Senate acknowledge that there were talks about the deal in the years leading up, but the plan that the White House put forward faced heavy criticism from lawmakers on both sides. Even California Democratic Senator Dianne Feinstein, the chairwoman of the Senate

Intelligence Committee admitted "there were very strong views and they were virtually unanimous against the trade… The White House is pretty unilateral about what they want to do and when they want to do it."[57]

The deal sent the five detainees to Qatar where they will be monitored by the Qatari government for up to two years, and then allowed to go free. As is the case with most of the detainees who have been released from Guantanamo, they are eventually allowed to go free, just not within the United States. The countries have to be willing to take them as well, and many Western countries really are not willing.

Many of the criticisms center around the question of what will happen once the time period that the foreign governments are required to watch the detainees is up. Will they be allowed to leave the country? Will they go back to their old affiliations? The problem is, we just don't know, but the intelligence community fears the worst.

Recent acts show that the President is now finally serious about closing Guantanamo Bay, but doesn't care about Congress' response. On the first of January in 2015, it was announced that President Obama released five more prisoners from Guantanamo Bay, after he had released five more in November. As the five released in the Bergdahl trade, these prisoners are sent to other countries to be monitored for a period of time so they do not come onto US soil. As of the January 1 release, the number of prisoners in Guantanamo Bay is reported to be at 127, according to Fox News. It still appears as though the President is not consulting Congress for these releases, but Congress isn't doing much to try to stop it either. They are blocking prisoners from being brought to the United States, but that is about it. Many expect the President to keep doing the same thing because he is facing little actual opposition besides rhetoric.[58]

Overall, this is likely to continue unless Congress makes an attempt to stop it, but it doesn't appear like they have any intent on doing so anytime soon.

The final point to make on the executive actions is the reports that came out at the end of 2014 that these actions are being passed under a different name, "Presidential memoranda." USA Today put together a comprehensive report on this story at the end of 2014 and actually found that with the compilation of executive orders and Presidential memoranda (which are essentially the same thing), President Obama has issued more Presidential memoranda than any other President. This shows us a clear attempt to hide the expansion of executive power.

The USA Today article titled *Obama issues 'executive orders by a different name'* cites Presidential scholar Phillip Cooper talking about the memoranda by describing them as "'executive orders by another name, and yet unique.'" This article by USA Today has brought quite a bit of attention to this matter, but not quite enough. Not many of the major news networks, including CNN or Fox News had picked up the story as of January 1, 2015. The report also notes that the President has issued 198 Presidential memoranda and 195 executive orders through his first six years in office.[59, 61, 62]

There is clearly a reason why this statistic is something that isn't advertised by the media and the White House; it doesn't fit with their rhetoric. President Obama campaigned on incriminating President Bush for his use of executive orders, so he is doing what he can to try to look like he is doing something while fulfilling his campaign promises. The use of Presidential memoranda shows that President Obama really has expanded his executive powers more than he is willing to admit to, showing the dishonesty in the case. There is more dishonesty in the idea that the President needs to call the executive orders something different in order to hide this.

There truly isn't too much to say about this, the facts are there in this case. It's clear the President was using this to hide his use of executive power. We would encourage you to check out the report by USA Today, as it shows all of the numbers that went into the study, and provides links to a few more. There are a few graphs and charts useful as well for analyzing the data.

We would also encourage you to watch the response from lawmakers and court officials in this case. Many states went on to take President Obama's actions on immigration to court since he announced he was making the executive order. In Pennsylvania, a federal judge examining a different case actually looked at the President's executive orders on immigration and ruled them unconstitutional. It will interesting to see where it goes from there, and how courts and Congress handle things from here on out. Overall, I understand times have changed, but there are still ways to avoid the use of executive orders. The President should be trying more to work with Congress instead of telling them he will work around them. Only then can we actually see more be accomplished in government.[60]

Conclusion

Not every case is completely evident, but most of the evidence put forth is self-explanatory. There are even some cases that we have not even covered, specifically the way the President has treated Republicans since he has been in office. Instead of really trying to work with them, the President has constantly tried to offload the blame on them when something doesn't go right. This is not the kind of example the President should be setting. President Obama came in as a man who had the chance to unite the country, but instead he has divided it in several different ways. We need a President who will take the chance to unite instead of divide, when something doesn't work out go back to the drawing board and admit to the mistakes, not blame the other side, only then will we see improvements.

To recap, we talked about Guantanamo Bay, Obamacare, the IRS, race relations and the use of executive powers. This is not an exhaustive list, more could have gone on here, but we simply didn't have the room. To be fair, of course there is more room for criticism for the President, simply because he is the President of the United States. He is the most watched man in the world, and every step he takes will be criticized. To expect anything different from any President would be unfair.

Unfortunately, the President has set the wrong example. The closing of Guantanamo Bay is unpopular and not really in the country's best interest, Obamacare has been plagued with scandals and controversies, the IRS scandal showed the President did not have as much oversight in the government as he should, the recent issues with race relations shows the President hasn't used his opportunity to unite the nation, and his use of executive orders has shown he is more concerned about his image than following the Constitution. These are all unfortunate, but not uncommon in politics today.

This is not meant to be a harsh criticism of the President, but to serve as a way to show the people what is truly going on in government today. Barack Obama has been elected to the highest positon in the country, by the people, and these are some of the most controversial moments during his presidency. At the end of the day, it is up to the people to decide how they feel about these acts, but I feel these cases show the President has not empathized with the common man and instead has lied and caused unnecessary division.

I hope that the President can actually prove me wrong in the last part of his term, but only time will tell.

III. Hillary Clinton

"The American people are tired of liars and people who pretend to be something they're not." Former Secretary of State Hillary Clinton

Hillary Clinton has been a prominent figure in American politics for quite some time now, and her time in the spotlight does not appear to be over. She has held many different titles including Senator, First Lady and Secretary of State. For our purposes, we will be using her title as Secretary of State to address her in this section, as we will be mainly focusing on her time as Secretary of State in the Obama Administration.

Secretary Clinton is on this list due to her current prominent role in the Democratic Party, as many consider her to be the Democratic nominee for President for the 2016 election cycle. She is well respected by colleagues on both sides of the aisle, but has her fair share of criticisms as well, including several incidents from her time at the State Department and comments she has made since leaving the State Department.

As with President Obama, we must look at Secretary Clinton's past to understand her motives during her time in office and to get a sense of where she is coming from. Also we again will not address any sort of rumors that are going around, our goal is to stick to the facts and be clear and concise.

Early Years[63,65]

Hillary Diane Rodham was born on October 26, 1947 in Chicago, Illinois to Hugh Rodman and Dorothy Rodham. Rodham was active in politics at a young age, participating in student government in High School and even volunteering in political activity before she graduated High School.

Rodham attended Wellesley College starting in 1965 where she majored in Political Science. Up until her college years she had been an active conservative, but Rodham's views changed when the Civil Rights Movement and the Vietnam War became more well-known. However, this did not deter Clinton from politics; she simply switched from being a Republican to a Democrat during her college years.

After she graduated from Wellesley College, Rodham attended Yale Law School. Rodham met her future husband, Bill Clinton, during her time there. During her time at Yale, Rodham also began to work in various political fields, including the campaign of Connecticut U.S. Senate candidate Joseph Duffey. She also interned at the law firm of Treuhaft, Walker and Burnstein during the summer of 1971 in Oakland, California, where she worked on various constitutional issues including civil liberties and child custody cases. In 1972 she campaigned in Texas for Walter Mondale's presidential campaign.

In 1973 Rodham graduated with a Juris Doctor degree, and began postgraduate work. In 1974 she was a member of the presidential impeachment inquiry staff which worked with the House Judiciary Committee during the Watergate scandal which led to President Richard Nixon's resignation. Afterwards, Rodham and Bill Clinton moved to Arkansas and became faculty members at the University of Arkansas Law School in Fayetteville. In 1975, Hillary Rodham and Bill Clinton married.

Arkansas

Most people credit Arkansas as being the place where Bill Clinton started his political career, but not as many people notice that his wife, Hillary Rodham Clinton, also started to do significant work in Arkansas. In 1976 Bill Clinton was elected as the Attorney General of Arkansas, a position seen as a springboard for a future run for Governor, while Mrs. Clinton started to work for the Rose Law Firm in Little Rock, Arkansas. There Mrs. Clinton would work on patent infringement, intellectual property law and continue her work in child advocacy.

In 1977, continuing her work in child advocacy, Hillary Clinton cofounded the organization Arkansas Advocates for Children and Families. The organization was founded to focus on expanding opportunities for children in health and education and attempting to create reforms throughout the state to help children. In 1978, President Jimmy Carter appointed Clinton to be on the board of the Legal Services Corporation, a group working for equal protection under the law for all, even those who can't afford it, where she served until 1981.[64]

1979 was an even bigger year for Hillary and Bill Clinton. In 1978, Bill Clinton won his first term as Governor, and therefore started his term in 1979. In that year not only did Mrs. Clinton become First Lady of Arkansas, but she was also named as Rose Law Firm's first woman full time partner. She continued to work for the law firm even when her husband was Governor.

During her husband's time as Governor, Mrs. Clinton also continued to work for the Rose Law Firm, and the Arkansas Advocates for Children and Families organization. Mrs. Clinton was also chosen to chair the Arkansas Educational Standards Committee, and then she was selected for the boards of the Arkansas Children's Hospital Legal Services and the Children's Defense Fund. In 1983 she was named Arkansas Woman of the Year and in 1984 she was named Arkansas Mother of the Year.[66]

White House-First Lady

In 1992, Bill Clinton defeated George H.W. Bush to become the 42nd President of the United States. During this 8 year, two term span, Mrs. Clinton was quite effective as a First Lady, with some accrediting her as being as influential as Eleanor Roosevelt. She played a very essential role during her husband's Presidency. Some of her accomplishments included establishing a way to help veterans of the Gulf War who were suffering from Gulf War Syndrome, working with the Justice Department to establish the Office on Violence Against Women, and continuing her work with child advocacy. Mrs. Clinton claimed her greatest accomplishment during this time to be the Adoption and Safe Families Act of 1997.

The Adoption and Safe Families Act of 1997 was aimed at fixing the foster care program, which many believed to be in disarray. The law provides more support for children in foster care, providing better options for healthcare and other necessities for children. It also provides incentives for families to adopt children. The act was adopted by Congress easily, and signed into law by President Bill Clinton. Mrs. Clinton would work on issues like this throughout her time as First Lady, and this became a significant highlight of her time as First Lady.[67,68,69]

Clinton was also well known for making trips around the world pushing for equal rights for women. She was well received, even in places like Asia and Africa where women did not have many rights. Mrs. Clinton was also well known for speaking out against the Taliban in Afghanistan as well, especially their poor treatment of women.

As expected of someone who is very politically active, Hillary Clinton also had her fair share of controversies as First Lady. Perhaps the most significant came in the form of an attempted healthcare law. One of Bill Clinton's main focuses in his Presidency was an attempt to fix the healthcare system that many considered to be broken. So in 1993 he appointed Hillary to head the Task Force on Health Care Reform. Many were skeptical of the plan in the very beginning, claiming that Hillary Clinton was too radical to take up health care reform.[71]

The plan faced heavy criticism, notably from Republican strategist William Kristol who noted in a memorandum on how and why to defeat the Clinton healthcare plan. Kristol noted "Passage of the Clinton health care plan in any form, would guarantee and likely make permanent an unprecedented federal intrusion and disruption of the American economy- and the establishment of the largest federal entitlement program since Social Security" (Kristol I). Other critics believed similar things that the Clinton healthcare plan would lead to an overreach of government and an excessive intrusion into the lives of everyday citizens.[70]

The conservative group The Heritage Foundation was also very critical of the Clinton healthcare plan. In an article from the Heritage Foundation about the plan, Dr. Robert E. Moffit notes "Emerging from the complex language of this huge bill is a massive top-down, bureaucratic command-and-control system that would meticulously govern every aspect of the delivery and financing of healthcare services for the American people" (Moffit). Those with very powerful voices were against the Clinton healthcare plan from the start, so passing it would be difficult no matter what.[72]

The plan that eventually came up for debate in the public sphere was one that the Republicans had warned about. The plan had several major points. The first is that every American was required to be covered under some sort of healthcare plan, private or public. If they could not afford the plan as determined by income level, the government would pay for the plan. Health providers were to work together regionally to set the best prices and fees for their clients, and the plan was meant to be a reform of the health insurance program as well.

However, the plan seemed doomed to fail from the start. Clinton faced heavy criticism when she testified in front of Congress towards the end of 1993. Although Congress was controlled by Democrats, the plan wasn't enough for them to support it. Republicans were able to gain enough support to keep the bill from even being voted on in the House or the Senate. In September of 1994, after a little over a year of work and debate, Senate Majority Leader George J. Mitchell declared healthcare reform dead for the time being. This failed attempt would continue to be used as a talking point against Mrs. Clinton for the years to come, and likely will even more so when people learn more and more about the Affordable Care Act.[73]

Several other small scandals came up during the Clinton administration that put Hillary into the spotlight. The first was known as the Whitewater scandal, which involved the Rose Law Firm, Hillary Clinton's former place of employment. The Clinton's had made an investment in Whitewater Development Corporation with another couple, and both ended up losing the investment. The other couple had been involved with a bank that retained the legal services of the Rose Law Firm. Critics claimed it was a conflict of interest for Clinton to work for Rose Law Firm while they represented the bank because Bill Clinton was Governor at the time, but an investigation turned up no sufficient evidence to prove wrongdoing in the case by Hillary Clinton.

Two other scandals that came up during the Clinton administration involved the possible misuse of files in the White House. The first was known as "Travelgate" which claimed that the Clinton's used misrepresentations in financial reporting by the Travel Office to hire friends from Arkansas in the government. Another claim was that Clinton ordered the removal of potentially damaging files from the office of former deputy White House counsel Vince Foster after his suicide in July of 1993. These claims were also found to be false or lacking in evidence. Another claim, known as "Filegate" claimed that Hillary Clinton used the FBI to access the records of several Republican officials, notably former White House employees. Again an investigation turned up no evidence to support the claim.[74]

While Hillary Clinton faced some heavy criticism during her time as First Lady that is expected of someone who was as politically active as she was during that time period. Hillary Clinton would also continue to face criticism during her time as a US Senator, presidential candidate and Secretary of State as well. As with all others on the list, the criticism continues as long as they are in the spotlight.

US Senate[75]

After the Clinton's left the White House, Hillary Clinton wanted to start her own political career separate from that of her husbands. She would always be known as "First Lady," but it was clear that Hillary wanted a career and title of her own as well. She was given the first opportunity very shortly after the Clinton's left the White House, and it even started while they still were in the White House.

In November of 1998, the longtime serving New York Senator Patrick Moynihan announced his retirement, he would finish out his term but not run for re-election in 2000. Many supporters urged Hillary Clinton to run for the seat, which she agreed to in 1999. However, there was one slight issue, the Clintons didn't live in New York. In 1999, the Clintons purchased a home in Chappaqua, New York to establish residency in the state.

As expected, Hillary Clinton faced heavy criticism for not living in New York. Her Republican opponent, Rick Lazio, and critics accused Clinton of "carpet bagging", or being a "parachute candidate," someone with no connection to the area they are running for elected office in. Clinton refuted this by vowing to visit every county in New York, and managed to do so before the election in November of 2000. Clinton campaigned on tax cuts and economic incentives, and in November of 2000 Clinton won the election handily, 55 percent to 43 percent.[74]

Hillary Clinton's time in the Senate was not as controversial as some others during that time period. Clinton was enthusiastic about focusing on health care reform once more and fixing some of the problems that were central to New Yorkers. However, after September 11, Clinton started to focus much more on national security and foreign policy.

One of the biggest criticisms against Clinton came in her support for the wars in Iraq and Afghanistan. In 2004 when Massachusetts Senator John Kerry ran for President against George W. Bush he faced heavy criticism for being "before it before he was against it," meaning Kerry supported the war efforts in Iraq and Afghanistan before he was then against it during the campaign. Clinton faced the same criticisms as she voted for both of the wars in Iraq and Afghanistan. In 2007 when she was running for President, Clinton made it clear she no longer supported those war efforts.

Clinton was also vocally against President Bush's major economic programs and the President's choices for Supreme Court, notably John Roberts and Samuel Alito. When it came to the Patriot Act, however, Clinton was a strong supporter, which was not a surprise at the time, as most politicians were in support of this after 9/11. When it came up for renewal a few years later however, Clinton worked to add in civil liberties reforms in the new bill.

In November of 2006, Clinton handily won re-election in New York. However, Clinton was again heavily criticized for excessive spending in the campaign, as she spent nearly $36 million in her re-election bid that year, more than any other candidate in that election cycle.

In her second term, which was short due to her candidacy for President and eventual role as Secretary of State, Clinton supported both the infamous bailout of the US financial system and the controversial Secure Borders, Economic Opportunity and Immigration Reform Act of 2007, which would have included a pathway to citizenship for around 12 million undocumented immigrants in the United States at that time. Clinton faced heavy criticism for her support of both.

Candidacy For President: Part I

"I'm in and I'm in to win." Senator Hillary Clinton, January 21, 2007

During her time as a Senator from New York, there was plenty of speculation if Hillary Clinton would run for President. What was curiosity for most became a reality in the early weeks of 2007 when she posted on her new campaign website "I'm in and I'm in to win." Although Clinton was not the first woman to run for President, she was noted automatically as the most famous and the one with the best chance to be the first to win. Clinton faced tough opposition from the start against Illinois Senator Barack Obama and former Vice Presidential candidate John Edwards. Edwards, however, would not play as much of a role in the election than Obama and Clinton did.

Through most of 2007, Clinton led the Democratic field in polling. However, towards the end of the year, Senator Obama started to close the gap. In the first Primary in Iowa on January 3, 2008, Senator Barack Obama would shock the party by winning the primary with 37.6 percent of the vote, with Edwards and Clinton taking a little over 29 percent each.

The rest of the election would only be uphill for Clinton who continued to face large amounts of criticism. One of Clinton's biggest problems was her support for the wars in Iraq and Afghanistan, which she openly voted for in the Senate. Senator Obama was able to combat this by stating he was against the war from the start. As Obama was not in the Senate for the initial votes, he was able to back this up with votes against the troop surge and claims that he wanted the troops brought home and the wars to end. Obama was able to clearly win over the anti-war crowd, and his message for ending both wars resonated well with voters. Although Clinton advocated for the wars to end in her second term, this did not help her with voters on that front.

Another criticism that Clinton faced was her inability to connect with average voters. The Clintons had never struggled financially, and Clinton was known for her high amounts of spending during her campaigns. As a matter of fact, Clinton's 2006 re-election campaign was the most expensive throughout all of the elections in that year; despite the fact that there was a party shift in the Senate. This would be another factor that would hurt her with voters in 2008, but may even come back to hurt her even more in 2016 with other comments made over the years.

The Bosnia Story[76, 78]

During Hillary Clinton's time as First Lady, she took several trips around the world in an effort to discuss the rights of women and children in various countries. One of those trips took the First Lady to Bosnia in 1996. The country had just been in the midst of a bloody war after the breakup of the Soviet Union, and was not in good shape. Clinton claimed that when she had stepped off the plane at an air base in Tuzla she was forced to run to the awaiting convoy to keep her from facing sniper fire. According to an article written for Reuters by Jeff Mason in 2008, Clinton specifically stated during a campaign stop on March 17 "'I remember landing under sniper fire. There was supposed to be some kind of greeting ceremony at the airport, but instead we just ran with our heads down to get into the vehicles to get to our base."' She retracted the statement about a month later in Pennsylvania when she stated "'I did make a mistake in talking about it, you know, the last time and recently.'"[78] Senator Barack Obama was sure to point this out on the campaign trail during the 2008 election, and the story only managed to turn into another PR disaster for the Clinton campaign.

The story has come back into the spotlight again with the recent story of NBC News anchor Brian Williams claiming the story he shared of coming under RPG fire in Iraq was false. Many have questioned why Williams was forced to resign over the lie, but Clinton has been seemingly given a second chance by the public. With the 2016 Presidential Election now in full swing and Clinton the frontrunner for the Democratic nomination, it would be little surprise to see the issue come to light again.[77]

Candidate to Cabinet Nominee

When it became clear that Barack Obama would win the Democratic nomination, Hillary Clinton ended her campaign and endorsed Barack Obama. Many were not sure where Clinton would go next; seemingly not ready to go back to the Senate. However, after Barack Obama won the election for President in November of 2008, he approached Clinton about serving as Secretary of State. She accepted the proposal, and was easily confirmed by the United States Senate in January of 2009. After she was confirmed, she resigned as a Senator from New York to resume her new full time job as Secretary of State.

Secretary of State-Reset In Relations?

Most Americans were actually quite excited with the brand new Obama Administration in 2009. President Barack Obama was set to bring many new bright ideas to try and reinvigorate the country and get people excited again. His message for "Hope and Change" had won over the hearts of many, and he continued to win more of the base with his selections for his cabinet positions. One of his most popular picks was Hillary Clinton as Secretary of State.

Along with President Obama, Secretary Clinton promised a new era of relations with many nations across the world, including Russia. During her first few months as Secretary of State, Clinton infamously stood with Russian Foreign Minister Sergei Lavrov and together pressed the "reset button." Clinton claimed that this would be the start of new relations between Russia and the United States. She also claimed the relations between the two nations would be better, and they would both be leaders on the world level again.

Secretary Clinton spent a lot of time, especially in her first year, traveling around the world to speak to world leaders and emphasize women's rights and human rights in countries all across the world. She was well liked during her first few years as Secretary of State, being in the low to mid 60's of polling popularity for her first three years in the position according to Gallup. Americans were generally approving of her handling of world issues.[79] They liked that Secretary Clinton was ready for a new start with world leaders, while also making sure the United States was a world leader itself. She was known internally for having strong stances during policy meetings at the White House, being a strong advocate for the troop surge in Afghanistan in 2009, despite Vice President Joe Biden's opposition.

During her first few years, Clinton was faced with several issues dealing with problems in Central and South American countries, but seemed to handle it without problems. Secretary Clinton was also heavily involved in the Israeli-Palestinian peace talks, in which she also tried to influence a "reset." Clinton finished 2009 and 2010 with high approval ratings, as her first two years had been decently quiet. However, it was after that point that things started to get quite controversial for the First Lady.

Wikileaks- Damage to State Department Reputation?

Towards the end of November of 2010 the hacker organization Wikileaks released a grand amount of data regarding actions by the United States government. Some of that information was in direct reference to the State Department. Many of the released documents were cables between diplomats across the world or cables about diplomats from other countries. The release of this information put the State Department in a tough position, although it was not a truly horrible scandal. Over 250,000 documents were released to some of the biggest newspapers in the world, some of these documents holding sensitive information withheld for national security purposes.

The State Department, and more specifically Secretary Clinton, were none too thrilled about the release of the data. Clinton took a very firm stance against Wikileaks and the release of the information as quoted in an article by Scott Neuman with NPR "'disclosure is not just an attack on America- it's an attack on the international community... There is nothing laudable about endangering innocent people, and there is nothing brave about sabotaging the peaceful relations between nations.'"[80] From a government and national security standpoint, Secretary Clinton had every right to be upset about the leak. Many felt that the leaks released information that was too valuable to American national security, and that it did more harm than good. Of course there were some instances in which they made valuable points, but there were several other points to consider.

It was discovered during this time that the State Department and the United States government had been monitoring several ambassadors from other countries. This was one of the more embarrassing points of the scandal. Some of the key figures who had been bugged included officials from Turkey, Brazil, and even Germany's Angela Merkel. While publically the issues were not addressed too much, the embarrassment for the Obama administration and Clinton State Department was unimaginable.

There was plenty of other information that was leaked too during this time, most of it having to do with the NSA spy program, the type of information that infamous whistleblower Edward Snowden leaked. However, the information regarding other diplomats was the information that affected the Clinton State Department the most. The question now becomes if Hillary Clinton is to hold another top position, like President for example, would other key world leaders be able to trust her? That is not a question for us to answer, but the American people and those public officials in question.

Arab Spring[81]

"The Arab revolutions have scrambled power dynamics and shattered security forces across the region." Secretary of State Hillary Clinton, January 23, 2013

We still remember quite vividly the start of the Arab Spring. Most of the major news networks had consistent live coverage of the protests in Tahrir Square in Cairo, Egypt from start to finish. The world was captivated by the idea of peaceful revolutions in several Arab countries, and people were sitting on the edges of their seats to see what would happen.

The Arab Spring first came to light in December of 2011 when a Tunisian street vendor set himself on fire in his hometown to protest poor treatment by the current government. Soon the outrage sparked protests which spread through the small North African country faster than wildfires in the western parts of the United

States. Within a month, the Tunisian President fled the country, and the people declared they had gone through a successful revolution.

The next country to be inspired by these protests was Egypt. Egypt had been ruled by military strongman Hosni Mubarak for almost 30 years, and the people decided it was the time for him to go. Even more than in Tunisia, the world watched the protests unfold on live TV. Modern technology and social media allowed the people of Egypt to connect with others across the world via Twitter, YouTube and Facebook, while media crews were blogging from the ground in Egypt trying to spread the word of the protests for Democracy.[82, 83, 84, 85]

Most around the world were quite supportive of the protests, including the Obama administration and the State Department. President Obama came out in early February in support of the protestors, noting that changes were necessary in Egypt. On February 1 President Obama had the following to say about Egypt's protests:

"Third, we have spoken out on behalf of the need for change. After his speech tonight, I spoke directly to President Mubarak. He recognizes that the status quo is not sustainable and that a change must take place…Now, it is not the role of any other country to determine Egypt's leaders. Only the Egyptian people can do that. What is clear -- and what I indicated tonight to President Mubarak -- is my belief that an orderly transition must be meaningful, it must be peaceful, and it must begin now."[88]

Former Secretary of State Hillary Clinton herself indicated in her book *Hard Choices* that she was also supportive of a change due to the young enthusiasm of the protestors who wanted Democracy. In the book she directly stated:

"some of President Obama's aides in the White House were swept up in the drama and idealism of the moment as they watched the pictures from Tahrir Square on television. They identified with the democratic yearnings and technological savvy of the young Egyptian protesters… I shared that feeling."[86, 98]

However, before the book came out, Clinton would admit in several interviews that she was hesitant about change in the Arab country. These feelings, if anything, were not unexpected, as Mubarak had been an ally to both the United States and Israel for many years, and a new regime would certainly bring uncertainty at the very least to relations between the three key countries. In the end, Secretary Clinton ended up supporting the Obama administration's positon in encouraging change in Egypt. And at the end of that February, Egypt and the world saw that change as Mubarak stepped down. In June of 2012, Mohamed Morsi of the Muslim Brotherhood would be elected President of Egypt and would serve until the Egyptian coup of 2013 in which Morsi was removed from power for expansion and abuse of his presidential powers.[85]

Not long after protests began in Egypt, protests began in neighboring Libya. Unlike Tunisia and Egypt, protests in Libya quickly got out of hand as the regime of longtime dictator Muammar Gaddafi had no intention of relinquishing power. The protests quickly turned violent as government forces opened fire on protestors, and the protestors turned into rebellion fighters who would be fighting a long and bloody civil war for their freedom. In March of 2011, the United Nations Security Council approved a no fly zone in Libya and approved authorization for use of force to protect the citizens of Libya, whom the Human Rights Council had previously expelled and condemned for abuses. In August of 2011, Gaddafi was captured and killed in Libya, ending the war, but not ending Libya's struggles. To this day, the country still struggles, and is a hotbed for terrorism. Although the main role of the United States ended after Gaddafi was killed, the burden of Libya on the United States would continue for a few years to come.[81,83]

While the violence escalated in Libya, violence also started to appear in the Syrian Arab Republic a few countries away from the current focus point of the Arab Spring. The Assad family had been in power for many years, with Bashar al Assad the current leader who had taken over from his father, Hafez al Assad. Protests started peacefully against the Assad regime in March of 2011, but turned violent by the end of the year when the Assad regime started to push back against the protestors. These protestors then turned into armed rebel groups, thus turning the Syrian protests into the Arab Spring's largest civil war. The conflict still continues to date, with no signs of it slowing down anytime soon. The death toll today is unconfirmed, but many believe it to be over 200,000. Syria has also seen the growth of ISIS, the Islamic State in Iraq and Syria, which has become a major problem for the Obama administration and the international community.[81, 83]

In an interview in August of 2014, former Secretary Clinton expressed her disappointment that President Obama had not agreed to arm the moderate Syrian rebels sooner in the civil war. Time Magazine's Sam Frizell notes Clinton stated that:

"the failure to help build up a credible fighting force of the people who were the originators of the protests against Assad — there were Islamists, there were secularists, there was everything in the middle — the failure to do that left a big vacuum, which the jihadists have now filled."[89]

According to this, Secretary Clinton was strongly for arming the Syrian rebels, notably the Free Syrian Army at the time. However, the question posed by many was how much did we know about the Syrian rebels at the time? Here a few quotes to answer that question:

"And finally, moderate groups have often sold their weapons or had them seized by the jihadist elements led by ISIS. According to the Carnegie Endowment, There are no neat, clean, secular rebels groups. They don't exist. They reiterate that this is a "very dirty war" with no clear good guys for us to ally with. The German Ambassador to the U.S. has fully admitted what our State Department tries to hide - that we can't fully control the final destination of these arms. Former officials are more forthright with their criticism. According to a former U.S. Ambassador to Iraq and Syria, 'We need to do everything we can to figure out who the non-ISIS opposition, is...Frankly, we don't have a clue.' The rebels have been all over the map. There are said to be 1500 different rebel groups. The largest coalition other than ISIS, Al Quada and Al Nusra, all jihadist extremists, is the FSA-- which has three people who claim to be the leader. There are estimates that half of the FSA has defected… Intervention aided and abetted the rise of radical Islam and intervention made us less safe in Libya and Syria and Iraq." Kentucky Senator Rand Paul September 18, 2014.[90]

Not convinced by Senator Paul's marathon speech on the Senate floor? Here are remarks by West Virginia Senator Joe Manchin, a Democrat, who made similar remarks on the Senate floor the day before:

"I cannot and will not support arming or training the Syrian opposition forces… But most importantly I studied our history, We have been at war in that part of that world for the past 13 years. If money and military might could have made a difference, it would have by now… we will be involving ourselves in a ground conflict we cannot resolve… No one's convinced me that they can identify friend or foe in that part of the world right now."[92]

And finally, Representative Raul Labrador of Idaho, one of 71 Republicans who voted against arming the Syrian rebels, had this to say:

"While Assad is a brutal dictator, I still believe backing rebels allied with al-Qaeda and on the same side as ISIS in this civil war likely would bring to power even worse elements in Syria… Our focus should not be on resolving an age-old religious civil war, but on bringing to justice those who took the lives of our citizens."[91]

We could provide more and more examples, but the common theme would be the same, we simply do not know who the good guys or the bad guys are in this scenario. Although Secretary Clinton is in favor of arming the "moderate" rebels, she does not know exactly who those "moderate" rebels are. This shows us she truly hadn't been doing all she can as Secretary of State, and that should come across as concerning to all of us. Secretary Clinton had consistently through the Arab Spring backed the wrong side. Although it was difficult to tell exactly who was the right or wrong side (well there really wasn't one) Secretary Clinton has not backtracked on her statements to admit her previous observations were wrong.

Secretary Clinton's actions during the Arab Spring fall under political dishonesty due to her poor handling of the situation and the fact that she attempted to handle it in a more political way. However, the incidents at Benghazi transcend the other incidents during the Arab Spring, as four Americans were killed…

Benghazi- The Attack Itself

"I will not be a part of a political slugfest on the backs of dead Americans. It's just plain wrong, and it's unworthy of our great country. Those who insist on politicizing the tragedy will have to do so without me," Hillary Clinton *Hard Choices*[98]

There is no question that the investigation into the highly controversial September 11, 2012 Benghazi terrorist attacks has become politicized, but that does not take away from the fact that the matter should be investigated fully and without bias and hesitation.

We will not be able to answer all of the questions in this section as the investigation is still ongoing, but we know enough at this time to accurately write about Secretary Clinton's role in the events leading up, the events during, and the events after.

There are two key facts of the case that should tell us most of what we need to know about the Benghazi attacks at face value. The first is the timing of the attacks, September 11, 2012, which happened to be the 11th anniversary of the September 11, 2001 terrorist attacks. American officials have speculated and feared for years that terrorists would attempt to use the anniversary as the day for another attack, and have been amazed that it hadn't happened up until this point. Therefore the timing of the attack, which we will describe further on, should not have surprised anyone too much. The second is the location of the attacks. The attacks took place at the American special mission complex in Benghazi, Libya. Benghazi had been the stronghold of the Libyan rebels during the civil war to oust Qaddafi only a few years before. The city was starting to become slightly unstable again as the new government was having trouble establishing legitimacy in the country.

The first problem in discussing Benghazi is that the facts of the day of the attack itself are quite fuzzy. Most reports indicate that the US Ambassador to Libya, Christopher Stevens, was in Benghazi for a few days on a diplomatic mission. Stevens had been in Libya for a few years now, as he had worked before to attempt to assist the Libyans during the civil war to oust Qaddafi. Needless to say, Stevens was both well-known and well-liked by the Libyans. For our purposes, we will be using the timeline in the declassified *Report of the U.S. Senate Select Committee on Intelligence Review of the Terrorist Attacks on U.S. Facilities In Benghazi, Libya, September 11-12, 2012.* During the evening, Stevens had been meeting with a Turkish diplomat at the "Temporary Mission Facility" or "TMF" (it wasn't a full consulate or embassy). Reports indicate that the diplomat left around 8:30 PM, and Stevens was preparing to settle in for the night. However, shortly after the diplomat left, armed men started to surround the compound.[97]

The report states that the attack started around 9:40 PM Benghazi time. "Dozens of attackers" gained access to the TMF and began to set fire to the barracks of the Libyan 17th February Brigade militia, the very same group that was supposed to be protecting the TMF and Ambassador Stevens. At that time, a Diplomatic Security agent working at the TMF noticed the attackers and activated the notification system, alerting CIA personnel stationed at a nearby Annex, the other members of the Libyan 17th February Brigade, the US Embassy in Tripoli and the Diplomatic Security Command Center in Washington DC. As to personnel at the TMF at the time the report states

"There were five DS agents at the Mission compound that night. Two had traveled from Tripoli with U.S. Ambassador to Libya Christopher Stevens (who was staying at the Mission compound in Benghazi) and three others were assigned to the Mission facility. In addition to the five DS agents on duty, there were three armed members of the Libyan 17th February Brigade militia, three Libyan National Police officers, and five unarmed members of a local security team contracted through a British company, Blue Mountain Group… In addition, six armed CIA security personnel operating out of the nearby Annex were able to respond quickly after receiving word of the attack" (United States Senate Select Committee On Intelligence).[97]

Once the CIA Annex was informed of the attack, they prepared to send a security team over to help evacuate the compound. The report states that the team left "approximately 20-25 minutes after the first call came into the Annex" (United States Senate Select Committee On Intelligence). While this was going on, a DS agent had secured Ambassador Stevens and State Department

Information Management Officer Sean Smith in the "safe area" in the main building of the facility. However, the attackers were in the process of setting fire to the building, forcing the agent to find a way out for himself, Ambassador Stevens and Sean Smith. The agent was able to open a window and climb out while hoping to empty some smoke out of the building, however when he looked back Ambassador Stevens and Sean Smith were gone.

The other DS agents at the TMF had ran to one of the other buildings to acquire heavy arms but encountered the attackers on the way back, and had to take cover. After the team regrouped, they made their way to the main building to find Ambassador Stevens and Sean Smith. They were unable to find Ambassador Stevens, but they found Sean Smith deceased by the building.

The report also states that the members of the 17th February Brigade refused to engage the attackers, noting they wanted to "negotiate" instead. By that time, the CIA security team had arrived at the TMF, and was assisting in the search for the Ambassador. They were unfortunately not able to locate the Ambassador, and made the decision to leave under the assumption the Ambassador had already been captured. By 11:30 PM Benghazi time, the team left the TMF for the CIA Annex.

A little before midnight Benghazi time, the attackers began a sporadic assault on the CIA Annex. In the initial assault, the security team took no casualties, while they estimated that the attackers must have taken some. The report states that the attacks over the next hour or so were sporadic and small, and when the security team returned fire the attackers dispersed.

Around 1:15 AM Benghazi time, a seven man team arrived in Benghazi from Tripoli to assist in evacuating the remaining American personnel in Benghazi. However, they were held up at the airport while attempting to negotiate with the Libyan government.

During the three hour time span they spent negotiating, the team learned that Ambassador Steven's body had been dropped off at the Benghazi Medical Center. Once the team learned this information, they decided to head to the CIA Annex to assist in the evacuation of personnel there. They ended up leaving the airport around 4:30 AM.

By the time that the security team arrived at the Annex around 5:00 AM, a third attack was launched on the Annex. This time the attackers were using mortar rounds to strike the rooftops. At that time, two security officers, Tyrone Woods and Glen Doherty, were killed on the roof of the Annex due to the mortar fire. Two other agents were severely wounded, prompting the team to decide it was time to evacuate the facility. About an hour later, a heavily armed Libyan militia unit arrived to help evacuate the remaining personnel from the Annex. Around 10:00 AM Benghazi time, all US personnel were finally evacuating from Benghazi.[95, 97]

Leading Up

One of the biggest criticisms that people have with the handling of the Benghazi attacks is that there are reports that there was plenty of notice and/or warning signs that an attack on American interests in the region was imminent. Not only was there intelligence of attacks in the Middle East region, but there was also intelligence of potential attacks against Americans in Libya, and even more specifically Benghazi.

The mentioned Senate report identifies several other reports in which American intelligence officials warned of terrorists and extremists looking at Western targets in Libya. The first report they mentioned was by the Defense Intelligence Agency, and it was titled "Libya: Terrorists Now Targeting U.S. and Western Interests." The report stated "We expect more anti-U.S. terrorist attacks in eastern Libya." The report was released in early June.

Another report by the Pentagon's Joint Staff stated "Attacks will also increase in number and lethality as terrorists connect with AQ associates in Libya." Part of this report, as with the one stated before and even more so the one noted after, are blacked out and not available for public view.

The next report, this one from July 2, 2012, by the DIA discussed the founding of Ansar al-Sharia, the group connected to al Qaeda that would eventually claim responsibility for the Benghazi attack. This report is not available for public view.

On July 6, 2012, the CIA produced a report stating "Al-Qa'ida-affiliated groups and associates are exploiting the permissive security environment in Libya to enhance their capabilities and expand their operational reach." The report also mentions the term "safe haven" for parts of Eastern Libya. Notably, Benghazi is the northeastern part of Libya.

That is consistent with a report from AFRICOM produced on September 5, 2012 in which they state "The threat to Western and U.S. interests and individuals remains high, particularly in northeast-Libya."

These reports noted by the Senate Intelligence Report are only the beginning of the evidence of the growing threat in Benghazi. There were an increasing number of actual attacks on Western interests in Benghazi itself that gave rise to concerns that were not only visible, but expressed by Ambassador Stevens and Sean Smith before the attacks took place on September 11.

As for these direct threats themselves, the Senate report indicates that "there were at least 20 security incidents involving the Temporary Mission Facility, international organizations, non-governmental organizations and third-country nationals and diplomats in the Benghazi area in the months leading up to the

September 11, 2012 attacks." These are only a few examples of these "incidents"

On April 6, 2012 a small IED was thrown over the wall of the Temporary Mission facility.

On April 10, 2012 an explosive device was thrown at a convoy in Benghazi carrying the head of the UN mission to Libya.

On May 22, 2012 the International Committee of the Red Cross building in Benghazi was attacked with an RPG.

On June 6, 2012 an IED exploded near the main gate of the mission facility in Benghazi, creating a significantly sized hole in the wall.

On June 11, 2012, assailants attacked the British Ambassador's convoy with RPGs and AK-47's, the Ambassador was not hurt but two security officers were. The British then end all diplomatic missions in Libya.

On July 29, 2012, a number of IEDs are found at a hotel in Benghazi that is frequented by foreign diplomats. It was also used as a base of operations previously by Ambassador Stevens.

These are only a handful of events that took place in Benghazi, Libya in the months leading up to September. There were other incidents targeted at Westerners across Libya, including in Benghazi, during the year 2012. So if the intelligence community knew all of this was happening, why didn't they have a better response? The British pulled out of Libya after the attack on their Ambassador's convoy, so why wasn't that evidence enough to do something to step up security? These are questions that remain unanswered, even as the evidence piles up.

The Senate report indicates that Ambassador Stevens himself submitted at least three different reports to the U.S. government raising concerns over the increasing violence in Benghazi and Libya, and asked for additional security for Americans in Benghazi. The Senate report also indicates that the ARB, the Accountability Review Board, reported that the government found it difficult to figure out who exactly was responsible for adding additional security in Benghazi. The report indicated that some security changes were made, but these changes were miniscule, and none were made to add personnel, which is what the original request from Ambassador Stevens was for.[97]

Looking at the numbers, the number of Diplomatic Security agents and CIA officers present in Benghazi during the attack also seems to be low given the circumstances. The Senate report indicated that there were five Diplomatic Security agents at the Mission compound on the night of the attack, with nine security officers at the CIA Annex. With the Ambassador in town, and threats growing every day, it seems like more emphasis would be placed on security for the trip. To this day we really aren't sure why more security wasn't added as the question was never actually answered.

The other fact that makes us question the lack of security during the attack was the timing of the strike. The attack occurred on September 11, 2012, 11 years after the horrible attacks in 2001. Intelligence reports that were released beforehand suggested that terrorists around the world were looking for ways to strike Western targets on September 11. A strike on the anniversary of 9/11 would be a significant propaganda victory for jihadist groups associated with al-Qaeda. In the end, these very same groups, including al-Qaeda and Ansar al-Sharia, hailed the attacks as a victory. It is hard to understand why the United States was not prepared for an attack on American interests on that specific day.[97]

Questions Regarding Day Of[97]

At this point, the only thing that no one truly disputes is the timeline of events regarding the attack itself. Otherwise, most everything else regarding the day of is in dispute, starting with why the attack occurred, and going to why was the official response to the attack so late. We will start by looking at the controversy regarding the response time and the official response from the U.S. government. The issues of a military response would need to be covered under another section(although you could make the argument both Secretary Clinton and President Obama should have been involved in making a decision on a military response to rescue those left in Benghazi). The long story short of that is the Senate report claims that there weren't sufficient military resources ready to respond in a timely manner to make a significant difference.

One of the most disturbing parts of the Benghazi attack was the response from Washington. We still remember that very day sitting in the doctor's office and receiving a "Breaking News" text alert from CNN about an attack at a U.S. consulate in Benghazi, Libya. We firmly believed right at that moment that it was an organized terrorist attack. The timing, the location and the details given led right to the assumption that it could have only been a terrorist attack. However, this was not as apparent to leaders in Washington, especially ones working in the White House and State Department.

There are still a lot of unanswered questions regarding the actions taken by President Obama, Secretary Clinton and others on the day of the Benghazi attack. The Senate Intelligence Report and other sources of information fail to identify any sort of action taken by either on that day. Several reports detail the actions of Secretary of Defense Leon Panetta, who made moves to send more support to be in the region in case there were any further attacks. The only thing publically released regarding Secretary Clinton's actions or comments on that day was this statement:

"Some have sought to justify this vicious behavior as a response to inflammatory material posted on the Internet. The United States deplores any intentional effort to denigrate the religious beliefs of others. Our commitment to religious tolerance goes back to the very beginning of our nation. But let me be clear: There is never any justification for violent acts of this kind."[96]

Secretary Clinton's statement was in reference to the acts in Benghazi, linked to an anti-Islamic video released a few days before on YouTube. This video would become the subject of controversy over the next few weeks, and even months, after the attack. Several government officials, including Secretary Clinton and President Obama would begin to denounce the actions of the video, while avoiding implicating the actions of terrorists in the attack.

Protested Video or Organized Attack?

There is no question that a few days before the Benghazi attack there was a derogatory video making fun of the religion of Islam uploaded to YouTube. The video, however, was posted and created by one individual, and had no support, help or endorsement from the United States government. The curious thing is that no one from the United States government acknowledged the existence of this video until the Benghazi attacks, which made many question what the government was blaming the violence on. This would cause controversy itself, as many would claim the United States government was directly blaming the video for "inciting violence." Comments made by Secretary Clinton, as shown in the previous section, and other comments made by President Obama and other members of the administration including Susan Rice in the days after the attack would add to this confusion, as expected.[100]

The Senate Intelligence Report attempts to also address this issue. The report attempts to answer the question regarding the possibility of demonstrations before the attacks started. The Report is able to disprove this claim. "On September 18, 2012, the FBI and CIA reviewed the closed circuit television video from the Mission facility that showed there were no protests prior to the attacks." The Intelligence Report also makes the recommendation that the Intelligence Community improve its information gathering and reporting due to this erroneous information. The poor information flow would only continue as it is used more and more by government officials over the next few days.[97]

The two officials who would continue to constantly avoid the terms "terrorist attack" or "organized attack" were Press Secretary Jay Carney and current National Security advisor Susan Rice. Rice had appearances on several talk shows in which she talked about the "hateful video." She told CNN's Candy Crowley:

"There was a hateful video that was disseminated on the Internet. It had nothing to do with the United States government, and it's one that we find disgusting and reprehensible. It's been offensive to many, many people around the world. That sparked violence in various parts of the world, including violence directed against Western facilities including our embassies and consulates."[100]

Rice then told CBS' "Face The Nation" that "We do not have information at present that leads us to conclude that this was premeditated or preplanned."

Hillary Clinton would be the very first public official, on September 20, to admit that the government felt the Benghazi attack was indeed, an organized terrorist attack. However, President Obama and other officials would still wait a full day before fully declaring it a pre-planned, organized terrorist attack. By October, they were stating it was a pre-planned attack.

So why was there such a mix up right away? Given all of the information, why weren't our officials, including Secretary Clinton, confident in giving a statement that this was a terrorist attack? There was plenty of evidence showing that the events were indeed an attack. The State Department allegedly knew the day of the attack that Ansar al-Sharia took responsibility for the attack, and that they were being praised by other groups such as al-Qaeda. Other past events in Benghazi showed that the area was a hot zone for terrorism and that attacks were likely. We will take the next section to describe how this affects Hillary Clinton specifically.

Secretary Clinton's Role- Or Lack Thereof

"It's 3 a.m. and your children are safe and asleep. But there's a phone in the White House and it's ringing. Something's happening in the world. Your vote will decide who answers that call, whether it's someone who already knows the world's leaders, knows the military — someone tested and ready to lead in a dangerous world. It's 3 a.m. and your children are safe and asleep. Who do you want answering the phone?" Hillary Clinton 2008 Campaign Ad[101]

Unfortunately, we still have some serious questions for Secretary Clinton regarding her role to responding to the Benghazi attacks. Where was she the day of the attacks? Was she trying to contact world leaders to ask for cooperation? Was she contacting the Libyan government to attempt to clear the way for U.S. military personnel to rescue Americans if necessary? Perhaps most importantly, why were all of the other requests for support previously unanswered. The Benghazi attacks and Secretary Clinton's role in the events surrounding the attacks are in this work because of those very questions. In 2008 Mrs. Clinton claimed she would answer the infamous 3 AM call. She had an opportunity with the Benghazi attack, and it appears she did not do so.

Because Christopher Stevens was an Ambassador, the State Department should have handled his requests for more security in Libya. The State Department also should have been aware of what was going on in the region, and coming up with ways to attempt to protect Americans there. However, it became apparent in hearings after the Benghazi attack that Mrs. Clinton did not respond to these requests. It is even possible that Mrs. Clinton never saw these requests. This is still not an excuse. We want a Secretary of State who is communication with our Ambassadors, all of them, no matter which country they are in. Isn't that the role of the Secretary of State? The Secretary of State should be reachable by the Ambassador to Mexico, or the Ambassador to Egypt, especially when there is a deteriorating situation in the country.

Mrs. Clinton clearly set a poor example in the lead up to the attacks, and the response after. Secretary Clinton should have been more aware of what was going on, and should have found a way to keep the Ambassador and others safe. She is not directly responsible for the deaths of Christopher Stevens, Sean Smith, Glen Doherty and Tyrone Woods, but she bears some blame for the failure to keep them safe that is on the United States government.

The actions taken after the attack, especially during the investigative process have also been quite poor from Secretary Clinton. Several investigations have already been launched regarding Benghazi, and several government committees in the House and the Senate have investigated and have held hearings. Secretary Clinton testified in one of those hearings to the Senate Foreign Relations Committee in January of 2013. A good portion of the testimony was back and forth between Secretary Clinton and Senate Republicans. Here are some of the most telling lines from her testimony:[103]

Senator Ron Johnson: "Madam Secretary, do you disagree with me that a simple phone call to those evacuees to determine what happened wouldn't have ascertained immediately that there was no protest… We were misled that there were supposedly protests and that an assault sprang out of that…"

Secretary Clinton: "…With all due respect, the fact is we have four dead Americans, was it because of a protest or was it because of a few guys out for a walk one night who decided they would go kill some Americans, what difference at this point does it make? It is our job to figure out what happened and do everything we can to prevent it from ever happening again Senator…"

Senator Rand Paul: "Had I been President at the time and I found that you did not read the cables from Benghazi, you did not read the cables from Ambassador Stevens, I would have relieved you of your post. I think it's inexcusable. I would think by anybody's estimation Libya has to have been one of the hottest of hot spots in the world… Their lives could have been saved had someone been more available.

Secretary Clinton: "…The ARB made very clear that the level of responsibility for the failures that they outlined was set at the Assistant Secretary level and below…"

Senator John McCain: "Four months after the Benghazi tragedy, there are many questions that are unanswered. And the answers that you have given this morning are not satisfactory to me… We didn't have a single Department of Defense asset apparently available to come to the rescue…"

Secretary Clinton: "…And we just have a disagreement in regards to the events…"

These were only some of the interactions between Senate Republicans and Secretary Clinton. There will likely be more controversial moments to come since Secretary Clinton last testified, as she will be testifying in front of the newly formed Select Committee on Benghazi, headed by South Carolina Congressman Trey Gowdy. Gowdy has already subpoenaed Clinton's emails regarding Benghazi and has requested her to testify in front of the committee. She has agreed, and will be testifying sometime in the future, the exact time is unknown as she has also declared her candidacy for President of the United States for the 2016 election cycle.[103]

Email Scandal

Since Representative Gowdy and the Benghazi Committee subpoenaed Secretary Clinton's emails, another scandal has emerged. It was uncovered that while Clinton was at the State Department, she was not using a secure government email; she was using her own personal email account. This was a strong cause of concern for many, as many believed that this would not be safe or smart. If the server is in Clinton's house, it is not secured by the government, which made many believe that it would be easy for the email account to be hacked.

Many have begun to question the legality of Clinton's use of a private email account during her tenure as Secretary of State, and the potential dangers it poses to national security. The government is constantly trying to ensure that states like North Korea, Russia and China are unable to hack our systems, which we know they are trying to do on a daily basis. It is hard enough to keep government servers safe, nonetheless a private server that the government doesn't know about, but government business is being conducted on it. Besides the fact that if a rouge state or a terrorist group were able to successfully access this information and steal it, TheBlaze's Chris Salcedo brings up another point in his piece on TheBlaze.com titled *Hillary's server: It's not just about her hiding things from the American people.* Salcedo notes towards the end "Not only do officials stress over foreign enemies gathering intelligence off the server, they also fret that they could have changed official documents that would have provided false data that caused then-Secretary of State Clinton to act on faulty information"(Salcedo). If something like this were to ever happen, the results could be disastrous, but the government may not even be able to realize such an impact for years to come.[104]

Again we point out that we do not believe Secretary Clinton meant to be misleading, but her negligence has again caused issues that we do believe need to be addressed.

Another concern came up when congressional leaders realized that Secretary Clinton did not hand over all of the emails sent during her tenure as Secretary of State. An article from Breitbart notes:

“Clinton supposedly turned over about 30,000 emails (totaling 55,000 pages) to State Department officials. But earlier this month, Clinton also admitted that she ‘chose not to keep her private, personal emails that were not federal records,’ which means that of the nearly 60,000 emails Clinton sent or received through her private server, approximately 32,000 other messages may have been withheld or deleted(Fitton).”[109]

Why did Secretary Clinton pick and choose which emails to send to the investigation? Judicial Watch is attempting to have that questioned answered by subpoenaing the rest of the emails. Secretary Clinton will likely also face these same questions by the Benghazi Committee, as they were the ones who started the investigation into the emails.

There are also reports that Secretary Clinton’s server was actually destroyed as well. That would also raise a certain amount of suspicions and questions that would need to be answered during the course of the investigation. At this point, the investigation could lead anywhere. The only thing that people know is that Secretary Clinton has a significant amount of questions to answer due to all of the suspicious activity surrounding these emails.

Now fast forward to the summer of 2015, where the scandal has only gotten worse for Secretary Clinton. In late July and early August of 2015, the FBI announced that they would be looking into the email scandal, and requested Secretary Clinton to turn over the email server. Currently the FBI is looking through the server for potentially classified emails, and the potential for security breaches to the server. Leaks throughout July and August of 2015 verified that classified information was indeed found on Secretary Clinton's server, and that some information that was requested by those investigating the server and the Benghazi attacks was not turned over properly when first requested. Not all of the classified data that was said to be found on the server was discussed, but some reports indicated that there was one or two emails that were deemed "top secret." This has not been completely verified.

Another concern is whether Secretary Clinton was the one who even sent the emails in question, or if she just received them, and those sending the emails didn't realize it was Secretary Clinton's private server they sent it to. This also has not yet been verified, as the FBI is still looking through all of the information. This would lessen the potential of wrongdoing with Secretary Clinton, but would raise more concerns over the safety of the information passed through the server.

An article by the Washington Post in early October of 2015 mentions that the FBI is now looking into a second private technology security company to see if they also had copies of the data they had protected for Secretary Clinton. Along with the FBI, Senate and House committees are also looking into the server, with the main goal of attempting to see if there were breaches that may compromise national security. Reports had come out that there had at least been attempts to breach the server, but there has been no confirmation on whether or not the server was actually breached and if top secret or classified material got into the wrong hands.

Also interesting is the continuing work of the House Select Committee on Benghazi in regards to the Clinton emails. The committee is continuing to look through the emails attempting to see if there is anything relating to the Benghazi attacks and Clinton's role in the response. The chairman of the committee, Representative Trey Gowdy, recently came out and stated that at least one email by a Clinton aide revealed the name of a CIA confidant working in Libya. This raises continued concerns of whether or not classified information was passed through the server or not.[105, 106, 107, 108]

The investigation is ongoing, but recent rumors suggest that Secretary Clinton has been given the advice to seek counsel to help her through the remainder of the investigation.

Out Of Touch

There is no question that a good number of Americans know who Hillary Clinton is. Of course, how could they not? She was the First Lady for eight years in the 1990s, and then was a Senator in New York for another few years until she ran for President in 2008. Even after that, Clinton stayed in the public eye as Secretary of State for a few years, and has reappeared in the spotlight not only as A Presidential candidate, but THE Democratic Presidential candidate. Many do not see a strong alternative to Clinton in the Democratic Party at this time, and many wonder if anyone will even step in to challenge her.

A poll conducted in the summer of 2014 just begins to describe how well known Secretary Clinton is. According to the poll, 91% of respondents were "familiar" with Clinton. This should come as no surprise to anyone; it would make sense for her to be almost as well known as the President of the United States.

With this familiarity, Secretary Clinton has attempted in the past to come across as in touch with the American people. Even with her new campaign video in which she announced her candidacy for

President for the 2016 election cycle, Clinton attempted to come across as in touch with the people. However, as hard as she has tried, Mrs. Clinton has not actually come across as in touch with the American people. And to be honest, there is no way she can. It's simple, she is one of the most famous public figures in the country right now, and she is not like the average American.

Mrs. Clinton really proved this in the summer of 2014 when she responded to a question by ABC News' Diane Sawyer. Sawyer told Clinton "It has been reported you've made $5 million making speeches, the President's made more than $100 million." (Referring to Bill Clinton). And Hillary Clinton's response was "you have no reason to remember, but we came out of the White House not only dead broke, but in debt. We had no money when we got there and we struggled to, you know, piece together the resources for mortgages for houses, for Chelsea's education, you know, it was not easy." It is hard to believe that the Clintons actually came out of the White House dead broke. Bill Clinton made over $300,000 a year while he was President, and the couple paid maybe $100,000 of that per year in taxes, at most.[110]

As Sawyer points out, the two would then go on and make a great deal of money through speeches. Hillary Clinton also launched her bid for Senate while still at the White House, and therefore was able to start her term right after Bill Clinton's second term was over. Therefore, the Clintons had a very steady source of income right after they left the White House. We reject the notion that the Clintons were "dead broke" when they left the White House. Hillary Clinton herself even states she rejects making these comments. However, she also then disproves her notion that she can be considered to be in touch with everyday Americans. Clinton will do more damage to her reputation by making statements like the "dead broke" one and attempting to show people she is something she is not rather than coming out and being truthful with the people.

Conclusion

Hillary Clinton begins the list of officials who are in various ways still up for re-election, or will be running for an election in some way. As mentioned before, Clinton has declared her candidacy for President, and she is now fully responsible to the voters. Some lawmakers, notably Kentucky Senator Rand Paul, have declared that Clinton should be ineligible to run for higher office due to her negligence during her time as Secretary of State, especially regarding Benghazi. That is something that the people will have to decide for themselves. However, this is something that the people are likely to hear quite a bit over the next few months as the campaign goes into full swing.

Clinton's negligence regarding the Benghazi attacks is something to consider when it comes to the election. We laid out the facts of what happened, the responses given, and how certain officials, notably Clinton, reacted. I firmly believe that Secretary Clinton had a hand in misleading the public not because they were attempting to cover up the deaths of four Americans, but because the government did not want to be found negligent in not properly protecting Americans abroad. Mrs. Clinton's remark during the Senate hearing of "what difference at this point does it make" gives us a glimpse into her real character. Four Americans are dead, Mrs. Clinton, and the families themselves don't feel they have received a proper explanation. That's the difference it makes.

Mrs. Clinton's negligence to speak out during the Arab Spring against the radical Islamist groups rising across the Middle East is also something to take into account. By sticking with the administration, whether she agreed with them or not, Mrs. Clinton helped to set a bad example, that America must pick a side and it must be the side that makes them look the best. That clearly did not work in Libya, Egypt or Syria, as all three turned out to be disastrous.

Also concerning is the scandal regarding Clinton's emails. Some have brought up the point if she can't handle two emails, how can she handle being President? It is a fair question to ask, and one that she needs to answer, and answer it soon. The scandal only seems to be continuing, and the Secretary will not be able to get through the 2016 election cycle without answering a good amount of questions regarding the situation.

Of course we expect most politicians to lie, but some of the lies Mrs. Clinton have told are completely unnecessary. The Bosnia shooting story was unnecessary, and the "dead broke" comments were highly misleading. Mrs. Clinton's lies have been to show she is in touch with the average American, but she clearly is not.

Overall, Hillary Clinton is now at the mercy of the American people. If they find her to be a strong, trustworthy leader, she will be elected President of the United States in 2016. However, if many people see what we have seen, they will be concerned about the direction Clinton would lead us in. We do not believe Mrs. Clinton has set a good example, and she will not continue to in the future. She was given a big role in government, and was negligent in her duties. It will now be up to the American people to decide if she gets another chance. In our view, she is dishonest, and sets a poor example for the American people.

I guess the people will have their decision made by November of 2016.

IV. Andrew Cuomo

New York State Governor Andrew Cuomo represents our wild card case for this edition. Although Cuomo is not in a direct leadership position within the Democratic Party, Governor Cuomo has expressed interested in higher office in the past. It is looking more and more unlikely that he will be running for President in 2016, but he could be a part of a Democratic administration if a Democrat wins in 2016, or he could seek the nomination in the future if a Democrat does not win the Presidency in 2016. However,

Governor Cuomo's uncertain future does not exclude his dishonesty or the actions he has taken over time.

Most of the evidence as to why Governor Cuomo is on this list comes from his time as Governor of New York, a title in which he still holds. Governor Cuomo has made several controversial acts that will be discussed, and it will be explained as to why this not only disqualifies Governor Cuomo from higher office in the future, but could also be grounds for a criminal indictment in the coming years.

Early Years[111, 112, 113]

Andrew Mark Cuomo was born on December 6, 1957 in New York City to Mario Cuomo, who would eventually be elected Governor of New York, and Matilda Cuomo. Cuomo would grow up in New York City, and graduate from Fordham University in 1979. Cuomo then went onto Albany Law School where he earned his Juris Doctorate in 1982.

During Cuomo's time in law school, he worked on his father's campaign for Governor of New York. After Mario Cuomo won the election, and Andrew Cuomo graduated from Albany, Andrew began working for his father. A few years later, Cuomo began working as an assistant district attorney in New York. During that time, Cuomo founded HELP, the Housing Enterprise for Less Privileged, in order to help the poor and homeless. This organization was able to help build and provide low income housing across New York. This led to Cuomo's appointment by New York City Mayor David Dinkins in 1991 to lead the New York City Commission on the Homeless.

In 1993, Cuomo was appointed the assistant Secretary of the Department of Housing and Urban Development under President Bill Clinton. In 1997, following the resignation of the Secretary of the department, Cuomo was appointed Secretary for the rest of

Clinton's term. According to Cuomo's personal website, Cuomo was able to clean up the HUD Department by ridding it of waste and fraud, while making it a powerful tool for economic development. Cuomo also earned the "Innovations in American Government" Award from the Ford Foundation for his work at the Department of Housing and Urban Development. Cuomo also worked to bring around 2,000 discrimination cases across the country to light during his time as HUD Secretary.

Cuomo faced heavy criticisms during his time as HUD Secretary as well. Critics today will point out that the subprime mortgage crisis started during Cuomo's time as HUD Secretary, and that he did not do enough to attempt to avert a crisis. Another criticism pointed out is that Cuomo was not Clinton's first choice to take over the department. Clinton's first choice, Seattle Mayor Norm Rice, was investigated by the HUD over false allegations during the time period. Rice was later cleared, but not until President Clinton picked Cuomo as Secretary. Other reports noted that Cuomo did not get along with the department's inspector general, Susan Gaffney. Gaffney's audits found mismanagement by Cuomo and the department, but Cuomo retaliated by launching a smear campaign against Gaffney, which appeared to work as the information never came to light.[114]

Cuomo and the HUD department also advocated for the mortgage groups Freddie Mac and Fannie Mae to purchase higher volumes of risky loans to offer to less accredited buyers. Although the Cuomo administration did not directly push this idea through, this idea was then discovered to be disastrous during the Bush administration. Cuomo was also known for pushing for federal subsidies and regulations, like his predecessor had before him. However, Cuomo would not be as criticized for these moves as he was only in his position for under 3 years as George W. Bush and the Republican Party won the 2000 Presidential election.[115]

First Campaign as Governor

After Andrew Cuomo left his position as Secretary of HUD, he announced he would run for Governor of New York State, challenging the Republican incumbent George Pataki. Cuomo would be ahead of his Democratic opponent for most of the election, up until he made a gaffe regarding Pataki's handling of the September 11, 2001 terrorist attacks on New York City. Cuomo stated "Pataki stood behind the leader. He held the leader's coat." Cuomo was widely criticized for this statement, and was even forced to drop out of the race as his poll numbers plummeted. Even so, Cuomo was trailing Governor Pataki in the polls, similar to the other Democratic candidate. Pataki would end up winning re-election, and Cuomo would take a step back from the public light for a few years.[111]

Cuomo's Comeback- Attorney General to Governor

After stepping back from the public spotlight for a few years, Andrew Cuomo announced that he would be running for New York State Attorney General in 2006 under Gubernatorial candidate Eliot Spitzer. Cuomo won both the Democratic nomination and the general election handily in 2006, receiving 65% of the vote in the Primary and 58% in the general election. Many considered this to be a significant comeback for Cuomo, especially since in most states the position of Attorney General is generally seen as a precursor to running for Governor.

Cuomo's tenure as Attorney General was relatively quiet on his part. The only true difficulty Cuomo had was when it was discovered that Governor Eliot Spitzer had asked the New York State Police to keep records on New York State Senate Majority Leader Joseph Bruno. Even then, Cuomo called out Governor Spitzer for these actions, and the Governor issued a public apology. Cuomo was also accredited for taking part in efforts to investigate poor student loan practices and internet usage regarding child pornography.

Cuomo was relatively quiet during Governor Eliot Spitzer's controversies. This is likely due to the fact that Governor Spitzer resigned rather quickly, and a thorough investigation was not necessary. After Spitzer stepped down, his Lieutenant Governor, David Paterson, took over as Governor. Paterson's tenure as Governor was short and relatively unsuccessful. Paterson was not popular in the state, and was marred in several scandals before he could even announce his plans to run for re-election. Paterson did attempt to run for re-election, but was convinced to drop his campaign by President Barack Obama. In response to this, Attorney General Andrew Cuomo picked up the mantle and declared his candidacy for Governor in May of 2008.

The 2010 Gubernatorial election was not a difficult one for Cuomo. Since 2002, New York State as a whole had become more liberal and therefore more likely to support a Democrat for Governor. Cuomo faced no challengers in the Democratic Party, while his eventual opponent for the general election, Carl Paladino, faced several Republican challengers. Paladino was well supported by his home city of Buffalo and the surrounding areas, and was well backed by the Tea Party Movement.

Cuomo campaigned heavily on changing the current status of New York. Cuomo campaigned against poor budgets, corruption in Albany and the continued increasing of spending by the state legislatures. Cuomo promised to "clean up Albany" and change how the state works for New Yorkers. At one point, Cuomo even noted that "New York doesn't work" but that he was the man to fix it.[117]

In the end, Cuomo easily won the election, winning a majority of the counties in the state, including those in New York City. Cuomo defeated Paladino by almost thirty percent, 63.05% to

33.53%. This came as little surprise to many in the state, as Cuomo had been the favorite since the moment Paterson dropped out of the race. The former HUD Secretary had completed quite the comeback, but no one was certain if he was done yet, or if he planned to run for higher office. His actions as Governor would certainly provide more answers to this question.

Governor Andrew Cuomo, 2011-Present

Although Governor Cuomo promised to personally clean up Albany, the Cuomo administration has been marred with problems and scandals from day one. Cuomo has become well known in the state for supporting a downstate mentality that is focusing on Albany, Westchester County and New York City, while ignoring a good portion of the rest of the state, Upstate New York in particular. There has long been the idea that most lawmakers only do what they can for New York City, and that they don't care about the rest of the state. They believe New York City is where all of the money and influence comes from, and the rest of the state is to be ignored. To be fair, even outsiders have this view. When you tell someone you are from New York, they often assume New York City, while forgetting the dozens of other cities, towns and counties north of Westchester County including Buffalo, Rochester, Binghamton, Syracuse, Utica and Watertown. (Similar complaints were made of Hillary Clinton when she was elected to the United States Senate). This divide is more evident in the 2014 gubernatorial election, which is to be explained later.

We must also look at the makeup of the legislature at the time of Governor Cuomo's election. The State Assembly Speaker at the time was Sheldon Silver, who represented Lower Manhattan. The Senate Majority Leader was Dean Skelos, who represented parts of Long Island. Since then, both have been removed, only to be replaced by other leaders from New York City. This contributes to the animosity most have towards the current administration in Albany.

Cuomo's first year as Governor was quite busy, as he went straight to work on his campaign promises. One of Cuomo's first major pieces of legislation was the Marriage Equality Act in New York State. The Marriage Equality Act legalized same sex marriage in the State of New York. The bill was passed by the state Senate and signed by Governor Cuomo on June 24, 2011. Many applauded the passage of the bill and its intentions, but there were many accusations that Cuomo's actions during the lobbying of the bill were brash, at times hinting that those who did not support his bill would not be supported in the future.[120]

Even more telling is Cuomo's rhetoric after the passage of the bill. In a statement released the night he signed the bill, Cuomo stated "The other states look to New York for the progressive direction…What we said today is, you look to New York once again. New York made a powerful statement, not just for the people of New York, but for people all across this nation." Cuomo's rhetoric suggests someone who wants to be noticed, someone who wants to take credit, not just someone who did something he believed was the right thing to do. This wouldn't be the first time Cuomo made similar comments, and it certainly wouldn't be the last.[120]

Cuomo's harsh tactics with other lawmakers was also seen with his tax code restructuring bill. The bill was to change New York's tax code, including increasing taxes on wealthier earners. During the debate, members of the State Assembly claimed that Cuomo threatened the lawmakers who were planning to vote against the measure, claiming Cuomo specifically told them he would campaign against whoever voted against his bill. The reports could not be verified, as the sources spoke anonymously, but the evidence of such tactics would continue to grow during Cuomo's tenure as Governor.[121]

In the eyes of liberals and progressives, Cuomo has been a strong Governor for the state of New York. Many of them like his no bull attitude that has allowed him to get bills such as Same Sex Marriage and the tax code restructuring done. However, some of Cuomo's other actions as Governor have been more heavily criticized. Some of these more controversial subjects include the SAFE Act, the Moreland Commission, the handling of Hurricane Sandy, New York's Common Core, the fracking debate and Start Up New York. All are to be discussed in the next section.

Controversies- Hurricane Sandy

One of the most underestimated situations that can have a lasting impact on a politician's reputation is that of a severe storm in a densely populated area. So we learned with Hurricane Sandy in both New York and New Jersey. New Jersey was arguably harder hit than New York, but the fact that New York City was impacted by a hurricane drew significant national attention. However, with national attention came both national funds and national criticism. President Obama and Congress would eventually approve billions of dollars in aid to New York and New Jersey to attempt to repair their states, but it would be up to the states to use that money properly.

The first issue that Governor Cuomo ran into was the creation of a "Superstorm Sandy Command Post" in Manhattan. A report regarding the reaction to Hurricane Sandy noted that there was already an emergency response group and command post in Albany, but creating another in New York City only stretched resources even more, notably personnel. This same report, cited in an article by James Odato with timesunion.com, notes that the creation of other reports by the state itself was also costly, and took needed financial resources away from dealing with the storm damages.[123]

Although the total costs are still not yet known, as efforts to rebuild are still ongoing, Cuomo's first estimate to Congress was around $33 billion, according to the New York Times. The final costs are likely to be significantly higher.[122]

In 2014 Cuomo's Republican opponent for Governor, Rob Astorino, also ripped the Governor for the use of Hurricane Sandy funds for television ads promoting the state of New York. Astorino claimed the ads were a misuse of funds, and instead should be going to the victims whose property was damaged during the storm. Cuomo's campaign responded by stating Congress did allow the Governor to use the funds to promote tourism to the state.[125]

Overall, this would be one of the Governor's smallest headaches, a talking point for Astorino during the 2014 gubernatorial election. Governor Cuomo would have far worse scandals to deal with throughout his administration than this.

New York State SAFE Act

On December 14, 2012, a gunman opened fire at the elementary school in Newtown, Connecticut, killing 20 children and 6 adults in the single deadliest grade school shooting in US history, second only overall to the Virginia Tech shootings in 2007. As expected, this sparked controversy and debate over gun control laws in the United States, and led many lawmakers to begin taking sides over the debate. While the public debate went on over both the legality of potential gun control restrictions and the sense of potential restrictions, Governor Andrew Cuomo went to work in New York to create new restrictions of his own in the progressive state.

On January 15, 2013, Governor Andrew Cuomo signed the Secure Ammunition and Firearms Enforcement Act of 2013, after it had been passed by the state Senate and Assembly. Cuomo would tout the SAFE Act, as it would be now called, as the "toughest gun law in the nation." Cuomo would also note that New York was the first state since Sandy Hook to pass such laws, and that he hoped other states would follow in the footsteps of New York. What Cuomo did not directly point out, however, is that the SAFE Act quickly became the most restrictive gun laws in the nation.[126, 128]

During Cuomo's State of the State Address in the days before, the Governor laid out this "seven point plan" essentially laying the groundwork for the SAFE Act:

"Number 1: Enact the toughest assault weapon ban in the nation period.

Number 2: Close the private sale loophole by requiring federal background checks.

Number 3: Ban high-capacity magazines.

Number 4: Enact tougher penalties for illegal gun use, guns on school grounds and violent gangs.

Number 5: Keep guns from people who are mentally ill.

Number 6: Ban direct internet sales of ammunition in New York.

Number 7: Create a State NICS check on all ammunition purchases."[133]

Each and every point made would be a heavy point of contention in New York, notably from conservatives, Republicans and the National Rifle Association. Though some of the points do not sound too contentious in this case, they would come out even more so in the law itself. Here are some of the main points of the passed law, though some have been subject to change.[127]

The definition of "assault weapon" was significantly expanded under the law, and now included any weapon that has a folding stock, a pistol grip or any other secondhand grip held by the non-shooting hand, a flash suppressor, or a bayonet mount, just among some of the examples. The New York State Police have a full listing of what is officially now banned.[131]

Any firearm that holds more than seven bullets was also banned under the new law. Seven bullets. The reasoning for this by Governor Cuomo was "no one needs ten bullets to kill a deer, no one hunts with an assault rifle." However, this provision of the law was recently struck down by a court in New York State, and is no longer valid. Common sense also forced the expiration of that part of the law, as there are no magazines that are designed to hold only seven bullets.

Another contested part of the SAFE Act was the database of registered assault weapons to be created in New York State. This would allow for background checks in the state to check the record of any gun owner to see if they are eligible for the purchase of certain firearms. The database would be kept and run by the State Police in New York.

Also contested was the mental health section of the law. This section of the law would require mental health professionals to submit to the state the records of anyone they felt should be disqualified from owning a firearm due to a mental health reason. Many have found this to be a significant invasion of privacy, and unfair to those who have been improperly diagnosed. Such a case was noted last year when a Navy veteran and retired police officer was told he needed to turn in his firearms when he was diagnosed with insomnia. The Navy veteran is fighting in the courts to get the Mental Hygiene portion of the law struck down. The veteran claims he was erroneously written down as an "involuntary" patient at the hospital, although he went there himself to seek treatment.[134, 135]

Another main criticism of the SAFE Act was its quick and sudden passage. Most critics note the SAFE Act was passed in the Senate in the middle of the night, with very little debate and little room for any possible amendments. The SAFE Act was then passed by the Assembly and signed into law by Governor Cuomo the very next day. In Cuomo's State of the State Address a few days earlier, he mentioned future gun legislation, but never addressed the SAFE Act by name and did not state it was coming up for a vote in the Senate in the coming days. Cuomo claims that he used the "message of necessity" to bypass normal debate procedures to get the law passed quickly, to ensure public safety and protections. Most critics still do not accept this point and claim it was unfair to pass such a restrictive law in such a restrictive manner.[128]

The SAFE Act however has run into a few legal challenges since its passage, but not as many as critics had hoped. Lawsuits were filed almost immediately after the public revealing of the SAFE Act, as many groups challenged the constitutionality of the SAFE Act. In December of 2013, Judge William Skretney of Federal District Court in Buffalo rendered his ruling on the case, striking down only the seven round limit, stating it was an "'arbitrary restriction' that violated the second amendment," according to an article by the New York Times.[136]

This however, has not kept lawmakers and everyday citizens from attempting to challenge the law through the political process. In the 2014 gubernatorial election in New York, Republican Rob Astorino ran on the promise of repealing the SAFE Act if elected. Although Astorino was not elected, current lawmakers have also made steps in scaling back the SAFE Act. New York's new Senate Majority Leader, John Flanagan, has also noted his interested in scaling back parts of the controversial law.

While lawmakers have debated the legality, businesses in New York are feeling the pinch. Several gun manufacturers, including Remington Arms, American Tactical Imports and Kahr Arms have all considered moving out of New York due to the restrictive laws. As of right now, none of them have made the official move, but plans have been discussed for the moves and steps have been made.

Some of the other criticisms of the SAFE Act include the fact that it just doesn't make any sort of sense. Why does Governor Cuomo think something this restrictive on law abiding citizens is going to help? It won't, and most New Yorkers realize this. Statistics have shown that crime in New York City has actually gone up since the passage of the SAFE Act. On April 6, 2015, the New York Daily News reported that the number of people murdered in New York City in 2015 was 82, up 16% from that time last year, which had increased anyway. This is added to the increases in attacks on police officers we saw at the end of 2014. The SAFE Act played little to no difference in preventing these rises in crime, and likely will not in the future as well.

So what can we truly do to stop gun violence? The answer certainly isn't to restrict the rights of law abiding citizens, or even those who are able to stop the violence legally. The SAFE Act was passed with such haste that originally, law enforcement was not even exempt from the seven round limit! This was quickly changed, but still proves the point about the law, it was passed too quickly, without proper debate, and isn't likely to do anything to change violence in the state of New York. The answer also isn't to have neighbors spying and turning each other in. There are reports in some parts of New York that is what is being encouraged, if someone has information about a violation of the SAFE Act, such as an unregistered weapon, they can call it in. Some believe that is encouraging people to turn on their neighbors in hopes of some reward. We can all hope that isn't the case, but unfortunately you never know.

The truth is, the SAFE Act was clearly motivated by Governor Andrew Cuomo's political interests. Cuomo said it himself when introducing the laws, "the toughest gun laws in the nation" "the first since Newtown." The SAFE Act doesn't make a lot of sense to law abiding citizens, but Governor Cuomo doesn't seem to care. In that same address, Cuomo also noted "no one needs 10 bullets to kill a deer, nobody hunts with an assault rifle." Well, that is correct, Governor, no one hunts with an assault rifle. However, with the crime rate up in New York City, should you be the one dictating how law abiding citizens can defend themselves?[137] We don't think so, and many others would agree. We do not see the full SAFE Act lasting longer than 5 years in New York, by 2020 it will be scaled back significantly, and many will look back and realize how much of a mistake it truly was.

Fracking in New York State

Since Governor Cuomo took office in 2011, there was significant debate on whether or not the state should allow the practice of hydraulic fracturing, or fracking. Fracking is the process of drilling and injecting liquid into the ground at a high pressure to fracture shale rocks and release natural gas that is inside. The debate has centered around the question of the safety of the practice in New York State. It has taken Governor Cuomo four years to finally make his decision on the matter, when he banned fracking in late 2014, becoming the second state in the country to do so after Vermont.[139, 142]

Opponents of fracking say they are concerned with the chemicals that get mixed into the water supplies of wells when fracking is conducted. They claim there are thousands of gallons of chemicals used each time a fracking operation is conducted, and that it is all potentially dangerous to water supplies. Another concern is that when the shale cracks, this natural gas then flows into the well water, the very same water many people use for drinking across the state. The website dedicated to exposing the dangers of fracking, dangersoffracking.com, claims there have been over 1,000 cases of health issues due to contaminated water. Although, the site did not specify if this was just in New York state or across the country. Opponents also claim they are opposed to the environmental damage that fracking can do to an area.[142]

During his announcement, Governor Cuomo claimed that "I've never had anyone say to me, 'I believe fracking is great.'" He cited a report by the New York State health commissioner, Dr. Howard Zucker, who noted the significant health risks of fracking.[142]

Supporters of fracking have since found significant frustration with Governor Cuomo's decision. It is no secret that New

York State is doing rather poorly economically (unless you're Governor Cuomo who believes the state is doing just fine) and supporters find fracking to be a way to add jobs to the New York economy. Others have pointed out that states that have supported fracking are now doing well, such as Pennsylvania and Texas, and are not reporting significant health problems. Supporters believe this would be a significant boost to the New York economy, and that the dangers are significantly overstated.[140]

When looking at the situation in New York, there are a few points that show why it is easy to understand why there is controversy in the case. If there are other states that have had success with fracking, why does New York see such a significant difference? Pennsylvania is not only a neighbor to New York, but they are the southern neighbor to New York, meaning the same regions of New York, the Southern Tier, that would benefit from fracking, border the same areas in Pennsylvania where fracking is taking place. One "border" cannot make that much of a difference in the safety of the practice. Another point is that Governor Cuomo waited until after the 2014 gubernatorial election to make his decision. The Governor claimed he was waiting on the health report, but the pressure had been on the administration since the beginning of his term in 2011 to make a decision.

Another interesting point is Governor Cuomo seemed to appease the minority of his party that didn't support him in the 2014 Democratic primary with this decision. Cuomo's opponent in the race, Zephyr Teachout, took approximately 1/3 of the vote in the election, far more than anyone anticipated. One of Teachout's main points was her opposition to fracking, which the Governor still hadn't taken a position. With this decision, Governor Cuomo seems to appease that group of individuals in the state.

We must also note that the Governor has overlooked a seemingly significant economic opportunity here. New York State has the worst economic outlook in the country, but Governor Cuomo does not seem to be taking significant steps to fix that, especially with decisions like this. The United States should be working on becoming more energy independent, and fracking would be a great way to do just that. Those who argue it isn't safe should be trying to find an alternative solution, or a way to help make it safe instead of arguing it to be banned. Instead, the Governor took a big government position, and banned the practice. The smarter decision would have been to attempt to find a solution, but instead Governor Cuomo took the political position that may in the long run harm New York's economy even more.

Startup NY- Another Failed Policy

With the 2014 gubernatorial election nearing in New York State, Governor Andrew Cuomo realized what many New Yorkers already knew, economic growth in the state was essentially nonexistent. Governor Cuomo knew this would be an issue, and began to formulate a plan to stimulate business growth in the state, especially in some of the poorer areas such as Buffalo. Cuomo began to tout the plan during the gubernatorial election, stating it would help grow the New York economy in the coming years.

The website for the plan, startup.ny.gov, has this to say about the plan:

"START-UP NY offers new and expanding businesses the opportunity to operate tax-free for 10 years on or near eligible university or college campuses in New York State. Partnering with these schools gives businesses direct access to advanced research laboratories, development resources and experts in key industries."[143]

The plan is advertised to bring in companies to work with colleges and universities to create economic opportunities for a community in a "tax free" environment. However, there are several problems with the plan. The first is the restrictive list of what companies can actually be a part of the program. These are just some of those who cannot take part in Start-Up NY, again taken from website: "Retail and wholesale businesses, restaurants, law and accounting firms, medical or dental practices, real estate management companies/brokers, hospitality and utilities/energy production."[143]

So if these companies can't take place in the program, who really can? And looking at that list, and thinking that the company would have to be near a college campus, does it really make sense to ban all of those companies? That's where most of the business would go, students working in a restaurant to pay for tuition, retail and wholesale businesses selling to the students, law and accounting firms, medical and dental practices and real estate companies taking interns. Why would you restrict companies from going to those areas? We don't have to ask too many of these questions, because the numbers end up speaking for themselves.

Lately, both economic experts and legislators have blasted the Governor's failed program. In early April, the state finally released the update for the progress of the plan, and it was not what the state would have wanted to see. According to reports, Start-Up NY created only 76 jobs in the past year. Some would say, well at least jobs were created, but when you look at the figures being spent by the state, you would then realize Start-Up NY has been a total failure for the state. Scott Beyer from Forbes lays this out in his article, *Cuomo's START-UP NY Highlights Failures Of The Empire State Development Corporation,* he states:

"The state has already spent $47 million on advertising, and overall public expenditures for the program's first three years are expected to be $323 million. Total job creation figures after five years are expected to be 2,085, but so far that figure stands at a whopping 76 jobs."[144] Some figures even have the state spending in the $1 billion range for the program altogether, only to come together to create a total of 76 jobs in the past year of its existence. It's clear now why lawmakers in New York are calling for Start-Up NY to be stopped, as it is only costing the taxpayers even more money, despite the claims of a "tax free environment."[145]

This shows yet again that Governor Cuomo truly has no proper plan for the State of New York, and that he is unfit to be Governor of the state. Failed programs such as Start-Up NY are things that the voters should be paying attention to when looking for qualities in an elected official at the ballot box. The Governor has failed in almost a term and a half so far to truly make New York better, and therefore voters should not reward him with another term or another position in a leadership role in the state.

Cuomo's Common Core

By now most around the country are familiar in at least some way with the new Common Core education standards. The very standards that came to the states through the infamous stimulus package set forth by the Obama administration during their first term. However, these standards were not created by the federal government; they were simply endorsed by the federal government. For most, this would be enough to say no, we don't want those kinds of educational standards. However, the common people had very little say in that decision, and most states were stuck with the Common Core Standards, and New York was no exception.

However, New York has been an exception in several other ways. At this time, New York is one of the leading states in the fight against Common Core, but not from the government. It's the common man who is leading the charge against these standards, the parents, the teachers and the students. They have done so by speaking out, going to Board of Education meetings, by choosing to opt out of the exams, by demonstrating and by contacting government officials. Some have had success in getting officials to listen, others have felt their cries have fallen on deaf ears. When it comes to Governor Cuomo and his administration, people have fallen into the second category.

Common Core has become an interesting topic in many different ways, but one of the key things to note for our purposes here is that it is not a typical Republican vs. Democrat or conservative vs. liberal debate. There are no party lines when it comes to Common Core, individuals on both sides acknowledge its problems, and want to be rid of it. Overall, Democrats tend to be more supportive, but not many have fallen back to liberal reasoning when attempting to defend it.

There are plenty of different reasons as to why parents, students and teachers are opposed to the standards. Some feel the government is too involved in the standards, others feel the standards are too much of a change from past standards, and that student and teacher performances will be negatively impacted by the sudden changes. Others claim the new standards are too difficult for some of the younger students. Other claims are that the government is collecting too much information on the students and their families through the testing. The testing itself, of course, is one of the biggest issues with Common Core, with many claiming the emphasis on more standardized testing just isn't going to help anyone. Opponents claim the "one size fits all" approach Common Core and its testing bring is simply impossible and will only hurt education. Most also cite the connection the tests have to the education company Pearson. Opponents claim Pearson created the standards and the tests, and will be making significant profits in New York when everything is said and done.[146, 149]

The New York State Department of Education and Governor Andrew Cuomo have come out in full support of Common Core, despite the significant public outcry. From the time of the implementation of Common Core until the end of his term in early 2015, former Education Commissioner John King had been a strong proponent of the standards. Despite many calls for either the delay of the implementation or the complete stop of the implementation, King and the state continued to push Common Core. At times King even stood in front of teachers, parents and elected officials, all opposed to Common Core, and stated he would not budge on the issue. Governor Cuomo for the most part has had the same stance, even though at one point he was for delaying the implementation, and then changed his mind.[151]

Some of King's earliest public support of Common Core can be traced to 2013, only about a year after the implementation of the standards (which unwisely occurred in the middle of the 2012-2013 school year) in which King stood in front of a crowd at Fayetteville-Manlius High School in Syracuse, New York to assure the crowd that "the commitment to the standards is unwavering," this of course despite the fact that most of the speakers before him, according to the article from Syracuse.com, had spoken out against Common Core and its implementation.[150] King's support of Common Core would continue until the end of his term in 2015. However, King's replacement, MaryEllen Elia has already stated her support for the Common Core standards, despite all of the protests over the past few years.[147] This also would not be the last time King would be in a positon to press for Common Core, as he has been selected by President Barack Obama to replace outgoing Education Secretary Arne Duncan.

Resistance to Common Core has been significant across the country, as several states, including Indiana, have already pulled out of the implementation of Common Core or have repealed the standards. According to a January 2015 poll conducted by the Siena Research Institute, 49% of New York voters want Common Core to be stopped, while 33% support the standards. The article the poll is noted in, *Poll: Nearly half of voters oppose Common Core* on capitalnewyork.com also claims that the number became nearly 2 to 1 opposed when it came to the upstate regions compared to the New York City region.[152] Most expect this number to grow even more in the coming years.

Even the teachers unions in New York State have turned against the Common Core standards. In April just before testing began, the United Teachers Union used robocalls to urge parents to opt their children out of the testing. Many others passed their opposition on through word of mouth, urging local parents in their districts to opt out of the testing. When it is all said and done, most expect the number of opt outs to be close to 200,000 across the state, while most estimates have it currently around 175,000, this is up significantly from the 2014 total of around 60,000.[146, 149]

Those who have taken the tests, or the teachers who have administered the tests and have seen the reactions from their students, do not have positive things to say about the tests or the process. An article from the Washington Post written by Valerie Strauss, *Educators alarmed by some questions on N.Y. Common Core tests* points out some of these issues. Strauss notes an article by Carol Burris, the 2013 High School Principal of the Year in New York. Burris notes some of these horror stories, these are just a few of the stories Burris shares, reports from educators across the state.

"These three days of ELA have been torture – I had only 23 students opt out and I had at least 3 times that number in tears. If we were permitted to talk about the content, it would be over so fast. Folks would be horrified at the vocabulary, the reading levels and the ambiguity of the questions. I was unable to answer at least 25 percent of them."[146]

"And all year they've [her students] been so proud of their academic growth, I've been congratulating them so much as of lately…they've blown me away. Now, they were in tears…and I heard… 'I thought I was smart, I guess not' 'I'm stupid I can't even take a test.' And more."[136]

I would encourage you to take a look at the article itself and read more of what Burris has to say, it's frustrating, but important to know what exactly is going on in the school system.

Heard enough of it yet? Apparently lawmakers haven't. New York State has still been incredibly slow to act on a repeal or at least delay of the implementation of the standards. However, if a school educator is claiming they're unable to answer around 25 percent of the questions, how would our lawmakers stack up? As a matter of fact, Jim Tedisco, a Republican Assemblyman in New York challenged Cuomo to take the math and English exams with the following statement:

"If you think the Holy Grail of improving our education is Common Core testing, I got a challenge. I want you to sit in the Red Room, I'll bring in the fifth-grade Common Core math test, the fifth-grade Common Core English test, and then we'll evaluate what your scores are and we'll release them to the public."[153]

No surprise, Governor Cuomo did not respond, not that anyone expected him to.

With all of the public outcry, most would think it is time Governor Cuomo did something about Common Core in New York. No he did not directly create Common Core, but his refusal to stand up for the students, teachers and parents in the state against the standards have earned the standards the name of "Cuomo's Common Core." In this case, it has also earned him a spot on our list of those who set the worst example. Everyone in the state deserves to be heard, including children, teachers and parents. Governor Cuomo has not given them the attention and respect they deserve. He has chosen to attempt to be a champion of liberal causes that will put him in the spotlight, but has not addressed the issues the majority of New Yorkers face. For this the Governor should be ashamed, however, this is not the most serious of the Governor's offenses in the state.

The Moreland Commission and State Corruption

If you ask just about anyone who covers state politics and has a good understanding of state politics for many states across the country to name the top five most corrupt states in the country, it is likely that around 99% of them will name New York in that list. For years New York has been riddled with corruption, to go back through all of the history would take far too long, and would be almost unnecessary since we have seen the same pattern over and over again. Since Eliot Spitzer became Governor in 2007, the Governor's office itself has been riddled with scandals. Spitzer himself resigned after being in office for a little over a year after being forced to resign after allegations of Spitzer's use of an international escort service emerged. His successor, David Paterson, was accused of ethical issues himself, although nothing serious enough to force him to resign before his term was up.

In the past few years alone, New York has seen both its long time Assembly Speaker, Sheldon Silver, and it's Senate Majority Leader, Dean Skelos, arrested for corruption charges in the state. This after Andrew Cuomo campaigned on ethics reform and "cleaning up Albany." However, Cuomo was not responsible for the arrest of either Silver or Skelos, Instead, the investigation that led to the arrest of the two men was led by Preet Bharara, the U.S. Attorney for the Southern District of New York. There are also now reports that Bharara is investigating Governor Cuomo as well. Cuomo himself has drawn suspicion to himself, notably with the sudden disbanding of the anti-corruption Moreland Commission. This will be elaborated on further in this section.

A report from stateintegrity.org towards the beginning of 2014 had New York ranked 37th on the state integrity scale, with an overall grade of a D. As stated, this was done around early 2014, before the Moreland Commission was disbanded and before Skelos and Silver were arrested. If we had to guess, we would put New York around 49th or 50th right now, with Cuomo's likely upcoming indictment being the icing on the cake that proves just how corrupt the state really is.[154]

Sheldon Silver, a Democrat from New York City, started his career as Assembly Speaker in February of 1994, and his career as Speaker only ended in January of 2015 when he was arrested on federal corruption charges. These charges included receiving payments from certain large law firms in New York, not disclosing these payments, and illegal investments through private vehicles. Reports are that Bharara picked up the investigation from the Moreland Commission after it was disbanded, adding to more suspicion as to why the commission was suddenly disbanded. The investigation is ongoing, and more charges are likely.

Dean Skelos, a Republican from New York City, started his career as Senate Majority Leader in 2008, and his career as Majority Leader ended in May of 2015 when he was arrested on federal corruption charges. These charges included using his position to extort and solicit bribes across the state. The investigation is ongoing, and more charges are likely.

Neither Skelos nor Silver has resigned from their elected positions in New York State, only their leadership positions. They continue to serve in the Senate and the Assembly, respectively, while they fight their pending criminal charges.

Governor Cuomo himself of course has not pressured either leader to step down completely, and has not offered to assist in the investigation. Cuomo campaigned on ethics reform, and attempting to "clean up Albany." Instead, it was done for him, and he may be involved in the very corruption he has been attempting to clean up, besides his erratic behavior during the investigations of Skelos and Silver, these are some of the other signs of Cuomo's guilt.

The Moreland Commission, formally known as the Moreland Commission To Investigate Public Corruption was created on July 2, 2013 to investigate the rampant reports of corruption throughout the government in the state of New York. The New York State website for the Commission claims that the Commission's investigation is focused on, but not limited to:

"Criminal statutes for corruption and misconduct by public officials, such as bribery laws;

Campaign financing including but not limited to contribution limits and other restrictions; disclosure of third-party contributions and expenditures and the effectiveness of existing campaign finance laws;

Compliance of outside organizations and persons with existing lobbying laws, including but not limited to organizations engaged in lobbying and other efforts to influence public policies and elections and the effectiveness of such laws;

Adequacy and enforcement of the State's election laws and electoral process including the structure and composition of the State and County Boards of Elections, the Board of Elections' enforcement and the effectiveness of and compliance with existing election laws."[155]

The website, publiccorruption.moreland.ny.gov, also notes that a preliminary report is to be issued on December 1, 2013, which it was, and additional reports by January 1, 2015. The latter however did not happen as the Moreland Commission was abruptly disbanded in March of 2014 by Governor Cuomo. Opponents then blamed the Governor of interfering with the investigation (there were other allegations of interference as well, which will be mentioned further on) and Cuomo's response was simply, "It's my commission. My subpoena power, my Moreland Commission. I can appoint it, I can disband it. I appoint you, I can un-appoint you tomorrow."[157] Cuomo's response as to why the Commission was disbanded was that ethics reform was passed through in the state budget that year, but watchdog groups were still not buying into it, rightfully so.

During the course of the investigation, the Governor was not afraid to make it quite clear that it was his Commission, and that he could do what he wanted with it. An article from the New York Times titled *Cuomo's Office Hobbled Ethics Inquiries by Moreland Commission* gives an example of this. The article details that a subpoena issued for a law firm, Buying Time, which had allegedly bought airtime for the Governor's campaign in 2010, was immediately pulled back once the Governor's office received word of it. The article details other instances of the Commission being blocked, both from outside and from within, from investigating anyone who had any ties to the Governor. Another story referenced the Real Estate Board of New York, who had supported Cuomo throughout the years. E. Dayna Perry, one of the veteran prosecutors on the Commission wished to serve the Real Estate Board with a subpoena, but a Cuomo ally, and one of the heads of the Commission, Regina M. Calcaterra, would not allow Perry and the Commission to do so. Rumors began to circulate that Governor Cuomo's Secretary Lawrence S. Schwartz, was doing the dirty work of interfering in the investigation. None of this would be completely proved, and the Moreland Commission itself would be shut down, until Preet Bharara picked up where the Commission left off, thus the investigations into Skelos and Silver. Bharara himself has also threatened to look into Cuomo if he impedes the investigation.[156]

All of this reportedly has Cuomo concerned, as Bharara has continued the investigation, without any fear of reprisal. Cuomo is noted as normally being a control freak, someone who feels the need to control everything that is going on. This has been supported by the common theory of "Three Men in a Room" referring to Andrew Cuomo, Dean Skelos and Sheldon Silver making all of the decisions in Albany. Bharara has noted he intends to break this up, and he has already completed 2/3 of that. But many close to Cuomo have claimed that in the past few months the Governor has been notably frustrated and concerned by the investigation. An article in the New

York Post by Fredric Dicker claims Cuomo's associates have noted he is "obsessed with fear." This was written back in February. Another piece from Dicker written in June details the Governor's growing paranoia even more. Those close to the administration have told the Post that not much is getting done, and that the Governor has gone into seclusion. Some note that recent personal troubles in Cuomo's life, including the death of his father and the health concerns of his longtime girlfriend have also had impacts, but that wouldn't explain the majority of the Governor's erratic behavior.[159, 160, 161, 162]

Cuomo, like several others who have found themselves on our list, is also known for being a political "bully." Many have described Cuomo's tactics as brash and they liken him to being a bully in politics, making sure things are his way all of the time. This has been seen in various times across the state, punishing those who vote against him with threatening to strip funding or close down state works in a legislator's district, or even his tactics with law enforcement and teachers unions. If proven true (which it is), it would not be hard for Bharara to find someone who is willing to provide evidence to prove the Governor's corruption.

There are even reports that those close to the Governor himself including aides, former coworkers and campaign donors are being investigated by Bharara and his staff. Nothing concrete has been released to answer that with certainty, but the behavior of the Governor adds to the suspicions.

Although there is no smoking gun right now to indict the Governor, most New Yorkers know that Andrew Cuomo is in some way guilty of corruption. Whether it was protecting political allies, interfering with the Moreland Commission, or some crimes of his own he is covering up, it is likely that Bharara will find something before Cuomo's second term is up. At this point, only time will tell.

Conclusion

Governor Andrew Cuomo has found himself on this list for various reasons, but the most important perhaps has been the last, his corruption scandal. If this is proven true, Andrew Cuomo has no place in leading anyone anywhere, and instead should be serving time in prison along with Sheldon Silver, Dean Skelos, and other Albany politicians who have been found guilty of corruption.

Governor Cuomo once said that "extreme conservatives" have no place in the State of New York. His exact comments were:

"Who are they? Are they these extreme conservatives who are right-to-life, pro-assault-weapon, anti-gay? Is that who they are? Because if that's who they are and if they are the extreme conservatives, they have no place in the state of New York, because that's not who New Yorkers are."

The Governor essentially seems to state that anyone who disagrees with him has no place in the State of New York, and that should be enough to tell anyone, no matter if they are liberal, conservative, libertarian, socialist or moderate, that Governor Cuomo himself has no place in being the Governor of a state. We cannot move forward as a society if we are not accepting of all points of view, and with this statement, the Governor seems to be willing to toss aside the point of view of many New Yorkers and Americans. Comments like this have just been some of the ways Governor Cuomo has shown he is an example of a poor political leader. Governor Cuomo is not a common man; he does not understand the problems that everyday Americans face. Cuomo is a dishonest politician who is also described as being very arrogant, and only in it for himself.

Cuomo, like Hillary Clinton, is now at the mercy of the American people. Cuomo has not announced he is running for President in 2016, but his political career is not likely over. There are rumors he intends to run for a third term for Governor in 2018 that is if he is not arrested for corruption charges by then. At that point, the people of New York can stand up and make a change. They can show that Governor Cuomo does not represent who New Yorkers are, and that it is time for someone who will listen to the people, and who will finally clean up the mess that is Albany.

V. John Boehner

"We're going to do everything — and I mean everything we can do — to kill it, stop it, slow it down, whatever we can." John Boehner, just before the 2010 Midterm Elections, referring to President Barack Obama's agenda.[163]

When John Boehner, a longtime Republican Representative from the state of Ohio was elected Speaker of the House in early 2011 after the Republicans won the House in the Midterm elections he came on quite strong. Boehner, along with Senate Minority Leader Mitch McConnell, swore to defeat President Obama's agenda and promote conservative principles. Boehner, along with House Majority Leader Eric Cantor and Majority Whip Kevin McCarthy held a lot of promise for Americans that were upset with Barack Obama's victory in the 2008 Presidential election and the passage of Obamacare in 2010. Not one single Republican had voted for Obamacare in the House or the Senate in 2010, and with the House now run by Republicans, you would think Obamacare would have been repealed, and the issues such as immigration, the national debt and some significant foreign policy debacles would have been settled. But you would be wrong.

Years later, the Republicans control both the House and the Senate, but we still have Obamacare along with a mess of an immigration system, increasing debt and a disaster in the Middle East. So what happened to those who were supposed to turn things around? Those who were supposed to stop President Obama's agenda like Speaker Boehner? In the eyes of many, Speaker Boehner has dropped his campaign promises and has betrayed the American people and his conservative base he claimed to represent for so long. Two attempted conservative coups for the Speaker position are just some of the biggest signs of the frustrations, but it is also important to note the aftermath of those attempts, as those involved were both openly and secretly punished by the leadership.

A great deal of blame has been placed on Speaker Boehner for the failed attempts to stop President Obama's agenda, but is it fair to place all that blame on the Speaker? The evidence will speak for itself, but there are significant reasons, including those already mentioned, as to why Speaker John Boehner is on this list among political leaders who have set the worst examples over the years.

Early Years

John Andrew Boehner was born on November 17, 1949 in Cincinnati, Ohio. John Boehner was one of 12 children born to Mary and Earl Boehner, a blue collar Catholic family. After graduating from High School, Boehner enlisted in the Navy, but was honorably discharged after eight months due to back complications. Boehner then decided to go to college, while also working part time. During that time, Boehner met his future wife, Debbie, and they married in 1973. In 1977, Boehner graduated from Xavier University, earning a degree in business. Boehner would run a small business in the years between his graduation from college and his entry into politics.

Only a few years later Boehner started his career in politics. He first served on the board of trustees of Union Township in Butler County, Ohio. A few years later Boehner was first elected to the

Ohio House of Representatives, where he would be for five years until he won his first election for U.S. Congress, defeating a Republican incumbent in the middle of a scandal.[166]

House of Representatives- Before Speakership

When John Boehner was first elected into the U.S. House of Representatives in the early 90's he was known as a rising conservative star. John Boehner, along with current Republican Presidential candidate Rick Santorum were two of the seven freshman members of Congress that year that were known as the Gang of Seven. The Gang of Seven were known for exploiting a banking scandal and a Post Office scandal within Congress. In the Banking scandal, 22 members of the House of Representatives were singled out by the House Ethics Committee for leaving their checking accounts overdrawn for at least eight months. 450 Representatives were implicated, but it was found most did not break any rules.

The Gang of Seven also was involved in investigating the Congressional Post Office scandal, in which the Congressional Postmaster conspired with several other Representatives, including Dan Rostenkowski, the head of the House Ways and Means Committee, to launder money through stamps and postal vouchers. Rostenkowski was convicted and sentenced to 18 months in prison for his role in the scandal.

Boehner arguably would go on to have the most successful career out of the members of the Gang of Seven. Santorum would go on to win two terms in the Senate, and Boehner would continue to serve in the House, while the others have retired by now. In 1995, Boehner began his position as Chairman of the House Republican Conference, the party caucus for Republicans in the House. He would also be known for working with Newt Gingrich on the infamous "Contract With America" in 1994. During the 90's, Boehner also helped to pass the Freedom to Farm act in 1996. From what it seems, John Boehner from the key state of Ohio was a rising conservative star, but that stardom doesn't always last for Congressional leaders.[165, 166]

In 2001 John Boehner became the Chairman of Committee on Education and the Workforce, and also became the House of Representatives sponsor for the now controversial education bill No Child Left Behind. If there was one bill that many could agree on was a mistake that was passed by Congress, it is No Child Left Behind.[167] Education experts from both sides of the aisle have come out against the bill in the past few years. However, when it was first passed, it was highly praised. Many were hopeful initially for an education bill passed by a Republican President, sponsored by a conservative Congressional leader, and passed with bipartisan support. However, many agree now that the bill has been an absolute disaster, and an overreach of government influence in education. Boehner and other Republicans in Congress praised the school choice portions added into the bill, but that has done little to please the many opponents. Since then, the House has voted multiple times to renew the act, most recently being in July of 2015, despite strong public outcry and disapproval.

During his time as Chairman of Committee on Education and the Workforce, Boehner also was able to pass school voucher reforms in Washington DC and the Pension Protection Act, which is hailed as the most sweeping reform of pension plans in over 30 years. His work during these years in Congress certainly did not go unnoticed, and earned him the positon of House Majority Leader during an election in February of 2006. Boehner replaced former Majority Leader Tom DeLay, who had been indicted on criminal charges, and defeated two other Republicans for the seat. However, that November the Republicans lost control of the House of Representatives. Boehner then took over as House Minority Leader, becoming the highest ranking Republican in the House. Boehner would serve as Minority Leader until January of 2011 when the Republicans formally took over the House yet again, and Boehner was unanimously elected amongst Republicans to serve as Speaker of the House. Many Republicans were hopeful that the new Speaker, a man noted as a conservative reformer in the past, would now help them to stop President Obama's agenda, just as he said he would.

Speaker of the House- Conservative Hopes

Since John Boehner has become Speaker of the House, there have been many tense moments between he and President Barack Obama. It is easy to tell at the President's State of the Union addresses, where Boehner sits behind the President, that Boehner is frustrated with the President and his plans. Boehner doesn't speak during the address, but his facial expressions tell all of his disagreement and frustration with the President. When Boehner was elected Speaker, many hoped that this disagreement and frustration would lead to a strong conservative voice speaking out against the President, working to stop the agenda many found to be quite radical.

As Speaker, Boehner himself does not take part in floor debates or House votes. Boehner would be the tie breaker, if needed, the 435th vote, but for the most part stays away from that kind of publicity. In a way, this makes sense. However, Boehner does have a strong say on the bills that do come to the floor for debate, come up to be voted on or how and when the bills are voted on or debated. Boehner and the leadership team also work to make sure they have the votes needed for bills to pass, which has caused some controversy over the years, and will be discussed further on.

One of the topics that has been at the forefront of Boehner's time as Speaker has been Obamacare. Some claim that as of early 2015 there have been around 50 votes in the House to repeal Obamacare. Members of the House claim it is much lower than that, but there is no question there have been quite a few attempts. If there have been around 50 votes, many of them successful, how is Obamacare still around? Often times when the House votes to repeal it, the Senate votes it down due to a higher percentage of Democrats in the Senate than in the House. It would also be difficult to bypass the 2/3 threshold needed to defeat the veto the President would issue if it were to come to that anyway. Boehner himself has even gone as far as to file a lawsuit against Obamacare, which was started in 2014. The House lawsuit claims the administration has used its executive power when it comes to Obamacare, including delaying certain portions of the law, which the House considers to be illegal. The lawsuit is still pending.[168, 169, 170]

Speaker Boehner has also been a strong critic of President Obama's foreign policy, often times claiming that his approach to the fight against the Islamic State in Iraq and Syria has been poor. Boehner has also been a strong critic of the President's negotiations with Iran over a nuclear agreement, and has vowed to make sure Congress fights the deal when it comes to them. Boehner also received a lot of praise from his own party, but criticism from Democrats, when he invited Israeli Prime Minister Benjamin Netanyahu to come speak to Congress in March of 2015 regarding the pending Iranian deal. Critics claimed Boehner did not have the power to do so and that he was undermining and disrespecting the President. Boehner and most Republicans disagreed, and Prime Minister Netanyahu came anyway. Many praised the speech, and compared it to the likes of Winston Churchill during World War II. Only time will tell if the comparisons are accurate or not, but to many conservatives, this was the right call by the Speaker of the House.[172, 173]

There were plenty of reasons for conservatives to have hopes for Boehner as Speaker. There was no doubt that he has been opposed to major parts of President Obama's administration, notably Obamacare, his use of executive powers and his foreign policy. We will likely never truly know all of what the Speaker has done to try and stop the President, as a good portion of what the Speaker does is done privately. However, despite his oppositions, there have been some things that have come to light that have frustrated conservatives and people across America, making many believe the Speaker has not been listening to the people. These criticisms have come from people on both sides of the aisle, and some of the criticisms have been quite severe.[174]

Speaker of the House- Controversies- Lobby Concerns

In 1995, John Boehner admitted to handing out checks on the House floor to other members of Congress from the tobacco industry as they were discussing a vote on tobacco subsidies. He would admit that this was a huge mistake, and would later work to make sure that kind of lobbying would never happen again. Boehner and others were successful in putting a rule in place that prohibited campaign contributions from being distributed on the House floor. However, the concerns about Boehner's connection to lobbyists would not go away after all of those years, in fact, they would continue even into his tenure as Speaker of the House.

In 2010, just before Boehner became Speaker, the New York Times ran an in depth article on Boehner's connection to several large companies. The article by Eric Lipton was titled *A G.O.P Leader Tightly Bound by Lobbyists,* and listed out several big companies that claimed Boehner was connected to, "including Goldman Sachs, Google, Citigroup, R. J. Reynolds, MillerCoors and UPS" (Lipton).[176] Lipton notes that the companies have contributed hundreds of thousands of dollars to his campaign, and that they admit their connections to Boehner and that they are lobbying the Speaker. Lipton also notes the lobbyists call several times a week seeking help, and they often receive the help they are looking for.

In the article, some of the lobbyists themselves defend their connections. One of Boehner's friends who was interviewed for the article, Mark Isakowitz admits Boehner has "a lot of relationships in this city… But I think all the good lawmakers do." Boehner himself defends the point in a similar fashion, noting he gets lobbied everyday by everyday people. His spokesman Michael Steel is noted in the article as saying that Boehner "often speaks with employers" because he understands the business background, having owned a small business himself in the past.[176]

To be fair to Speaker Boehner, the New York Times hasn't always been known to be the most accurate or fair to Republicans, so there are some points that may be a stretch. But it is well known by the American people that most, if not all politicians do have some sort of connections to lobbyists. It is not illegal, but in some cases it is a betrayal of trust of the everyday people that voted to put them in office in the first place. According to opensecrets.org, a website that claims to be a Center for Responsive Politics, Boehner's top contributors were people connected to organizations like Murray Energy, FirstEnergy Corp and Comcast Corp. The website notes the organizations themselves did not donate, just people connected to them. Again it is important to note this is not illegal, but we hope at the end of the day the politicians remember they represent the everyday working people, and not the lobbyists who will spend money to get what they want done. This is something not just Speaker Boehner, but all politicians need to remember.[175]

Questionable Support

Although Speaker Boehner often does not vote on bills on the House floor, he does occasionally vote, and he almost always has a say on the procedures of the House votes and the bills and amendments that are voted on (Mitch McConnell in the next section provides a different issue, as McConnell also has a say on the procedures of the Senate and he often votes on the bills and amendments). This has given Boehner enough spotlights to take heavy criticism from conservatives unhappy with his tenure as Speaker of the House. Sure, Boehner has done some things that have pleased conservatives and the Republican base, but not enough for him to have full confidence from his fellow Republicans in the House, and the everyday people on the outside. In his three elections for Speaker so far, Boehner has faced two strong attempts by conservatives to oust him from his Speakership. One in early 2013, the other in early 2015 when the first House session was opened and Speaker elections were being held, those will be discussed more in depth later on. Several websites and organizations that track the votes and procedures by members of Congress including Heritage Action and Conservative Review have given the Speaker rather low ratings, with Conservative Review giving John Boehner a 35% for his record on the past 50 key votes in the House of Representatives.[181, 182]

So what has led to all of this? How did a Representative who was seen as a rising conservative star, someone who was unanimously voted Speaker of the House the first time around, and someone who strongly promised to stop President Obama's agenda turn from a strong conservative to one of the most hated men in politics? First, we look at the bills and issues that the Speaker has supported or not supported since he first became Speaker in 2011.

One of the biggest fights to always come to Congress is the fight against the debt limit. As of August of 2015, we are over $18 trillion in debt, and the estimated debt per citizen, yes per citizen, not per taxpayer, is over $57,000. Many Americans have opposed raising the debt ceiling for years, and that trend is continuing. A poll by Reason-Rupe in 2013 showed that 70 percent of Americans do not support raising the debt ceiling.[179] However, this does not to appear to have affected Speaker Boehner too much. Boehner supported debt ceiling increases in 2011, 2013 and 2014, including a bill in 2014 that suspended the debt limit until 2015. Another one of these votes, the one in 2013, actually involved the funding of Obamacare, and with the passage of the debt ceiling deal, Obamacare was also funded by the House of Representatives yet again, despite Speaker Boehner's promises to fully repeal the measure. Many conservatives have found the constant raising of the debt limit to be irresponsible by Congress, and a move that will hurt future generations. Polls have shown that the American people did not want the increases either, but the House and the Senate still passed these measures, multiple times.

In 2012 Speaker Boehner also supported raising the fiscal cliff tax, which increased taxes on those making over $400,000, and it raised the payroll taxes of over 77% of Americans while extending tax breaks to corporations. This angered many conservatives as well as many Americans who did not wish to see any more tax increases, at all.

In 2013, Speaker Boehner supported the Ryan-Murray budget. This budget increased spending and taxes over the next few years, with promises of decreasing taxes and spending in the long term. Again, it was not what the American people wanted to see, and it was a step in the wrong direction for the country. There comes a point where federal spending has to stop, but Speaker Boehner has not done a very good job in attempting to rein it in during his time as Speaker.

One thing that the passage of many of these deals has in common is the back room deals that are made to pass the bills. Many argue that the House Republican leadership and the Democratic leadership will often meet behind closed doors to come up with a deal, and then come out and tell the rest of their caucus to get behind the deal. The American people did not elect these leaders to go behind closed doors and make secret deals, they elected them to protect their interests and best represent them. Some Representatives and Senators have made steps in attempting to call out the leaders for these backroom deals, but are often faced with harsh criticism for doing so. So what does that really tell us? Do these leaders really have our best interests at mind when they make these deals? It doesn't always seem like it.[178, 180]

January 2013- First Attempt To Oust Boehner

In January of 2013, during the opening session of the 113th Congress, John Boehner faced his first challenge to his Speakership. It wasn't too much of a secret at the time that Boehner and House Leadership had angered some conservatives, and some of these conservatives were ready to strike back. Faced with frustration of having been betrayed by Boehner's votes in the past, and several conservatives being frustrated after being removed from their committee assignments due to voting against the Speaker, 10 House conservatives voted against John Boehner for Speaker of the House. This doesn't seem like much, but when you look at the House rules for the Speaker election, you realize if only a few more Republicans had voted against Boehner, he would have lost.[183]

In order for a Representative to win the Speaker's election, they must win an absolute majority of the votes cast, not the number of Representatives in the House at the time. Therefore, the Speaker does not always need 218 votes to win the majority. As the minority party will likely always rally around one candidate, who automatically becomes their minority leader, the Speaker must rely on all of the votes to come from within their own party. In this case, Speaker Boehner needed 214 votes from Republicans to win, as there were six Representatives who did not vote on that day, including Boehner himself, and the Congress started with 433 members, 233 who were Republicans. Representatives can then vote for anyone they wish, and there was a variety of names mentioned during the vote. At the vote, 10 Republicans voted against Boehner.

Jim Bridenstine(Oklahoma), Steve Pearce(New Mexico), Ted Yoho(Florida), Paul Broun(Georgia), Louie Gohmert(Texas), Justin Amash(Michigan), Tim Huelskamp(Kansas), Walter Jones(North Carolina), Tom Massive(Kentucky), and Steve Stockman(Texas). Boehner received 220 votes, and therefore was able to win re-election.[184, 186]

There were rumors after the election that punishments would be given out to the Republicans who voted against Boehner, with some of the Representatives, including Tim Huelskamp, openly telling supporters that he feared punishments from the House leadership for voting against Boehner. Boehner would later publically state that he would not be punishing those who voted against him. This however would not be the last time that concerns of punishment from House leadership would be discussed by Republican Representatives, with the peak being the reason for an even stronger challenge to Speaker Boehner's position in January of 2015.[187]

Cromnibus

Having been frustrated with the actions of conservatives in fall of 2013 to fight the excessive funding of the federal government, Speaker John Boehner, his leadership team and President Barack Obama became worried when the issue would come back up again, most notably towards the end of 2014. Debate in the previous year in regards to the funding of Obamacare had led to a government shutdown that had frustrated both sides of the aisle, and many Americans. In regards to the 2013 shutdown, it was the Senate and Minority Leader Mitch McConnell who caved first and gave up the fight to defund Obamacare, but John Boehner and his leadership team, including Majority Leader Eric Cantor and Majority Whip Kevin McCarthy also caved and brought the Senate "compromise" to the House. The new compromise, which really didn't include any of the concessions the Republicans had previously asked for, passed the House by a vote of 285-144, with all 144 no votes coming from House Republicans.[188]

In the aftermath, it was Senate conservatives who were publically humiliated for the shutdown, although they were not the ones who had conceded defeat while losing sight of the original goal. Most conservatives would acknowledge that this would only set up another fight in the future regarding the funding of the federal government and the strings that could possibly be attached. However, this would also add to the tension between John Boehner and the conservative wing of the House, as they felt the compromise was completely unnecessary.[188]

With this in mind, Speaker Boehner knew that in 2014 another fight like the one that had ensued the year before could be disastrous. Therefore, the Speaker began working on a plan to keep the government funded. In December of 2014, this plan, noted was as the "Consolidated and Further Continuing Appropriations Act, 2015," or "Cromnibus" for short. However, there is nothing short about Cromnibus, as it is 1600 pages of spending and regulations. While a lot of frustration came about with the size of the bill and the amount that it funds, there was one issue that stuck out to those opposed to the bill, the funding of President Obama's immigration plans.[189]

When opponents to the President's immigration plans realized at the end of 2014 that they had a chance to defund the plans through the next spending deal, they hoped to do just that. However, the Cromnibus bill took that idea away. The section of the bill that became the hot topic centered on the funding of the Department of Homeland Security, the agency that would be responsible for immigration control and border protection. The Cromnibus bill planned to fund DHS until the spring of 2015, where more noise could be made on funding the agency and fighting President Obama's immigration plans. However, many felt this was just another way to delay the fight, and then when the time comes, come up with a new deal to avoid another fight. When it came to the floor debates and vote, there was disagreement from both sides of the aisle. The final vote was 219-206, with 67 Republicans voting against the measure. Conservatives and Liberals were frustrated with extra policy riders added into the bill, including one for campaign finance regulations and one that softens the Dodd-Frank Wall Street

Reform Bill. Others were opposed to the massive spending that Cromnibus allows for, with many pointing to the 1.1 trillion dollars that are given to the federal government in the bill. Either way, the bill barely passed, but this was hardly the last time the House leadership would hear about the egregious spending bill.[190, 191, 194]

Just days after the passage of the Cromnibus bill, reports started to come out of Congress that the House leadership had lied about the contents and intention of the Cromnibus bill. The vote had initially been much closer than 219-206, but Boehner and his leadership team went around to Republicans in the House and asked for more votes, and successfully managed to pick up a few. At least one Republican Representative, Marlin Stutzman from Indiana, came out publically and stated that he was lied to by a member of House leadership, but did not identify whether it was Speaker Boehner, newly elected Majority Leader Kevin McCarthy or newly elected Majority Whip Steve Scalise. Stutzman claimed he was told that Cromnibus would be replaced by a short term measure, and that when Republicans formally took control of the Senate, the battle would be brought up again. That proved to be untrue. According to an article from Breitbart News, other sources backed up Stutzman's claim, and noted that other Representatives were told the same thing. Other promises were allegedly made to Representatives to convince them to vote for the egregious Cromnibus bill.[192, 193, 195]

What exactly did House leadership have to hide in this bill? Why did they feel they had to lie in order to get it passed? Did they know that if the American people truly knew what was in it, they would overwhelmingly reject it? Anything is possible, but by then, a pattern of this type of behavior was growing with Speaker John Boehner. There had been multiple votes where members were intimidated into voting one way or another, against their beliefs or against what the people wanted. Only two groups of people had the ability to actually do something about Boehner's tactics, the people of his district, or the Republican members of the House. Since Boehner had already been re-elected in his district, the aftermath of the Cromnibus bill would spill over into January of 2015, where Boehner would face the next, but not final, attempt to oust him as Speaker of the House.

January 2015- Second Attempt to Oust Speaker Boehner

Following the vote on Cromnibus, the 113th Congress was ready to come to a close. Many conservative Representatives were frustrated with Speaker Boehner and the leadership, and they knew it. Many of them believed the Speaker had betrayed the American people and the conservative base to work with President Obama to pass a spending bill that really made no sense, and that would turn out to be an absolute disaster. They were frustrated with the way it was done, and how sneaky the Speaker was to get the votes needed for it. The end of the 113th Congress meant the 114th session of Congress would be coming up in early January, which also meant there would be elections for the leadership positions. Before the year 2015 even started, several Representatives were voicing their opposition to John Boehner for Speaker, with a few even putting their own names forward as replacements. The most vocal of these Representatives was Louie Gohmert of Texas. Rep. Gohmert had often caught the ire of the leadership, and has always been a vocal opponent of Speaker Boehner. Gohmert was one of the 10 in 2013 that was willing to vote against the Speaker in the first failed coup attempt. Two other Republican Representatives, Daniel Webster and, Ted Yoho, both of Florida, also offered themselves as alternatives to Speaker John Boehner.[196, 197]

This time the battle was much more public. Gohmert had announced his intentions to run a few days in advance, with Yoho announcing shortly after. Even before the vote began, Representatives were announcing their support for the other candidates or their opposition to John Boehner. The following are statements from several Representatives, including Louie Gohmert and Ted Yoho, on why they voiced their opposition to Speaker Boehner.

Representative Louie Gohmert: "After the November elections gave Republicans control of the Senate, voters made clear they wanted change. There have been numerous examples of problematic Republican leadership, but we were hopeful our leaders got the voters' message. However, after our Speaker forced through the CRomnibus by passing it with Democratic votes and without time to read it, it seemed clear that we needed new leadership. There had been much discussion. But, until yesterday, no one had stepped up.

I applaud my friend Rep. Ted Yoho for putting his name forward as an alternative to the status quo. Ted is a good man for whom I could vote, but I have heard from many supporters and also friends in Congress who have urged me to put forward my name for Speaker as well to increase our chances of change. That is why I am also offering my name as a candidate for Speaker."[197]

Representative Ted Yoho: "In order to do this, strong leadership is required. The American people have spoken loud and clear by their choice to elect conservative Representatives to serve them in Washington. It's our turn now, as Members of the People's House, to echo their demands by electing a new Speaker. The American people have allowed us to choose who is best suited to lead the House by electing a deep bench of diverse and qualified members. Our Republic is built on choice, and if needed, I would stand up to give our members that option."[196]

Representative Justin Amash(Michigan): "Speaker Boehner has been the leader of our party in the House for eight years. We have welcomed at least three large waves of new representatives during that time. Republican conference rules limit chairmen to six years in their offices to promote fresh thinking and new priorities. We should apply those same principles to all our party's leaders.

The speaker of the House has one of the most challenging jobs in government. Speaker Boehner has given his best to our conference, and I thank him for his service. But it's time for Republicans to change our leadership. This afternoon, I will vote for a new speaker."[198]

Representative Jim Bridenstine (Oklahoma): "The CR/Omnibus legislation sufficiently undermines the checks and balances enshrined in the Constitution that it warrants my pending vote against the Speaker, Speaker Boehner went too far when he teamed with Obama to advance this legislation. He relinquished the power of the purse, and with it he lost my vote."[199]

Conservatives were unsure if they were going to have the votes to oust Speaker Boehner, as they needed more this time around then they did in 2013, as the Republicans had more of a majority this time around. Again, the Speaker only needed to win a simple majority of the votes cast, meaning normally he would only have to receive 218 votes. However, this time around there was around 20 members missing from the House for various reasons, lowering the threshold significantly for Speaker Boehner. This time there would be 408 votes cast in the election, Boehner himself again not being one of them, although he was present. In the end, 25 votes were cast against Boehner, who received 216 votes, clearly a majority given the number of votes, conservatives figured before the vote was to occur, they needed 29 votes to defeat Speaker Boehner. They were also counting on a number of freshman Representatives to cast their vote against the Speaker, but it did not happen.[201, 202]

Votes were cast in the following way, 12 for Representative Daniel Webster, 3 for Representative Louie Gohmert, 2 for Representative Ted Yoho, 2 for Representative Jeff Duncan, 1 for Senator Rand Paul, 1 for former Secretary of State Colin Powell, 1 for Representative Trey Gowdy (who had been begged by conservative groups before the election to run for Speaker, but refused to do so), 1 for Representative Kevin McCarthy, 1 for Senator Jeff Sessions (who was one of the leading voices in the Senate against President Obama's executive amnesty, so no doubt another protest vote against Cromnibus) and one member voting present.

The 25 Representatives to vote against Boehner were Rep. Dave Brat (Virginia) (the Representative who defeated Eric Cantor in the Republican primary, and therefore automatically an enemy of the leadership team), Rep. Gary Palmer (Alabama), Representative Mark Meadows (North Carolina), Rep. Jim Bridenstine (Oklahoma), Rep. Justin Amash (Michigan), Rep. Jeff Duncan (South Carolina), Rep. Louie Gohmert (Texas), Rep. Thomas Massie (Kentucky), Rep. Tim Huelskamp (Kansas), Rep. Curt Clawson (Florida), Rep. Scott Garrett (New Jersey), Rep. Rod Blum (Iowa), Rep. Randy Weber (Texas), Rep. Marlin Stutzman (Indiana), Rep. Scott DesJarlais (Tennessee), Rep. Paul Gosar (Arizona), Rep. Bill Posey (Florida), Rep. Steve King (Iowa), Rep. Richard Nugent (Florida), Rep. Walter Jones (North Carolina), Rep. Ted Yoho (Florida), Rep. Daniel Webster (Florida), Rep. Scott Rigell (Virginia), Rep. Chris Gibson (New York) and Rep. Jim Cooper (Tennessee).[200]

It was the strongest attempt yet by the conservative wing to oust Boehner, but it would no doubt not be the last time they would attempt to defeat the Speaker. There was clear frustration among those who voted against Boehner with other Representatives, including Raul Labrador (Idaho), Mick Mulvaney (South Carolina) and Steve Pearce (New Mexico) who had voted against Boehner in 2013, but did not in 2015. It is unknown why those Representatives did not vote against the Speaker this time around. There was also frustration with strong conservative favorites such as Jim Jordan (Ohio) and Trey Gowdy (South Carolina) who did not vote against Speaker Boehner. Again, it cannot be explained why they supported him this time around.

Even though the vote was over, the backlash was not yet over. With more eyes on Boehner than before, the Speaker and his leadership team still went forward with punishments for those who voted against the Speaker, a tactic that would be brought more and more into the light in the coming months.

Speaker Boehner's Punishments For Opposition

Another habit the Speaker had begun to be called out for around that very same time was what he and his leadership team would do to Republican Representatives who broke ranks from the leadership and were active in opposition to their bills, punishments. Representatives who voted against Boehner and his allies could be stripped of Committee posts, publically shamed, have their bills or amendments blocked from entering the House floor for debate or a vote or in the long run become an enemy to GOP leadership and become the target of nasty smear campaigns leading up to an attempted Primary challenge. The leadership team may have gotten away with it for a few years, but in 2015, people really started to notice and call out the ploy.

According to the National Journal, there was rumor that House Republicans were planning a rule change in September of 2014 that would punish those who vote against the party's nominee for Speaker of the House. The nominee is normally first chosen in a closed door session in November, and then the actual vote takes place in the first session in January. However, the session in November is private and closed door, so no one knows exactly how many Republicans voted for Boehner or against him at that time. The plan would reportedly then strip the committee assignments from anyone who chooses to vote against Boehner or whoever the Speaker nominee is in January. This essentially would take any form of dissent away from the Speaker vote, forcing everyone to agree on one individual. This also would not allow those who would dissent from speaking their minds.[203]

However, the rule was not formally put in place for the 2015 Speaker election. Therefore, if punishment was to take place, it would be up to the Speaker and his leadership team to take the action. As it should be of no surprise to anyone at this point that is exactly what happened. However, this time, the actions taken were far more public, and the media actually used the words "punishment" "dissenters" and "revenge." In the days after the vote, several different news sites, including Breitbart, Politico, and Bloomberg, reported that Boehner had begun to give out punishments to dissenters. Two Representatives that voted against Boehner, Florida Representatives Daniel Webster and Richard Nugent, were both kicked off the influential Rules Committee. Another Representative, Randy Weber of Texas, who also voted against Boehner, was not allowed to sponsor a bill headed to the House floor because of his vote against Boehner.[204, 205, 206]

As the punishments built up in the aftermath of the failed coup against Boehner, more past punishments were coming to light. Bloomberg also noted in the same article discussing the aftermath of the 2015 Speaker election that in 2012 Representatives Justin Amash, Tim Huelskamp, David Schweikert (Arizona) and Walter Jones were all pulled off of some of their committees as well. All four are noted to be strong opponents of Boehner and Representatives who are not afraid to vote against leadership. Huelskamp also reportedly told Bloomberg that he lost out on a subcommittee chairmanship that he was promised in 2015 due to his vote against Boehner.

A different form of punishment was given to Freshman Representative Rod Blum of Iowa who had taken over the seat of a Democrat in the 2014 Midterm election. Boehner had backed Blum, and had even gone to Iowa to campaign for him. Blum, however, stuck to his principles and promised his constituents he would not vote for John Boehner as Speaker of the House. When Blum followed through on that promise in January of 2015, Boehner dropped his support of Blum. Blum was dropped from the list of Representatives to be financially supported in the next election due to their district being Democratic leaning. Blum also reported that he was picked over for a seat on the Financial Services committee, a committee he believed he would have been perfect to serve on due to his business background.[203]

The same article from National Review that noted Blum's punishment, also noted that Representatives Louie Gohmert (Texas) and Steve King (Iowa) were stripped of funding for travel due to their opposition to the Speaker in the election. These are all just examples of punishments for those who voted against Boehner in the 2015 Speaker election, there are even more punishments that likely were not reported, that occurred later, or have yet to occur. All of this comes as House conservatives who didn't vote against Boehner, including Ohio Representative Jim Jordan, warned Boehner from giving out punishments to those who voted against him. Others warned that excessive punishments, or more than have already been listed, could result in an escalating war within the House Republican caucus.[203]

In June of 2015 another controversial piece of legislation came up to be voted on in the House, the Trade Promotion Authority, or TPA. This time 34 House Republicans voted against the legislation that was heavily backed by Boehner. Again, dissenters were punished. This time, Representatives Trent Franks (Arizona), Cynthia Lummis (Wyoming) and Steve Pearce (New Mexico) were removed from the House Whip Team for voting against the Speaker and his leadership team. However, these were not as public as the other House member who was punished for voting against TPA, Representative Mark Meadows of North Carolina. Meadows was removed from his chairmanship position on the House Oversight subcommittee overseeing government operations. However, after days of public backlash against Boehner and the House Oversight Committee Chairman Jason Chaffetz, Meadows was reinstated to his position. There were also rumors leadership was planning on removing Ken Buck, a Representative from Colorado as President of the House Freshman class, but decided not to after public backlash.[209]

So with all of these examples of punishment by leadership for simply voting against them, we have to ask, what is driving this? The leadership team denies being the driving force, and Boehner allies have come out and stated that it is the rank and file Republican members, the 200 or so who often vote with leadership, who have stated their desires for members who break ranks to be punished. No matter how the leadership team attempts to justify it, it isn't right. A Representative should not be punished for voting the way his or her constituents want them to vote. If Representatives campaign promising their people they will vote for a new Speaker, and the people vote for the Representative for that reason, it is their duty to stick to that promise and vote for a new Speaker.

The point of a Democracy is to be able to have disagreements, and for everyone's voice to be heard, and for everyone to have their own opinion. The House of Representatives should be the representation of that. When we elect these men and women to go to Congress we should expect them to vote for their people, and not what other members of Congress or the leadership told them to vote for. They are not responsible to other members of Congress, they are responsible to the people. It is absolutely disrespectful to the people of the United States that Representatives are being punished by other members of Congress for believing they are voting for their constituents. These are allegations that need to be looked at very seriously, and hopefully stopped before they get more out of hand. Again, Congress represents We The People, not the Republican or Democratic party.

The Trade Debate

In the late spring of 2015, and pushing into the summer, another major piece of controversial legislation came up in the

House and the Senate, this one involving trade authority. This was actually split into two parts, which managed to cause quite a bit of confusion for people, and made it difficult to follow. The two parts were TPA and TPP. TPA, or Trade Promotion Authority, was the legislation made to create a fast track plan, or a quick way to get trade deals passed through Congress and the President. In order for any treaty or trade deal to become active or law, the Constitution requires that it is accepted by both Congress and the President. TPA speeds up that process. TPP, or the Trans Pacific Partnership, was the specific legislation that the United States Senate was working to invoke TPA on in 2015. TPP and TPA were both being pushed heavily by President Obama, and backed by Senate Majority Leader Mitch McConnell and Speaker of the House John Boehner. However, there are different sides to the story, as there were very different outcomes in the each chamber, with the Senate passing TPA and TPP easier than the House did.[212, 214]

Opponents of TPA, coming from both sides of the aisle, were concerned that TPA gave the executive branch too much power. They were not just concerned with President Obama, but with anyone else who would hold the office of President in the future, and now hold more power over trade negotiations that TPA offered. Despite objections from Democrats and conservatives, TPA passed in the House by a vote of 218-208. After the vote, Speaker Boehner was reportedly unhappy with Republicans who voted against the measure, and voiced his frustration. As stated before, Boehner then punished several members who voted against the trade deal.[212, 215]

Boehner himself admitted he supports TPA because he believes it will lead to the creation of more jobs in the United States. In a video posted on the Speaker's website, with the Speaker narrating, this is what he had to say about TPA:

"Right now, we have a big opportunity to pass a good, bipartisan jobs bill for the American people. It's called TPA – Trade Promotion Authority – and here's what it does, one letter at a time.

T stands for Trade.

Trade is good for America. It supports some 38 million jobs, and saves the average family more than $13,000 a year. This bill ensures that we make the best trade agreements possible.

P stands for Promotion.

This bill is going to promote jobs and economic growth. In my home state of Ohio alone, trade supports some 261,000 retail jobs.

A stands for Authority.

The way things work now, the president can negotiate a trade agreement on his own, without any direction from Congress. Our bill flips the script. Now any agreement will have to meet goals laid out by Congress, and it will have to withstand unprecedented scrutiny. That means more transparency, which means more authority for the American people.

But if you're looking for the short answer, TPA stands for jobs. Good-paying, high-quality American jobs. That's why it's important for us to pass this bill."[210, 211]

That is indeed the short answer, and to be fair, it's a good answer. Supporters of the trade deal believe it will bring in more jobs for the American people. However, not everyone feels that way. There are many that support the idea of promoting trade, but do not support giving the executive branch more authority in the negotiating and approval process, which is where the debate has to come to light. The truth is, TPP could have been passed without TPA, but Congress attempted to state that both needed to be passed in order for them to be relevant, and that is how they both ended up passing. At this point, we do not know everything about the trade deal, as now it heads for negotiations with the other countries involved. It will take quite a bit of time to find out whether or not the economic impacts are positive or negative. However, the measures taken to pass both TPA and TPP are questionable and shady. Why would both need to be passed? Why did the Speaker punish those who voted against it? These are the types of questions that the people should be asking and looking into, and that the Speaker should be answering. Without question, this will not be the last time the American people hear about TPA or TPP.[209, 213]

A 3rd Attempt To Oust Boehner- Vacate The Chair

With 2015 full of examples of Speaker John Boehner waging what seems like an all-out war on Republicans who have dared to oppose him, it was only a matter of time before there was push back in another form besides the January Speaker elections. On July 28, 2015, North Carolina Republican Mark Meadows, the very same Representative who had been punished for voting against TPA, took the important first step against Boehner's actions. Meadows filed what is called a Motion to Vacate the Chair, or essentially un-elect the Speaker of the House during the legislative session. Meadows laid out quite serious charges against Boehner, but none that should be any sort of a shock to those who have followed the situation very closely. Stated below is everything from the motion itself:

"Declaring the office of Speaker of the House of

Representatives vacant.

Whereas the Speaker of the House of Representatives for the

114th Congress has endeavored to consolidate power and

centralize decision-making, bypassing the majority of the

435 Members of Congress and the people they represent;

Whereas the Speaker has, through inaction, caused the power of Congress to atrophy, thereby making Congress subservient to the Executive and Judicial branches, diminishing the voice of the American People;

Whereas the Speaker uses the power of the office to punish Members who vote according to their conscience instead of the will of the Speaker;

Whereas the Speaker has intentionally provided for voice votes on consequential and controversial legislation to be taken without notice and with few Members present;

Whereas the Speaker uses the legislative calendar to create crises for the American People, in order to compel Members to vote for legislation;

Whereas the Speaker does not comply with the spirit of the rules of the House of Representatives, which provide that Members shall have three days to review legislation before voting;

Whereas the Speaker continues to direct the Rules Committee to limit meaningful amendments, to limit debate on the House floor, and to subvert a straightforward legislative process; and

Whereas the House of Representatives, to function effectively

in the service of all citizens of this country, requires the

service of a Speaker who will endeavor to follow an orderly

and inclusive process without imposing his or her

will upon any Member thereof: Now, therefore, be it

Resolved, That the office of Speaker of the House of

Representatives is hereby declared to be vacant."[217]

Notice that there are even some charges here that have not been discussed in this piece, including the voting of controversial legislation via voice vote with few members present. Most of it however does tie into what has been discussed in previous sections. Meadows specifically notes Boehner's punishments of those who do not comply with how the Speaker wants them to vote. He also notes that the Speaker uses the calendar to create crises to force members to vote one way or another; we have seen this with issues such as the 2013 government shutdown, and the 2014 Cromnibus bill. Long story short, it is often done when it comes to a budgetary issue. The House can choose to deal with the issue ahead of time, but Meadows makes a valid point when he states they do wait until the last minute to deal with important issues.[220]

House Democrats would agree with Meadows at the very least on the breaking of the three day rule, with Democrats noting that in the 113th Congress the House broke the three day rule at least 18 times, including with the Cromnibus spending deal in 2014.

Other members have stated at other times that their bills and amendments, which they believe would have been valid, have been kept from going to the House floor for a debate or a vote. It actually happens quite frequently in the House Rules Committee. The same accusation is often leveled in the Senate towards leadership, but it doesn't make it more right or wrong. The point is, most, if not all, of what Meadows stated in his motion truly can't be disputed. There are public records and facts that point to each of the cases that he has stated. However, the question is, is it enough to convince Republicans to vote to remove John Boehner as Speaker of the House?

Speaker Boehner publically does not seem too concerned with the matter, stating that the measure "isn't even deserving of a vote." With the measure going to the Rules Committee, which is stacked with Boehner supporters, the chance of the measure moving forward is rather low anyway. However, how much does the measure even need to move forward? Meadows himself even stated that he hoped this would at the very least generate a discussion with the Speaker, even if the vote doesn't occur.[219]

Other reports, including one from Breitbart, state that the Speaker was actually considering bringing the measure up for a vote before the August recess, but was unable to find the votes to safely overcome the measure. Meadows himself stated he had talked to Representatives who were contacted by Speaker Boehner's allies who confirmed they wanted to vote on the measure before August recess, but decided not to instead. The measure has been co-sponsored by Representatives Thomas Massie and Ted Yoho, two of the Representatives who opposed Speaker Boehner in January. It is unknown how many plan to vote against the Speaker again, but it would not be a surprise if the number was close, or even higher, than what it was in January of 2015.[218]

Boehner's Resignation

Many tried to write off the Meadows motion as being non-important during August and September. Allies of Speaker Boehner would repeatedly come out and speak against the measure, often calling it childish, or ridiculous. Conservatives, including Meadows, would hold strong for that period of time, and in the end would win. In a move that appeared to shock most of the political world, John Boehner announced on Friday, September 25, 2015 that he would be resigning as Speaker of the House at the end of October. The announcement came shortly after Pope Francis had spoken to Congress, which Boehner found to be quite inspirational.

Boehner gave several reasons for his timing of his resignation. In his speech, Boehner stated "last night I started thinking about this and this morning I woke up and I said my prayers -- as I always do -- and I decided today's the day I'm going to do this. As simple as that." He would add to that by stating, "I got plenty of people following me but this turmoil that's been churning now for a couple of months, it's not good for the members and it's not good for the institution. If I was not planning on leaving here soon, I can tell you I would not have done it." Boehner would also then continue to deny that his leaving was a result of the Meadows motion, but future actions can only show more evidence that the motion and the growing discontent with the Speaker played a large part in the timing of his departure. The Speaker would admit he wanted to retire before, but felt he couldn't due to Eric Cantor's election loss the year before.[221]

In a move that was of little surprise to anyone, the House Majority Leader Kevin McCarthy was the first to announce that he would be seeking to replace Boehner as Speaker. Boehner gave his full support to McCarthy, and worked behind the scenes to get McCarthy those votes. However, Boehner and McCarthy missed one very key point, many inside and outside of Washington have always associated Kevin McCarthy with John Boehner and the leadership team. Utah Congressman Jason Chaffetz, who would enter the Speaker race against McCarthy along with Florida Congressman Daniel Webster would state in an interview with Fox News that there were 50 Representatives willing to vote against McCarthy. Other Representatives stated their opposition to McCarthy because they wanted the status quo to change, not continue. McCarthy could not lose more than 30 Republicans to become the next Speaker of the House.

On Thursday, October 8, 2015, the day of the closed door vote within the Republican caucus, Kevin McCarthy stood up and told Republicans "I am not the guy," and officially dropped his bid for Speaker of the House. Since then, Boehner has postponed the Speaker election as the leadership searches for a new candidate to back. Republicans in the House then turned to Wisconsin Representative Paul Ryan, the Chairman of the Ways and Means Committee and Mitt Romney's Vice Presidential candidate. Ryan would face a significant amount of opposition in the closed door debate, only receiving 200 votes, with Daniel Webster receiving nearly 40 votes. On October 29, 2015 the new election was held, and Paul Ryan was elected Speaker with 236 votes, while Webster received 9 on the floor. It is our hope that Ryan will lead by example and change the way the House is run to reflect the will of the people.

Conclusion

When John Boehner became Speaker of the House in 2010, he came in with a lot of promise. There was a lot of hope from Republicans that maybe he would change the status quo in Washington, and that they would be able to get things done and pass meaningful reforms. However, Speaker Boehner has proved them wrong. Boehner's attempt to make himself look better has only created a more divided House than before, and has alienated the side he was supposed to lead. Throughout all of this, Speaker Boehner has also forgotten about his promises to the American people, and has led improperly.

Speaker Boehner has become the type of leader that rules by strong arming, by punishing those who disagree instead of working to find a compromise. Boehner may claim that he wants to have a united House Republican caucus, but no group of individuals can be united if they are not allowed to express their own views. By alienating members of the House by attempting to shut down their views, he has also alienated the American people. In 2014, the people went to the polls and elected a Republican majority to Congress. However, they did not all vote for John Boehner. Members of his district did, while members of a district in North Carolina voted for Mark Meadows and his conservative values, members of a district in Texas voted for Louie Gohmert and his conservative values as well. The same could be said for moderate Republicans elected across the country, and Democrats elected across the country. Life and politics isn't all about black and white or red and blue, there are many different points of view, and they should have the chance to be heard.

In the end, the grassroots and the people of the United States won this election. The Speaker of the House has no right to punish those who vote against him, which is exactly what Speaker Boehner was doing far too much. Boehner may deny that the Meadows motion had any part to play in forcing him to step down, but if you look at the numbers of those who were willing to vote against him and those willing to vote against McCarthy, it shows Boehner likely would not have been able to keep the gavel in a floor vote. The search is currently on for a new candidate for Speaker, and no date is set for the election. One thing is for certain, the next Speaker must be responsive to the people of the United States, and the Representatives who were elected by the people, for the people. The next Speaker should learn from John Boehner's mistakes and lead the House in an open and honest way, or else things will only continue to get worse.

VI. Mitch McConnell

"It's time Congress got its priorities straight."
Senator Mitch McConnell

Senate Majority Leader Mitch McConnell and Speaker John Boehner are similar in many ways, but also quite different in many ways. We've already seen some of the comparisons when talking about Speaker Boehner, and we will see more coming up here. However, we will also see the differences between the two in this section as well, notably McConnell's more blatant disregard for the conservative wing of his party. While Speaker Boehner at least claims to embrace it, and be a conservative himself, Majority Leader McConnell uses conservatives to win elections, and then tosses them aside afterwards, as he did in Kentucky in 2014, a topic that will certainly be brought up in this section.

McConnell has also been in Congress longer than Speaker Boehner has, having been in office for 30 years, since McConnell was 42 years old. This is a similarity that McConnell will have in common with our final example, Arizona Senator John McCain, being in Congress for far too long. However, McConnell, like Boehner, has come onto the scene promising to work for the American people time after time, but consistently has let the people down with empty promises and backdoor deals that end up hurting the people instead of helping them.

For the most part, McConnell had remained a moderate Republican throughout his career and managed to stay under the radar, avoiding controversies and public ire. However, since he has been drawn into a leadership role that has changed for McConnell and he has been thrust into the spotlight. McConnell has been noted for his opposition to President Obama while working with Senate Democratic leader Harry Reid on many occasions, and drawing the ire of Senate conservatives such as Texas Senator Ted Cruz and Utah Senator Mike Lee. Most of the criticism aimed at McConnell has come from the last few years, and there are explainable reasons as to why that is the case, which will be discussed further on.

Early Years

Mitch McConnell was born on February 20, 1942 in Sheffield, Alabama to Addison and Julia McConnell. When McConnell was eight, he and his family moved to Georgia. When McConnell attended high school, he moved to Louisville, Kentucky. He also chose to attend university in Louisville, where he graduated from the University of Louisville with a B.A. in history in the year 1964. McConnell then went onto law school at the University Of Kentucky College Of Law. Also during McConnell's time at law school he enlisted in the U.S. Army Reserves, but was discharged shortly after joining due to a medical condition.

During his school years, McConnell interned for Senator John Sherman Cooper of Kentucky. It was then that McConnell was convinced he wanted to enter into politics. Before he entered the Senate he was an assistant to Senator Marlow Cook, also of Kentucky, and was an Assistant Attorney General under President Gerald Ford. In 1977, McConnell officially entered politics when he was elected the Jefferson County, Kentucky Chief Justice/Executive, a position he held until 1985, when he would begin his Senate career. In 1993 McConnell married his current wife, Elaine Chao, who served as President George W. Bush's Secretary of Labor.[222, 224]

McConnell's Early Senate Career (Pre-Leadership Positions)[222, 224]

In 1984 Mitch McConnell defeated Democratic incumbent Walter Dee Huddleston by 0.4% to win his first Senate election. McConnell would go onto win each general election for the next 30 years by significant margins, with his most serious challenge coming from a Primary challenger in 2014. Throughout his career, McConnell has been noted as a moderate Republican who tends to follow the party lines, although he attempts to show himself as a conservative at times.

McConnell has been noted over the years to be a "villain" in the political landscape. Some have declared his politics to be rough, and his campaign styles to be nasty (noting that McConnell is not afraid to launch attack ads against his opponents or to back up his allies). This has had impacts on both Democrats and Republicans, some positive and some negative for both sides.

For his first few years in the Senate, McConnell was rather quiet. However, his first big fight came in the early 90's when the Bipartisan Campaign Reform Act came into play. McConnell opposed the act for years, including in the Supreme Court in 2003, by stating that it was a violation of the First Amendment. The Act placed limits on political contributions by interest groups and political parties, as well as other restrictions on campaigning. McConnell lost his challenges over the years, including his Supreme Court case, noted as McConnell v. Federal Election Commission.

McConnell was also noted early in his career to have been the "go to guy" for foreign aid for other countries by a member of the George H.W. Bush administration. During the 90's, McConnell served on the Senate Foreign Relations committee, and was instrumental in making sure aid was sent to Egypt, Israel and Ukraine (after the fall of the Soviet Union), while also engineering new funding for the International Monetary Fund as well, which certainly was not an easy task with the opposition of Russia, who wanted little or no IMF funding for its former states such as Ukraine.[225]

For his reputation with foreign aid, McConnell was awarded his first leadership positions starting in 1998 when he was selected to head the National Republican Senatorial Committee, a position he held for the 1998 and 2000 election cycles. This was noted as a success for McConnell, as Republicans held onto a majority in the Senate in both election cycles. At this point, McConnell would begin to stand out more in the political scene, and he would begin to move into leadership positions in the Senate, which many note to be his desire all along.

The 2000's- McConnell's Early Leadership Career

At the end of 2002, Mitch McConnell was selected to be the Majority Whip in the Senate for the 108th Congress, a position he would hold again for the 109th Congress. It was then that McConnell started to become more of a public figure, and his stances and votes were becoming more public. At that point, just about everything in American politics had started to become more public, with CSPANs constant coverage, and the internet era housing plenty of websites that track and explain each and every vote, it would be nearly impossible for a Senate leader to be unknown.

Several key bills and votes that McConnell would be noted for were the Common Sense Medical Malpractice Reform Act of 2001, the Small Business Liability Reform Act of 2003, and his vote for the Iraq War in 2002. None of them would seem to be too controversial at the time (although it is common today for people to bring up any Senator's vote for authorizing the Iraq War in a critical manner), and would only help to aide McConnell's rise to the top. McConnell would continue to fight against campaign finance laws, including in his 2003 Supreme Court case (in which he lost). All of McConnell's work would eventually lead into him being chosen for the top leadership position for the Senate Republicans in 2006. In the 2006 elections, the Republicans lost their majority in the Senate, and their Majority leader, Bill Frist, who decided not to seek re-election. At the start of the new Congress, Republicans elected Mitch McConnell to lead them as the Senate Minority Leader, and McConnell has been leading the Republicans in the Senate ever since.[222, 224]

Senate Minority Leader and President Obama

Being in a very similar position to John Boehner, Mitch McConnell had quite a bit of support from Republicans and conservatives when he first became Senate Minority Leader, but even more when Barack Obama was elected President in 2008. Republicans knew that McConnell's hands would be tied at least until 2011 due to the Republicans being in the Minority in both the Senate and the House. For the majority of the 111th Congress (2009-2011) the Democrats held a majority of 58 seats in the United States Senate (taking into account vacancies and the two Independents caucusing with the Democrats), meaning it would nearly impossible for Republicans alone to stop anything Barack Obama wanted to pass through, with a similar situation in the House as well.

In the 111th Congress, Barack Obama's first as President, President Obama's signature legislation, Obamacare, was passed. This would not only continue to define Barack Obama's Presidency and legacy for the years to come, but it would set up a consistent battle in both chambers of Congress between Democrats and Republicans, Republicans and Republicans, and Democrats and Democrats over how to handle the bill. At first, all Republicans in both chambers voted against the bill. Obamacare passed in the House 219-212, with some Democrats voting against it. Obamacare passed in the Senate 60-39, with all Democrats and Independents voting for it, and all Republicans voting against it, with one Republican not voting. With the Democrats having the 60 vote threshold at the time, it was impossible for Republican to even force a veto. However, with the election of Scott Brown from Massachusetts in the special election around the same time, many believe he would have been the vote that could have kept the Democrats from receiving 60 votes, but he was not sworn in in time for the vote. For now, the Republicans, including McConnell would have to wait for another strategy to appear, or at least for the numbers to change, before voting down Obamacare.[228, 229]

Also like Boehner, McConnell came out very publically against Barack Obama in his first term. In 2010, McConnell even stated that he believed it was important to make Obama a one term President. His exact words to the National Journal were "The single most important thing we want to achieve is for President Obama to be a one-term president."[227] One has to wonder if this really is the job of the Senate to meddle in the affairs of a Presidential election, but McConnell added after "our single biggest political goal is to give our nominee for president the maximum opportunity to be successful." The follow up was a better way to phrase it, but there is no doubt that this would set a tone of animosity between the two sides for years to come. The Senate and the House should be focused on doing what they can for the American people legislatively, not making their electoral decisions for them. As expected, McConnell would take a lot of criticism for the comment, and many to this day do not let him forget those words.

In 2010, the Republicans began to take back more seats in the Senate and completely took over the House. The numbers this time were 53 seats held by Democrats and Independents in the Senate, and 47 seats held by Republicans in the Senate. The House of Representatives was now held by a sweeping Republican majority of 242-193, quite a significant change from the term before in the Democratic held chamber. Republicans were now starting to feel that they could do more to advance their ideas, and stop things such as Obamacare. When more of these plans seemed to fail, including what seemed like a failed battle over the government budget, the focus then turned to taking over the Senate and the White House in 2012 for the next Congress.

In the 2012 election the balance of power remained mostly the same, with Democrats and Independents holding 55 seats in the Senate and the Republicans holding 45 seats, with the Republicans still holding a strong majority in the House. Yet again, the argument was that with a democratically controlled White House, the Republicans would need to capture the Senate in 2014 in order to advance Republican plans and stop Barack Obama's agenda. So this would continue to be the argument throughout the Congress, Republicans must have the Senate. However, things were starting to change, some Senators, like their counterparts in the House, were starting to see maybe it just isn't the party that is the problem, maybe it's the leadership. Minority Leader McConnell would continue to see his poll numbers and favorability drop in this session, and would even face a significant primary challenger in the 2014 election cycle. However in the end McConnell kept his seat and Republicans gained the majority they had wanted for so long in the Barack Obama presidency.

So now things would change for the better, right? Wrong. Conservative Review and the Heritage Foundation, two organizations that keep scores of members of Congress (noted when discussing Speaker Boehner as well) have had McConnell's scores go down each year for the past few years; his numbers for 2015 are not pretty, sitting at 52% and 58% for each. What exactly caused many to lose faith in Mitch McConnell during his years as Senate Minority Leader? Here are some of the reasons why conservatives and Americans began to lose faith in the elder statesman.[230, 231]

McConnell and Obamacare, Yes but No

Like with all Republicans, Mitch McConnell was strongly opposed to Obamacare when it first came out. McConnell led the Republican effort in the Senate in 2009 to block the President's healthcare plan, which turned out to pass anyway. However, over the years there would be countless (literally) other attempts to get rid of Obamacare, from straight votes of repeal, to efforts to defund either the whole law or parts of the law. Both House and Senate conservatives would consistently give leadership plenty of options to stop Obamacare, risky, but options that could potentially succeed. All this being said to this day we still have Obamacare in full effect, so what exactly happened? Leadership didn't like the ideas.

Here is a just a brief history of Mitch McConnell's voting record on Obamacare in the Senate, noting the key votes regarding the healthcare law. In 2009 McConnell voted with Senate Republicans to block Obamacare, this vote failed. In 2011 there were two key votes. The first came in regards to an amendment to reject Obamacare, and McConnell voted for the measure to advance. This motion also failed, unsurprisingly. Later in the year the Omnibus spending deal came into play (note this is different than the 2014 Cromnibus), and part of the deal was to fund Obamacare. McConnell voted against the spending measure.

In 2013 the issue was raised again in the form of defunding Obamacare in both March and September. In March it was a smaller fight, with very little publicity. McConnell voted in this instance to fund Obamacare and the government in full (McConnell had co-sponsored a bill with Senator Ted Cruz to defund Obamacare, but when the amendment failed, McConnell voted for the bill without the amendment, whereas most other conservatives voted against the measure in its entirety). In September a similar tactic came into play, but was a much larger fight. This is when the issue of the government shutdown came into play. McConnell voted against defunding Obamacare in this instance as well. The next major vote came in late 2014 in regards to the Cromnibus spending bill that has been discussed, part of the spending was in regards to Obamacare. McConnell voted for the Cromnibus spending bill, and therefore again voted to fund Obamacare.

When McConnell became Senate Majority Leader at the end of 2014, McConnell doubled down on his rhetoric to repeal the law, telling reporters in an article in the Washington Times by David Sherfinski "We certainly will have a vote on proceeding to a bill to repeal Obamacare. … It was a very large issue in the campaign. We're certainly gonna keep our commitment to the American people to make every effort we can to repeal it."[232]

At face value, it appears that McConnell is for voting to eliminate Obamacare, but when it comes to funding Obamacare, McConnell voted in favor for it. Why is there such a discrepancy? Some would argue that those who have voted to fund Obamacare but voted to repeal it are worried about the effects of a government shutdown, and that they know that the President and Senate Democrats would never allow Obamacare to be repealed. However, it hasn't just been the public votes that have people concerned with McConnell's stance on Obamacare, many are concerned with the behind the scenes actions McConnell has taken against those who have vowed to fight the healthcare law, no matter what, including Utah Senator Mike Lee and Texas Senator Ted Cruz. McConnell and Cruz's feud deserves its own section, but there will be some overlap here.

The truth is, on several occasions Mitch McConnell has worked behind the scenes to ensure that conservatives attempting to repeal Obamacare in any other method rather than a full bill repealing it would fail, and these actions have made the fight very public for Majority Leader McConnell, much like Speaker Boehner's fight with House conservatives has become public. This was most evident during the 2013 government shutdown fight, as this would represent the start of the public fight between Senate conservatives and Mitch McConnell. Even before Mike Lee and Ted Cruz began their tactic in 2013 to defund Obamacare, McConnell came out publically against the plan.

Overall, the plan to defund Obamacare really wasn't a complicated one; it was just a controversial one that had to be played just right by conservatives in both the House and the Senate. The architects of the plan, Utah Senator Mike Lee and Texas Senator Ted Cruz knew that Obamacare was set to kick in on September 30, and that a vote on funding would be due up just before that. With lack of options from other Senators, Lee and Cruz knew their plan was the only one available that could actually work. Cruz himself lays out the strategy in his new book *A Time For Truth.*

"When the continuing resolution funding the government expired in late September, Congress should fund the entire federal government-but not Obamacare. This strategy was based on the principle that the Constitution is designed with checks and balances. The most significant check that Congress possesses is the power of the purse, and so we urged that Congress should continue to fund everything in the government-except Obamacare" (Cruz 273).[237]

Cruz would then go onto explain that the plan was to encourage Americans to support the plan by organizing a grassroots movement, then convincing the House of Representatives to pass the funding resolution, then convince Senate Republicans to support it, and then finally start convincing Democrats, notably those in red states who would be vulnerable in 2014 and 2016, to support the plan. Lee and Cruz knew it was going to be difficult, and that they would likely have to overcome a veto as well, but they felt they had to fight it somehow.

Cruz also notes in his book that as Lee and Cruz described their plan to colleagues they were told that they "just didn't understand how Washington works" (Cruz 274). This would be a common phrase thrown at Lee and Cruz throughout their careers, because they don't play the game the same way others do, and maybe that's not a bad thing.[237]

To the disappointment of certain others in Congress, over 2 million people signed the online petition to defund Obamacare, and then called their Representatives in Congress. The House then voted to go along with Senator Lee and Senator Cruz's plan, and passed a continuing resolution that did not have funding for Obamacare. However, when it came to the third part of the plan, convincing Senate Republicans from going along with the plan, that is where the issues came up. Not only did Cruz and Lee find it difficult to convince certain Senate Republicans to support their plan, Senate Republican leadership, notably Minority Leader Mitch McConnell, came out publically against the plan, and against conservatives who backed the plan.

Cruz states in his book there were several potential reasons why McConnell came out so aggressively against the plan. "Perhaps they wanted to discourage conservatives like Mike and me from ever again rebelling against the party line. Or perhaps they were simply angry that a handful of senators would have the temerity to take our case straight to the American people" (Cruz 276).[237] Sounds quite familiar to Speaker John Boehner right? Congressional leadership does not like dissent, and whether the idea was good or bad, leadership was bound to be opposed because it might make them look bad, and they don't want any bad publicity coming back on them.

McConnell, speaking before Cruz's filibuster on September 24, 2013, made this statement. "I just don't happen to think that filibustering a bill that defunds Obamacare is the best route to defunding Obamacare. All it does is shut down the government, and keep Obamacare, and none of us want that."[233] However, just before that McConnell had stated they could invoke cloture and then vote to defund Obamacare. However, this never happened. If Senate leadership, including McConnell want to really get rid of Obamacare, why won't they support the options on the table? They didn't support the defund movement that came to them, and they never made a full push to invoke cloture either.

Over the next few weeks, Cruz would take quite a bit of criticism from Senate Republicans who blamed him for the shutdown of the government, although he was not the one to blame. Instead of standing with Cruz, McConnell and others choose to try and shut down his plan that was already in play. Matthew Boyle with Brietbart stated in an article before Cruz's speech that McConnell and Senator John Cornyn, McConnell's number 2 in the Senate, were actively whipping votes to deliberately shut down Cruz's speech and arguments before they even started. Therefore, the public campaign against Cruz would continue.[234]

In the end, McConnell met with Senate Majority Leader Harry Reid and a deal was made to fund Obamacare and the government, and no concessions at all were made for the Republicans. McConnell would then continue to use phrases like "it was not a smart play" and it was a "tactical error" when describing

Cruz's plan, although he really didn't have one of his own to use. There have been heavy criticisms of the deal that McConnell cut with Reid, especially since the Republicans got nothing out of it, well except for McConnell. The Senate Conservatives Fund reported that McConnell was able to get something out of the deal, $3 billion for a dam project in Kentucky, something he could boast about in his upcoming primary election in Kentucky.[235, 236]

To this day, over two years later, Obamacare is still the law of the land. This other plan McConnell claims that could have worked better, was never truly discussed. There have been several show votes to attempt to repeal Obamacare, but still nothing has "worked." Because of this, McConnell's poll numbers have started to plummet, and rightfully so. However, the 2013 fight would only be the start of the public outcry against McConnell. This would be the first major instance, in which McConnell seems to have gone against the support of the public for his own personal gain, but it would not be the last, and many would take note of this.

2014 Kentucky Republican Primary- Lies, Lies, Lies

By the time the 2014 election cycle started (early 2013), many were starting to question the strength of the infamous Tea Party that had been responsible for the election of Senators like Ted Cruz, Mike Lee, Rand Paul and Marco Rubio along with Congressmen Mark Meadows and Jim Bridenstine in 2010 and 2012. Before the cycle even started, there were two new sides to the battle, those who felt the Tea Party was still relevant, and those who argued the Tea Party was on its way out and would not have a strong impact on the 2014 Midterm elections. From the side of the Tea Party, there was little doubt which state would serve as the battleground for this cycle, the state of Kentucky for the seat of Senate Minority Leader Mitch McConnell.

Conservative groups and commentators had begun to warn McConnell several years before that if he continued down his current track, they would make an attempt to remove him from office in the next election cycle. McConnell only seemed to get worse, and conservatives followed through on their threat to remove McConnell. In the early months of 2013, several candidates began declaring their intentions to run for the Republican nomination for Mitch McConnell's Senate seat. McConnell also faced a challenge from the Kentucky Democrats in current Kentucky Secretary of State Alison Lundergan Grimes. McConnell's most significant challenger during the Primary, and what many considered to be the election of his career, was Kentucky businessman Matt Bevin. Matt Bevin was strongly endorsed by key conservative figures, including radio hosts Mark Levin and Glenn Beck, and key conservative groups such as the Senate Conservatives Fund. These were all endorsements Bevin would certainly need even just to get his name out to the public, as Bevin would be facing one of the most dirty and nasty political machines seen recently, as well as squaring off against the Republican establishment that heavily supported Minority Leader McConnell in the election.

Although Bevin started out with low name recognition and low poll numbers, he was still presented as a significant threat to McConnell, one that McConnell would be forced to address. Although McConnell would go on to win the Primary, Bevin would be McConnell's most significant Republican challenger to date, and would bring up many issues that McConnell would not only be forced to address in the election, but also issues that would continue to follow McConnell in the coming years. While Bevin did not hold back in his criticism of McConnell, he was able to do so in a respectful manner. However, before Bevin even announced his candidacy, there were reports that McConnell and his allies had been attempting to convince Bevin not to campaign against the Minority Leader.

The Huffington Post, in an article titled *Mitch McConnell Allies Allegedly Threatened Matt Bevin Over Primary Challenge: Report* went on to note a piece by Katrina Trinko of the National Review in which she stated:

"'Mitch McConnell's people reached out to Matt for several months through all different avenues trying to convince him not to run,' the adviser close to Bevin tells National Review Online… 'First they tried to threaten him," the source added, "and then they tried to dangle shiny political prizes.'"[238]

Of course the article also stated that the McConnell campaign denied the allegation. Obviously the dialogue did not work to dissuade Bevin, who still launched his campaign with a clear intent to remove the Minority Leader who he did not believe could continue to lead Republicans in the Senate or the American people any further. If these reports are true, which given what many have said about McConnell's campaign style in the past, it likely only strengthened Bevin's resolve to run and defeat McConnell. This is the kind of behavior that we should not be accepting as Americans. In a Democratic society debate and request for change should always be welcomed, but Minority Leader McConnell does not seem to be following that idea as closely as he should.

When Bevin did enter the race, the McConnell campaign, without surprise, went on the attack rather quickly. However, in this strategy there were conflicting reports. The same above noted Huffington Post article also notes that the McConnell campaign noted that Bevin's challenge was '"nothing more than a nuisance.'"[238] However, others would anticipate that Bevin would be a stronger opponent then McConnell would really like to see, and that while he may not win, he would at the very least damage McConnell enough to make the general election even messier.

Bevin's first ad against McConnell was what was expected being directed at someone like McConnell. The Weekly Standard noted the ad in their article by Michael Warren *And They're Off: Kentucky Republican Senate Primary Begins with Dueling Ads* that Bevin criticized McConnell's "'30 years in Washington,'" along with McConnell's support for "'higher taxes, bailouts, debt-ceiling increases, congressional pay raises and liberal judges.'"[240] McConnell then responded by criticizing Bevin's record as a businessman in Connecticut, where the McConnell campaign reports that Bevin received taxpayer bailouts, but did not pay taxes; Bevin disputed this claim, instead stating he received a loan from the city of East Hampton after a storm damaged some of his property. Bevin also noted McConnell was desperate to hang on to power, and that all of the mudslinging and lies would not be helpful for the people of Kentucky. However, the mudslinging and lies would only continue throughout the entire campaign, with the majority of it coming from the McConnell campaign.[239]

In an interview with US News, Bevin would state the following:

"We're tired of the bail outs, we're tired of the amnesty, we're tired of the votes against our 2nd Amendment rights, we're tired of the votes that repeatedly allow the federal government to spy on law-abiding citizens, we're tired of the pay increases for you... He constantly brags how he'd like to be the Senate majority leader, but he's not even doing a very effective or good job as the minority leader and the people of Kentucky are saying, 'what about us?'"[241]

These are all valid points that Bevin would continue to bring up throughout his campaign, while McConnell would continue to make empty promises that he has even to this day not followed through on.

One of the biggest obstacles for Bevin's campaign was the support that Mitch McConnell received from fellow Kentucky Senator Rand Paul. The two had formed a strange alliance in 2013 for the election despite Paul defeating McConnell's choice for the Senate seat in the years before. Before Bevin entered the race, Paul endorsed Mitch McConnell, and refused to change his endorsement even after Bevin had entered the race. It is likely that if Paul had thrown his support behind Bevin that Bevin would have stood a better chance against McConnell. He may not have won, as McConnell has racked up a lot of permanent support in Kentucky being a 30 year Senator and the future Majority Leader, but the election could have been even closer if Paul had backed Bevin and campaigned against McConnell. Many found Paul's actions to be strange, as the biggest things McConnell and Paul have in common are political party and state of residence, they often disagree on major issues such as foreign policy and domestic surveillance programs, and have openly argued on the Senate floor.

Although McConnell received the backing of Rand Paul, he was quick to bash some of Paul's strongest supporters, the Tea Party and conservatives. In a statement also referring to the challenge of Republican incumbents in Kansas (Pat Roberts) and Mississippi (Thad Cochran) McConnell stated "I think we are going to crush them everywhere… I don't think they are going to have a single nominee anywhere in the country."[242] Again McConnell is showing the idea that he believes it is his way or the highway, if you do not agree with McConnell, then you are wrong. However, McConnell, Roberts and Cochran have served a total of 116 years in Congress, with Pat Roberts serving 44 years, Thad Cochran serving 42 years and Mitch McConnell serving 30 years. Their conservative challengers, Dr. Milton Wolf, State Senator Chris McDaniel and Businessman Matt Bevin were all relatively young, and would have represented fresh ideas coming to Congress.

If this election showed anything, it is that the older members of Congress are afraid to lose their power, and will go to extreme lengths such as threatening to "crush" a part of their party, and their constituents, to win re-election. McConnell's backing of Thad Cochran during the election is another issue itself, as Cochran won his primary against Chris McDaniel by using the vilest tactics of the campaign season, including extreme lies and race baiting.

Other attacks McConnell would launch against Bevin would be calling him a "traveling salesman" and saying he has a laughable pitch, comparing Bevin's speech to a John Lovitz comedy video in which he calls himself a pathological liar, and in many cases a phony conservative. McConnell would also try to hit on a report that Bevin had once attended a cockfighting event, and that made Bevin someone who was not eligible to be a United States Senator. Such silly arguments just helped to show that McConnell really didn't have anything credible against Bevin, and that he knew he could potentially be in trouble. These types of attacks against Bevin would continue even as Bevin would attempt to call for real debate.[243]

McConnell would then attempt to save his own reputation by declaring himself a true conservative. He attended the Conservative Political Action Committee event in 2014, and even brought a rifle with him to attempt to show how much of a supporter of the 2nd Amendment he really is (although that was one of the few issues not in dispute for McConnell). At CPAC McConnell stated he would fight for "conservative reform," apparently ignoring the fact he was willing to bash those same principles around that time. He has also at times attempted to state that he "loves the Tea Party," and wants their support for the election, and would help them if he could as well. As expected, McConnell also campaigned on stopping President Obama's agenda, including Obamacare. McConnell had stated in previous years, and on the campaign trail, that Obamacare could be defeated, even with just 51 votes. However, after

McConnell defeated Bevin, and only a few weeks before the general election, he made this statement to Fox News: "It would take 60 votes in the Senate. Nobody thinks we're going to have 60 Republicans. And it would take a presidential signature. No one thinks we're going to get that." Again McConnell stated one thing before his election, and then yet another after he felt he was in the clear.[244, 245, 246]

Another notable point with McConnell and his campaign was that he promised to change how the Senate functioned. There was no question that Harry Reid often attempted to block or slow down bills he didn't want to come to the Senate floor, which often were bills by Republican
Senators. McConnell would state that he would allow fair and open debate on the Senate floor. He also promised to have Senators working harder. A report by Erica Werner with politicsusa.com referenced a promise McConnell made to hold more Friday votes. In the article Werner states McConnell allowed more votes in January then Reid had in the past, McConnell was still allowing long weekends for Senators. This seems to be a smaller issue compared to some of the other issues, but it still speaks to McConnell's record and the wonder if he can be truly trusted or not. Several of his campaign lies, flip flops and promises seem to suggest otherwise.[247]

McConnell would continue the negative attacks on Bevin, most of which were proven false, up until the Primary election. When that day came, McConnell defeated Bevin by over 24 percentage points, 60.2 to 35.4. This seems like a significant margin of victory, but it was the closest primary race McConnell ever had. When it came to the general election, McConnell defeated Alison Lundergan Grimes by over 15 points, 56.2 to 40.7. The race between McConnell and Grimes was even a bit nastier than the primary battle, as expected. Today, McConnell still faces plenty of criticism from Republicans and conservatives, while Matt Bevin is the

Republican nominee for Governor of Kentucky, and is expected to defeat Democrat Jack Conway in November.[249, 250]

So where does the primary fit into this narrative? McConnell made plenty of campaign promises, but to this day really has not followed through on any of them. McConnell campaigned on the idea of crushing the Tea Party because they promised new ideas, and when new ideas came up in the Senate, McConnell tried to shoot them down there as well. McConnell isn't willing to try new ideas, but will campaign on being the best option. Obamacare still has not been defeated, and there are still notable issues within the Senate regarding the process of debate and votes. Many still describe McConnell as "spineless" and not willing to fight for important issues because it might make him look bad. Others note McConnell's negativity on the campaign trail as something that should not be tolerated. As Senate Majority leader, McConnell should be a leading example for the kind of ethics the voters want to see in Congress; however McConnell has become one of the leading examples for the kind of ethics people are disgusted with in Congress. This kind of behavior has drawn quite a bit of ire from other conservatives, notably Utah Senator Mike Lee and Texas Senator Ted Cruz. This of course would lead into Mitch McConnell's biggest challenge at this time, Texas Senator Ted Cruz.

Senate Majority Leader Mitch McConnell's Worst Nightmare- Ted Cruz

Mitch McConnell may have skated by the 2014 elections, and he may have been able to keep some of his strongest supporters in office, but eventually McConnell's poor leadership style, and dishonesty to the American people was going to catch up with him. Two major changes have made McConnell's job and style significantly harder, his position as Majority Leader, which has thrust him into the spotlight, and the Senate career of Ted Cruz, a vocal conservative who is not afraid to back down from a fight, the last thing Mitch McConnell wanted to see.

Senator Cruz has several things that Matt Bevin did not, which makes Cruz an even stronger adversary to McConnell. The first is that Cruz is in the Senate with McConnell, and that McConnell is the leader of the same party Cruz is in. Therefore, all of the behind the scenes talk and deals that Matt Bevin was not privy to during the 2014 election, Ted Cruz has heard countless times, and is not afraid to speak out. Cruz also has a bigger platform to stand on then Bevin. Bevin and McConnell were fighting for a Senate seat, an important one, but one that was still mainly focused around the state of Kentucky. Due to McConnell's position it drew national attention, but not the same kind a public debate in the Senate would. Cruz on the other hand being a sitting Senator has drawn public attraction to what is going on, forcing McConnell to address Cruz and the present situation. Cruz also has his current position as "presidential candidate" going for him. More people know who Cruz is because of his campaign for President of the United States, and this allows him to not only get his name out there, but tell the entire nation stories he knows from the Senate that Bevin or other challengers may not have known about McConnell, or simply could not prove.

We have seen the same case with Speaker of the House John Boehner. The strongest opposition has not come from Democrats or primary challengers, or even special interest groups. The strongest opposition has come from members of the House in the Republican Party, men like Mark Meadows and Louie Gohmert. The same is said for Mitch McConnell, with his strongest critics being Mike Lee and Ted Cruz, with Cruz being the most evident and vocal.

In Ted Cruz's new book, *A Time For Truth,* Cruz opens up the entire book by noting an experience he and Mike Lee had with Mitch McConnell that just show how out of touch the Majority Leader is with the American people. Cruz describes the setting as being at a Republican Senatorial lunch in February of 2014 during the debt ceiling crisis. Cruz noted that McConnell had mentioned that in order for a debt ceiling bill to pass, the House and the Senate should add something else into the bill that would be beneficial to the American people. President Obama, however, wanted a clean bill. Cruz then notes the strategy of the Republican leadership.

"In the Senate, any rule can be changed by unanimous consent, which takes, as the name implies, the affirmative consent of all one hundred senators… the members of the Republican leadership stood before us and asked every senator to join with the Democrats in granting unanimous consent to lower the 60-vote threshold to take up the debt ceiling to just 50 votes… None of us should oppose this, we were told… if we lowered the threshold, the 'clean' debt ceiling would pass… And second if we consented to lowering the threshold, Democrats would then have the votes to raise the debt ceiling on their own. We could all vote no. This way, we could return home and tell the voters that we had opposed raising the debt ceiling" (Cruz xiii).[237]

Just take a look at the last few lines, the most telling parts of that message. According to Senator Cruz, Republican leadership asked Republican senators to cave simply so they could tell their constituents they tried. Cruz's response was this:

"It was too much. I raised my hand and said, 'There's no universe in which I can consent to that…' 'If I were to affirmatively consent to making it easier for Democratic Senate leader Harry Reid to add trillions in debt-with no spending reforms whatsoever- I think it would be dishonest and unfaithful to the voters who elected me'" (Cruz xiv).[237]

Cruz then notes that Mike Lee was the only other senator in the room who stood with him. Unfortunate, but not too much of a surprise. Cruz then notes that the yelling started after that, with fellow Republicans becoming angry with him for going against the status quo, or what has become the status quo under Mitch McConnell's leadership. Cruz specifically notes:

"When I made my case to my colleagues, they looked at me like I was a fool. I heard more than one variation of 'that's what you say to folks back home. You don't actually do it…' *Don't you understand what we are doing?* Senators thundered. *Why are you forcing us to tackle this? Why can't you just go along?...* The response from the Republican leadership was firm- they didn't want us to fight for anything" (Cruz xviii).[237]

Cruz then notes that the vote was held the next day, and the votes were not read aloud like they usually are, this allowed Republican leadership to attempt to find one or two more senators to vote for the debt ceiling increase. Only about an hour later, the Democrats had their vote, with 12 Republicans voting yes with the Democrats. Cruz notes that after the initial vote, only 4 Republicans had voted yes. Senators Cruz and Lee made a strong case in the days leading up to convince some of their colleagues to stand by their principles and campaign promises and vote against the debt ceiling increase, and Republican leadership had worked hard to ensure that Republicans voted against their campaign promises. It's also worth noting those very same "leaders" including McConnell, voted for this measure.

Throughout the very same section of his book, Cruz notes that Congressional leadership has several ways to punish members who "speak the truth" (Cruz xx). One he notes is withholding campaign funding, and the other is the use of "public flogging," essentially making them look bad in the public spotlight, and Cruz notes that McConnell himself has been responsible for some of the flogging, including making sure Cruz was called selfish during the Sunday morning news shows. At this point Cruz is used to these attacks, as many have begun to note the feud between Cruz and

McConnell. This is no surprise, as McConnell represents those in Washington who have been in too long, and are in it for the power and prestige, while Cruz, a newcomer to Washington, has been fighting for his constituents without fear of attack.[237]

While McConnell may not be punishing dissenters as publically as Boehner is, it's still wrong for a sitting Majority Leader to attempt to punish senators for doing what they believe is the right thing by telling the truth. Although those who have been in Congress for a long time may not believe this, telling the truth is the right thing to do, and it is what the American people want to see more politicians do.

In July of 2015, Cruz himself went after McConnell on the Senate floor for lying to Senate Republicans over the revival of the Export-Import Bank. Cruz stated in the speech that in May he asked McConnell during a meeting if the deal recently cut for the TPA bill including a way to reauthorize the Export-Import Bank, Cruz then states in the speech that McConnell told him three times that there was "no deal." Cruz began the speech due to the fact that the reauthorization of the Export-Import Bank was added to the highway spending bill the Senate was about to vote on, he also criticized McConnell for not allowing amendments to be added to the bill, which meant an amendment to remove the Export-Import Bank reauthorization could have been added. Cruz also stated McConnell was visibly angry with him for daring to ask that question. Many criticized Cruz for the speech on the floor, claiming that it wasn't the time or the place, and that calling out another Senator for lying was disrespectful.[251, 252, 253]

However, if what Senator Cruz said is true, it is McConnell who has shown disrespect, yet again, to the American people and his Republican colleagues. If McConnell told Cruz there wouldn't be a deal to reauthorize the Bank, but then two months later a deal is made, that is indeed a lie by the Majority Leader. As to McConnell's anger with Cruz, everyone has the right to ensure there are not added deals to bills being passed, and McConnell has no reason to be angry. How is Senator Cruz, or any other Senator just to start, supposed to trust McConnell after something like this? Also it brings up the question, how many times has this happened before under McConnell's watch? And finally, how are the American people supposed to trust McConnell as well if this is true, or even if there is the slightest hint of truth?

Many in politics, whether it be public policy, the media or other Senators and Representatives, have noted since Mitch McConnell became Majority Leader that Cruz has been, and will continue to be, problematic for McConnell. An article by CNN is even titled *Ted Cruz Poised to Make Life Miserable for Mitch McConnell*. Some of the other issues that Cruz has opposed McConnell on, but they have not had public debates on, have been the 2013 government shutdown, the defunding of Obamacare, the defunding of executive amnesty, the Cromnibus bill, and the TPA. Cruz even stated that the second time TPA came up for a vote he voted it down because of the extra deals that were added to the bills, noting them as "corrupt deals."[253]

In reference to the shutdown, while McConnell worked against Cruz, he also worked to come up with a deal to end the shutdown, but a deal, as stated before, that would not give Republicans anything. McConnell hailed the deal as a success, but the deal both funded Obamacare and raised the debt ceiling; the two things that Republicans were attempting to make sure did not happen in any deal that would be made. This would only add to Cruz's frustration with McConnell, and McConnell's poor public perception.[254, 255]

The fighting between Cruz and McConnell has only escalated in the last few months, notably with the instance of Cruz calling McConnell out on the Senate floor. To McConnell, it seems like a personal attack, but to Cruz and his supporters, it's a way of hitting back at the old ways of Washington that they find to be corrupt and dirty. With a Senator as outspoken as Cruz and a Majority Leader like McConnell who is old fashioned, it was only a matter of time before the two clashed, and Cruz became a significant problem for McConnell. There is no question that Cruz has indeed become a problem for McConnell, but many wonder who is right, the seasoned veteran or the outspoken newcomer. The fact that McConnell is the subject of this section notes our answer here.

McConnell's Other Critics-Caving Too Easily

During McConnell's time as Minority Leader and during his time as Majority Leader he has had plenty of other examples where conservative critics have been upset with him. Note that McConnell's most serious primary challenger came in the 2014 election, before McConnell even became Majority Leader. This shows that a good portion of the Republican Party was upset with McConnell even before he won his current leadership position. Boehner at the very least was able to keep the support of the entire party before he became Speaker. One of the most common criticisms of Mitch McConnell has been over his negotiations, with many noting that McConnell caves too easily and cuts deals with Senate Democratic leader Harry Reid and President Obama. It was McConnell who caved first on the 2013 shutdown which gave Boehner the position to cave in as well. Some of the other examples of McConnell's caving include on Cromnibus and the trade debate. Some of the other criticism McConnell has received has been over his support for controversial programs such as the NSA surveillance programs and the Patriot Act.

The situation in regards to the Cromnibus bill is somewhat similar for Mitch McConnell to what happened with John Boehner. However, there were several key distinctions. The first is that when Cromnibus came up in the Senate in December of 2014 the

Republicans did not yet have the majority in the Senate. It was also unusual in the sense that McConnell did not speak too much on Cromnibus or offer too much of an argument for or against. This, however, does speak to the concern of McConnell caving too easily. McConnell could have led an effort to try and defeat the measure, but he did not. McConnell also voted for the measure, which passed in the Senate 77-19, showing that he also supported it. Many conservatives, including those who voted against the measure, felt that voting for Cromnibus was a vote for President Obama's amnesty. Of course in the Senate Republicans and Democrats found a way to blame Senator Cruz for Republicans not being able to stop the bill, but in this case it was Senate Minority Leader Mitch McConnell who chose not to step up and lead the opposition.

In February of 2015 conservatives promised to attempt to stop President Obama's executive amnesty by not allowing it to be funded through the Department of Homeland Security, whose funding was not settled in the 2014 Cromnibus. They promised the fight in February would be to allow the DHS to received funding, but not funding for immigration. This time the Republicans had their majority, and promised they could do what they swore to do before. However, at the end of the debate, Mitch McConnell again offered a "clean" DHS bill, one that funded everything, despite the fact that conservatives promised to defund the executive amnesty. McConnell's response was that conservatives could offer their own bills to defund the amnesty on its own. However, Republicans were given a possible out before the vote, as a federal judge paused the immigration plans while a group of states appealed the actions. However the bill passed, again with McConnell doing nothing to stop it.[256, 257, 258, 259]

Also like John Boehner, Mitch McConnell played a role in the passage of TPA and TPP. As stated before, the argument against TPA is that it gives the President too much authority in negotiating trade deals, and does not give the Senate enough. The issue is the Senate is supposed to have the final say in regards to the passage of treaties (as stated clearly in the United States Constitution), but many fear TPA takes some of that power away from the Senate in trade agreements. The website Conservative Review, one of the places that the rankings for members of Congress comes from, stated their concern is that TPA does not allow for full disclosure of information regarding trade agreements, directly stating "There is no reason to pass fast track authority without releasing more details about these trade agreements to the public." McConnell noted in an interview with Fox News Host Bret Baier that the TPA will be "completely transparent." However as stated before, several Republican Senators voiced their concern to what else was in TPA, including Texas Senator Ted Cruz and Kentucky Senator Rand Paul. Paul was also among those who criticized McConnell for using the same tactics he accused Harry Reid of using in the previous Congress. In the end, TPA managed to pass, and McConnell was one of the main pushers of the deal.[260, 261]

Others have criticized McConnell for his support of Attorney General Eric Holder's successor, Loretta Lynch. McConnell was among several Senate Republicans who were willing to support Lynch simply because she was not "Eric Holder." Others felt that McConnell should have taken a stance against Lynch, noting that during her confirmation hearing she would not declare President Obama's immigration actions unconstitutional. Lynch would pass the Senate nomination process to become the next Attorney General, with little fight from McConnell.

Another criticism McConnell has received is his support of programs such as the NSA surveillance and the Patriot Act. However in both of these instances, McConnell's fellow Kentuckian, Rand Paul, has prevailed in the fight. This is one of the reasons why many are surprised at the alliance between Senator Paul and Senator

McConnell, as limited government is one of Paul's strongest stances, while McConnell has voted in several occasions to actually expand government. Many recall Rand Paul's strong opposition to the reauthorization of the Patriot Act in May of 2015, and that the Patriot Act was not reauthorized mainly due to Paul's strong opposition to it. Many Republicans were frustrated with Paul, including McConnell, but McConnell did not call out Paul by name. Paul also blocked efforts by McConnell to extend some of the NSA surveillance programs. As Paul came out on top, McConnell was criticized heavily for backing the programs, and Paul received decent public backing.[262, 263]

Conclusion

Senate Majority Leader Mitch McConnell follows a similar pattern to that of Speaker of the House John Boehner, those who have been in Congress for a significant amount of time, and has isolated certain parts of the Republican Party who have become not only frustrated with them but tired of them in leadership positions. While McConnell does not face the internal threat that Boehner does, McConnell may find it continuously more difficult to keep a grasp on his respect in the Senate if he continues to alienate conservatives. While today it may only be Mike Lee and Ted Cruz who are vocally opposed to McConnell, no one knows when the next vocal conservative will win a Senate seat and join them. If McConnell continues to alienate conservatives he may also frustrate other Republican members of the Senate who are generally quieter, and they may also start to speak out against McConnell.

Overall the general public is not fond of McConnell either. According to a poll by Rasmussen in August of 2015, Mitch McConnell has a 22% favorability rating and a 55% unfavorable rating among people across the country.[264] People are sick and tired of career politicians, and the leadership is not doing a very good job at instilling confidence in the public. McConnell will only continue to lose public support if he does not change his ways. McConnell promised that more would be done in the Senate and the House if the Senate was given a Republican majority, this has not happened yet. The several cases noted above, including McConnell's failure to repeal Obamacare, the passage of massive spending bills such as Cromnibus and the failure to stop President Obama's executive amnesty have frustrated the general public, and they have lost faith in the current leadership in Congress.

McConnell, like Boehner, also has lost faith in the public due to his treatment of the conservative wing of the Republican Party. A leader in the party cannot get away with bashing the conservatives and stating that he would "crush" them. McConnell may have won the election, but in the process he alienated an entire group of people across the country, something those people will not forget when advocating for politicians and voting.

McConnell has made his way onto this list for these various reasons. While many believe McConnell to be a strong leader who is often dealt a very poor hand in dealing with President Obama, most people see an ineffective and dishonest leader who has not led like he should have. McConnell has left the American people with empty promises, and many lies. He has not been a good example for the American people, and has only added to the frustrations of the American people. Many people find McConnell to be "weak" and do not support his style of leadership. Again we have a leader who came in with promise, and has not lived up to that promise. It is up to the American people to decipher the truth for themselves, and decide whether or not to allow Mitch McConnell to keep his leadership position or not. However, McConnell is not up for re-election until 2020, but his leadership position could change every two years. Only time will tell how the people view McConnell's leadership going forward.

VII. John McCain

"We cannot forever hide the truth about ourselves, from ourselves." Arizona Senator John McCain

If a political scientist was asked to name three to five of the most influential members of the Senate in recent history, there is very little doubt that they would name Arizona Senator John McCain right next to Nevada Senator Harry Reid and Kentucky Senator Mitch McConnell. McCain has made quite a name for himself over the years, one of those namely being his infamous Presidential run against Barack Obama in 2008, in which he was the Republican nominee for the election. McCain is not only one of the most senior members of the United States Senate, he is one of the most highly respected and highly decorated members of the Senate. He is also commonly noted for his time as a POW during the Vietnam War. In order to be his party's nominee for the Presidential election, he must command a certain amount of respect from within his own party, and even among Independents. This is all fact, undisputable fact. However, it is also fact that this famous Republican Senator is now trailing a Tea Party challenger in the latest polls for his 2016 race for re-election in Arizona. Why is there a Tea Party challenger to McCain in the first place if he has become so well respected? The answer is simple, Senator McCain has been in Washington for too long, and the people have recognized how much of a politician he has become.

McCain has never been shy about his harsher foreign policy standpoints and his willingness to push the United States into intervention in certain situations, including the recent Syrian civil war. However, McCain's recklessness on the issue may have inadvertently caused some issues, including supporting the wrong side in a war where no side looks to be the good guys at this time. McCain has also been quoted as have a strong dislike for the Tea Party and conservatives, notably fellow Senators Mike Lee, Ted Cruz and Rand Paul, Senators who are far less inclined to support a hawkish foreign policy. McCain has even resorted to name calling in the cases of Cruz and Paul.

McCain himself even knows that many in the Republican Party and in the state of Arizona have a problem with him. A few months before he even received a challenger, McCain stated he knew he was the top target of the Tea Party in 2016. He even made moves in Arizona to shut down the Tea Party so a challenger would not stand against him. However, someone has risen to the challenge, and may present a significant problem for McCain in 2016, while providing a solution to frustrated constituents of McCain who are tired of same old thing for over 30 years now. For these reasons, John McCain has found himself to be the sixth and final politician on this first list.

Early Years[267]

John Sidney McCain III was born to John S. McCain and Roberta McCain on August 29, 1936 at Coco Solo Naval Air Station in the Panama Canal Zone, where his family was stationed while his father, a four star Admiral, served in the U.S. military. It is little surprise that McCain spent quite a bit of his childhood moving across the country and world from base to base. McCain however did eventually graduate from Episcopal High School in Alexandria, Virginia in 1954. McCain then went to the United States Naval Academy at Annapolis in which he graduated from in 1958. McCain also went to flight school, in which he graduated from in 1960.

Vietnam[267]

McCain has two key distinctions that differentiate him from the other candidates. The first, and most obvious, is that McCain is the oldest, now almost 80 years old. The other is that McCain is the only combat veteran listed here, and McCain's service record is certainly long and respectable. When the Vietnam War started, McCain volunteered almost immediately for combat duty. McCain's responsibility as a pilot was to fly bombing missions during the war. On McCain's 23rd air mission on the day of October 26, 1967 McCain's plane was shot down over Hanoi, Vietnam. McCain was severely injured and captured by the North Vietnamese forces that were in control of the city. Two months later, McCain was moved to the Hoa Loa Prison, known as "Hanoi Hilton" one of the most infamous prisons in Vietnam during the war.

McCain's captors quickly learned he was the son of a four star admiral, and offered him early release. McCain reportedly refused, not wanting to allow his situation to be used as propaganda for the Vietnamese. Subsequently, McCain would spend the next five and half years in Vietnam as a prisoner of war. During this time McCain would continue to suffer even more injury, but would be able to last until the war was over. McCain rightfully was awarded the Silver Star, Bronze Star, Purple Heart and Distinguished Flying Cross.

When McCain returned from the war, he wanted to continue to serve in the United States Navy, but was unable to serve in a combat role due to the severity of his injuries. McCain would continue to serve in the United States, but did not fly anymore combat missions. McCain continued to earn the respect of those around him during this time as well. In 1976 McCain was promoted to be the Navy's liaison to the United States Senate. In 1981, McCain married his second wife, Cindy Hensley, and moved to Arizona. McCain would then start to work for his new father in laws business, and would become well respected in the community. McCain would at that time then set his sights on a political career that is ongoing to this day.

McCain Enters Politics[267]

Driven by his new interest in politics and the popularity he had earned in the years since he had returned from the war and had moved to Phoenix, McCain decided to run for a seat in the U.S. House of Representatives. In 1982 McCain won a long and hard fought primary battle, and then was able to easily win the general election in the heavy Republican area. McCain started his time in the U.S. House of Representatives in 1983, seen as a growing figure for the Republican Party. He was also elected to lead the group of incoming Republican freshmen, a position that is often seen as a launching pad for leadership positions. During his time in the House, McCain had a great amount of respect for President Ronald Reagan, and found himself in line with Reagan most of the time, notably on foreign policy. However, McCain was not afraid to criticize and speak out against the administration as well, something many respected. At this time, McCain was seen as a strong conservative voice in the House.

McCain won re-election to the House in 1984, but decided in 1986 to take a different route. With the retirement of Barry Goldwater, the very same Senator who ran against Lyndon Johnson in 1964, Representative McCain decided to run for the open Senate seat. McCain defeated his Democratic opponent by 20 percentage points in the 1986 election, and began his time in the Senate at the start of 1987. McCain would be elected as a strong conservative who many have respected, but almost 30 years later, the same cannot be said for his next upcoming election.

U.S. Senate

With McCain's background in the United States Navy, there was little question he would be a strong advocate for the military during his time in the Senate. McCain was placed on the Armed Services Committee, and would continue for years to be a strong voice regarding U.S. foreign policy. In 1993, McCain was selected to be the chairman of the International Republican Institute, which promotes and supports the emergence of Democracy worldwide. McCain also continued to work to improve the lives of Native Americans across the country, and would be an advocate during his time in the Senate. McCain also was supportive of budget cuts, especially in regards to deficits. This is shown by his support of the Gramm-Rudman legislation during the late 1980's.

McCain and a few other Senators would get caught up in a small scandal during the late 1980's regarding campaign donations he had received from businessman Charles Keating Jr. The scandal, known as the Keating Five would focus on campaign donations and small favors some politicians had received from Keating and his associates. Other reports noted that McCain had flown on Keating's jets. The trouble for McCain came when questions arose if he and other Senators had attempted to interfere with a federal investigation by regulators in Keating's actions. McCain would state he only met with the regulators a few times to discuss the investigation. McCain would eventually be cleared by the Senate Ethics Committee, and would apologize for the association. The committee only reprimanded McCain by suggesting he exercised poor judgment with the situation. The matter would be dropped and hardly ever brought up again, even in McCain's upcoming elections.[265, 266]

McCain would also come to be known for his actions to push forth campaign finance reform. In the mid 1990's, McCain worked with Wisconsin Democrat Russ Feingold on what would be known as the McCain-Feingold Act. After years of debate, the act would never come up for a vote. However, McCain was able to make a name for himself through all of the debates as a maverick in the Senate. McCain also built a name for himself by opposing pork barrel spending. McCain even pushed for the use of a line item veto, but the act supported by McCain was ruled unconstitutional by the Supreme Court. As a result of McCain's growing influence, he was named chairman of the Senate Commerce Committee in 1997. Shortly after, McCain would be noted for daring to take on the tobacco industry, something many Republicans would not dare to do during this time.

During the 1990's, notably the Clinton era, he came under fire for voting to confirm President Bill Clinton's nominees to the Supreme Court. McCain's defense of his vote was that a nominee is a President's call to make. This would be something he would carry on and support for years to come, whether it was the feelings of other Republicans or not. McCain also stated he voted with the same intentions for Ronald Reagan and George H.W. Bush.

At the start of McCain's third term in the Senate, in which he won with ease, McCain and Senator Feingold received accommodation for their attempts to push campaign finance reform. McCain also voted in favor of NATO action in the Kosovo War, and criticized the Clinton campaign for not doing so. Also during this time McCain released his first book, *Faith of My Fathers.* This would be noted as an extremely popular book and would be noted as potentially setting up a run for President in 2000. As expected, McCain did run for President in 2000, but lost to George W. Bush, who would end up winning the Presidential election. This Primary was a particularly nasty one, and McCain would be dealing with the ramifications for years.[272]

When George W. Bush became President, he and John McCain differentiated on many different issues including climate change, gun legislation and tax cuts. McCain even went as far as to oppose the Bush era tax cuts, one of two Republicans to do so. Many also suspected that there was tension between Bush and McCain over the primary battle that had ensued in the years before. The tension between Bush and McCain was so bad at times that some figured McCain may leave the Republican Party. An article on AZcentral.com titled *John McCain Report* discusses the issue in-depth, and quotes author Elizabeth Drew's 2002 book *Citizen McCain.* Drew reports that McCain was "upset" about the reports he considered changing parties. However, after the September 11 terror attacks, Bush and McCain found themselves back on the same side, as McCain was a strong advocate for military action in Iraq and Afghanistan. McCain was also a strong influence in the creation of the 9/11 Commission.[270, 272]

Things also started to look up for McCain in 2002 when recent issues among big businesses, notably Enron, allowed McCain and Feingold to reintroduce the McCain-Feingold Act regarding campaign finance reform. In February of 2002 the House passed a similar bill, which was then adopted in the United States Senate. In McCain's speech to the Senate regarding the bill, he stated "Mr. President, the proponents of this legislation have had, and continue to have, one purpose: to enact fair, bipartisan, campaign finance reform that seeks no special advantage for one party or another." Eventually President Bush did sign the bill, finally making all of John McCain's hard work on the issue pay off.[271]

McCain would also be consistently noted for his opposition to the Republican Party on the issue of climate change. In 2003, McCain worked with Senator Joe Lieberman to create the Climate

Stewardship Act which would attempt to reduce greenhouse gas emissions. Rarely have we seen Republican Senators work so hard on such a bill, most as a matter of fact oppose any attempts to regulate such matters.

In McCain's next term, he would begin his work on comprehensive immigration reform, which would become a major criticism of McCain's time in the Senate. McCain would be a part of teams in both 2006 and 2007 that would attempt to put forth comprehensive immigration reform plans. The Comprehensive Immigration Reform Act of 2006 would pass in the Senate but fail in the House, while the Comprehensive Immigration Reform Act of 2007 would be taken down by conservative grassroots organizations. McCain would help to take up immigration reform yet again in the 2010s when he joined the Gang of Eight, a group of Senators working on immigration reform. However, this again would fail due to conservative opposition in the House of Representatives.[273]

In 2007 Senator McCain decided again to make a run for President. This time McCain won the GOP nomination, but lost to Democratic nominee Barack Obama in the 2008 general election. After President Obama assumed office, McCain would become one of the few Republican Senators the President would speak to at first for consolation on issues. However, the two would of course eventually find themselves at odds, with McCain being vocally opposed to the President's signature healthcare law and the President's decision to scrap the missile defense system in Poland.[274]

In 2010 John McCain faced a primary challenge from a J.D. Hayworth, a former radio talk show host. Hayworth considered himself to be the conservative alternative to McCain, but did not receive significant backing from all of the prominent Tea Party groups that would help so many others achieve campaign victories during that election cycle. McCain would go onto win another term, but this term would be the start of many of McCain's controversies, notably with foreign policy. In McCain's 5th term, he would face some of his greatest challenges yet, notably young conservatives who McCain would become visibly frustrated with many times. McCain would also be drawn into the most significant foreign policy debates of the 2010's, most of which regarded the Arab Spring and the rise of ISIS. It is McCain's reactions to these challenges that has yet again drawn the ire of conservatives and even another challenge from the Tea Party for his sixth run as a United States Senator.

Running for President- 2000, 2008[274, 275, 276]

With McCain's popularity at a significant height in 1999, the bold Senator decided to make a run for President of the United States. The stakes were against McCain from the start as Texas Governor George W. Bush was the favorite to win the election that year. McCain ran with the intention of being anti-establishment and as an alternative to those who were almost certain to win their nominations, especially George W. Bush. McCain stated in his announcement that he was intending on fighting special interest money, directly stating "we must take the corrupting influence of special interest money out of politics." However, the campaign would be rough for McCain even from day one, as Governor Bush was able to secure the endorsements of McCain's predecessor in the House John Rhodes, and the current Republican Governor Jane Hull.[272]

Despite McCain's tough start, he ended up defeating Bush in the New Hampshire primary by 20 points, a significant margin for any candidate in a primary. After that, the campaign started to not only heat up, but get dirty as well. Some leaked reports had accusations that McCain's wife, Cindy, was a drug addict. McCain at one point responded by comparing George W. Bush to Bill Clinton, a move seen as a huge negative for a politician to do to another in their own party. John McCain ended up losing South Carolina to Bush, which many were not surprised to see. However,

McCain was able to bounce back a few weeks later by taking Arizona and Michigan from Bush. The race at that time was more even than anyone had anticipated, until many looked at the financial aspect. McCain was really hurting for money, and wouldn't be able to last past Super Tuesday if he didn't have a good showing. As expected, McCain was clobbered by Bush on Super Tuesday, with Bush taking nine out of thirteen states, and McCain only taking four. Bush managed to take New York and California, severely taking delegates from McCain. After Super Tuesday, McCain dropped out and supported Bush for the election.[272]

However this would not be the end of Senator John McCain's presidential ambitions. In what appeared to be the start of a small pattern for the Republican Party, McCain decided to run again in the 2008 Presidential Election. This time McCain was in better shape in the polls, as both he and former New York City Mayor Rudy Giuliani shared the status of frontrunner throughout the course of the election. McCain would continue to emphasis the threat of too much influence from big businesses, but also spent a majority of time focusing on his experience, as an article by the BBC quotes McCain stating "I'm not the youngest candidate, but I am the most experienced." McCain would face difficult times during the early months of the election, as fundraising would be a significant challenge for the Senator. McCain also choose not to put much emphasis on the Iowa caucus in January, instead aiming for the first primary in New Hampshire again. As expected McCain lost the Iowa caucus to Arkansas Governor Mike Huckabee. However, McCain was able to focus on South Carolina and Florida, where he defeated former Massachusetts Governor Mitt Romney, Mayor Giuliani and former Tennessee Senator Fred Thompson. Before Super Tuesday, Giuliani dropped out of the race and endorsed McCain.[272, 276]

McCain was able to overcome his Achilles heel from 2000 and win Super Tuesday with a clear majority. McCain by that time had also been able to escape significant challengers, as former Massachusetts Governor Mitt Romney also dropped out of the race in February, clearing the way for McCain to win the Republican nomination.

When it became clear that Illinois Senator Barack Obama would be the nominee for the Democrats, the race became experience and a continuation of a Republican presidency versus youth and new bold Democratic leadership. McCain added youth to his ticket by selecting Alaska Governor Sarah Palin as his running mate, and Obama added experience to his ticket by selecting Delaware Senator Joe Biden as his running mate. While the Palin addition helped McCain at first, Obama and Biden surged ahead of McCain in the polls again rather quickly. By the time the debates began, it was clear that Obama had the upper hand. In the end, Obama defeated McCain by a margin of 53 percent to 46 percent of the vote, and 365 electoral votes to McCain's 173. This would be the final time that Senator John McCain would run for President of the United States, although he would continue his Senate career at least until 2016.[274, 277]

Controversies- McCain's Dangerous Foreign Policy

Ever since John McCain had entered the United States Senate, he had been a strong advocate for national defense and a strong foreign policy. He had been hit several times, notably by Barack Obama in 2008 for his support of both the Iraq War and the Iraq troop surge in 2007. These votes have given McCain a reputation for being one of the most significant hawks in the United States Senate. While the intentions of the wars in Iraq and Afghanistan are often heavily debated as legitimate or not, the current situation in the Middle East is a different story.

As discussed with Barack Obama and Hillary Clinton, the Arab Spring easily became the most significant foreign policy situation of our time during the 2010's. While before we focused on the impact of the Obama administration on U.S. actions towards the Middle East during the Arab Spring, the United States Senate, notably John McCain and Lindsey Graham, also played just as important roles in the actions of the United States.

When the Arab Spring began in Egypt, McCain was one of the most vocal Senators regarding the matter. McCain was one of the first American lawmakers to call for longtime Egyptian leader Hosni Mubarak to step down, despite the fact that Mubarak was a U.S. supporter, and no one knew who would replace him if he did step down. McCain is quoted in a CNN article by Dana Bash as stating "The rapidly deteriorating situation in Egypt leads me to the conclusion that President Mubarak needs to step down and relinquish power."[278] While McCain was correct in stating that the situation was continuing to deteriorate in Egypt, and that one way to fix things was for Mubarak to step down, it was unclear exactly how a transition of power would take place, and that would cause trouble in and of itself. Once Mubarak did step down, he handed power over to the army. Over a year later, Egypt would hold free and fair elections, with Muslim Brotherhood candidate Mohammed Morsi winning the election. However, things would deteriorate under Morsi quickly, causing the military to step in yet again. At this time former military leader Abdel Fattah el-Sisi, is President of Egypt. Many question whether those in the United States, including McCain, who pressured Mubarak to step down so quickly made the right decision or not, as Morsi only added to the tensions in the country when he was elected President in 2012.

As it would turn out, Egypt would be the least of John McCain's concerns with the Arab Spring. After Mubarak stepped down in Egypt, McCain, like many others, turned his attention to neighboring Libya. Egypt would be a cakewalk in comparison to what happened in Libya as Libya would deteriorate into a full blown civil war when longtime dictator Muammar Qaddafi refused to step down and declared war on his own people. Throughout the war, McCain would be a strong advocate of not only arming the Libyan rebels, but providing key military support to them in their attempt to oust Qaddafi. McCain would even go as far as to visit the rebel leaders in Libya, staying at a hotel in Benghazi, Libya, where he would be quoted calling the Libyan rebels "heroes."[279, 280] McCain advocated for arming the rebels, and providing support via drones. Eventually the United States and NATO would end up instituting a no fly zone and arming the rebels. After the aid was started, the Libyan rebels would quickly capture Qaddafi and end the violent war.

However, Libya did not turn out like Egypt did unfortunately. In the post Qaddafi era, Libya has descended into absolute chaos, and is a hotbed for terrorism and extremism. There is not one set group in control of the country, as certain parts of the country are controlled by certain groups. Some are loyal to the government, some are terrorist groups associated with al Qaeda and ISIS looking for another stronghold. Worst of all, Benghazi, where John McCain stayed and professed his support for the Libyan rebels was the site of the assassination of Ambassador Chris Stevens, along with Sean Smith, Glen Doherty and Tyrone Woods. There are also rumors that the weapons the U.S. had given the Libyan rebels to use against Qaddafi's forces have not been recovered, and worst yet may have been used in attacks across the Middle East.

While we cannot blame John McCain or anyone in the United States for the aftermath of the conflict in Libya, each official that advocated for the support of these groups should have shown more caution in not only their support but their tracking of them after the war ended. If it is ever proven true with complete certainty that the Libyan rebels McCain backed are now associated with al Qaeda and ISIS, the Senator would have quite a bit to answer for. As a matter of fact, in order to get find out the truth, the Senator, other elected officials and the Obama administration all have quite a bit to answer for in their support of Libyan rebels. While their intentions may have been noble in helping Libyan civilians, unfortunately reckless acts only added fuel to an already intense fire.

If anyone thought the situation in Libya had gotten pretty severe, they would be horrified to now see what has happened in Syria. While the President of Syria, Bashar al Assad reacted similar to Qaddafi by sending the military out against his civilians, Assad managed to take things even farther by using chemical weapons against his own people. As discussed in the section about President Obama, the threat of the use of chemical weapons prompted the Obama administration to state that the actual use of the weapons would be a red line for the Assad regime. When the chemical weapons were used, Obama faced pressure from the international community and his own Congress to do something about the attacks because of the red line comment. McCain was one of many in the United States Senate to attempt to press the administration to authorize U.S. military support and action in Syria against Assad. The types of action that McCain advocated for did not pass in Congress, as conservatives like Ted Cruz and Justin Amash teamed up with liberal Democrats to oppose such measures, but other measures McCain advocated for did go through, and have caused some tension today.

Like in Libya, McCain was involved in a hands on manner. In May of 2013, McCain visited with members of the Syrian rebel groups near the Turkish-Syrian border. The trip was unannounced to the public, but when the details did come out McCain came under heavy fire from the American people and the media. Especially because of what had happened in Libya, many were cautious about sending arms to "moderate rebels." McCain attempted to ease those concerns by stating "the people I met with and talked to directly were well-vetted. Their names and their duties were outlined to me. They came from all over Syria." This did very little to ease the concerns of many in the United States, as the public was still against getting involved in Syria.[283]

According to a poll by Gallup in September of 2013, which was shortly after Assad used the chemical weapons, 51% of Americans were against intervention in the conflict. 36% supported action, while 13% had no opinion. These numbers were even lower when McCain made his pitch in June to arm the Syrian rebels.[281]

Before McCain's trip to Syria, the Senate Foreign Relations committee, including McCain, voted to arm the Syrian rebels, despite opposition from the Obama administration at the time. The vote was 15-3, with Kentucky Senator Rand Paul, New Mexico Senator Tom Udall and Connecticut Senator Chris Murphy voting against the measure, raising concerns that they did not know where exactly the arms would be going. Udall summed up the vote by stating "We're providing arms, I think, into a very chaotic situation." Rand Paul continued the voicing of concerns by stating "I know everyone here wants to do the right thing, but I think it's a rush to war," both were quoted in an article by The Hill.[282]

After the Assad regime used chemical weapons against civilians, the Obama administration began to side with McCain and those in Congress who supported action in Syria. Congress would end up debating the measure after the chemical weapons attack with the support of the Obama administration. However, enough conservative and liberal opposition to the bill would prevent direct actions from taking place, and the bill would not come up for full vote on the Senate floor. In the coming months, conservatives would take aim at McCain for backing extremist groups in Syria and Libya. Texas Congressman Louie Gohmert at one point would refer to McCain in a speech as "a guy that's been to Syria and supported al Qaeda and the rebels… And I know that senator would never intentionally hurt this country. But he's made mistakes that have hurt it, but certainly never intentionally."[284]

Gohmert's words would not hold much weight at that time, but when reports came out that factions of the Syrian rebels were not as moderate as many had first believed, the criticism against McCain and others who supported arming them began to mount. According to an article by the Economist, ISIS made their first significant move in 2012 with the capture of Raqqa. By the beginning of 2014, they were more prominent. By the end of the summer of 2014, everyone knew who ISIS was and that they were a significant threat. Also at that time more support for funding moderate rebels in Syria grew, as everyone now knew that both Assad and ISIS would be a growing threat.[286]

The biggest problem for the Obama administration and its allies in the Senate like McCain regarding the situation were the growing concerns of those who had opposed action from the start. Kentucky Senator Rand Paul, who McCain would have very public fights with over Syria, would go as far as to state that the U.S. has armed ISIS allies in Syria. Paul would directly state the following: "I think one of the reasons why ISIS has been emboldened is because we have been arming their allies. We have been allied with ISIS in Syria."[285]

Other sources have collaborated Paul's concerns by reporting that the CIA has been arming and training rebels in Syria. The debate would evolve over the years, with many claiming ISIS has inadvertently received aid from the U.S., whether it be by posing as moderates to receive weapons, or taking them from moderates they defeated. Now the United States is more involved than it was before in the conflict, with direct bombing missions in Syria and Iraq to attempt to stop ISIS and the Assad regime.[287, 288]

With the United States even more involved in the war now, we return to Congressman Gohmert's previous statement. Did the actions of McCain, the Obama administration and others who supported arming the Syrian rebels get us into a situation we could have avoided? Or was intervention simply inevitable? Could we have done a better job vetting the recipients of American aid? Or did we do the best we could? These are the questions that should be asked when evaluating the role of men like McCain regarding this conflict. Unfortunately with the situation the way it is now, things are not looking positive for the Senior Arizona Senator.

McCain's Poor Treatment of Other Lawmakers

While everyone is absolutely entitled to their own opinions, and can say whatever they want, our public officials should be setting a high standard as they are often in the public eye. Well, of course our public officials should be setting a high standard for many things, and they end up disappointing us in the end. In regards to respectful speech, John McCain is no exception.

McCain has faced plenty of opposition from both sides of the aisle, liberals and conservatives alike. However, McCain's recent treatment of his fellow Republican Senators and Congressmen has been nothing but a show of utter disrespect for their opinions. The most obvious case was McCain's heavy criticism of Rand Paul, Ted Cruz and Justin Amash for their plans to filibuster the nomination of John Brennan to the CIA over the use of drones in targeting terrorists. Senator Paul ended up waging a successful filibuster which resulted in the Obama administration sending the Senator a letter stating they would not target Americans in the strike. Seems like a significant victory for liberty, right? Not according to Senator McCain.

McCain stated in early 2013 that "they were elected, nobody believes that there was a corrupt election, anything else… But I also think that when, you know, it's always the wacko birds on right and left that get the media megaphone." McCain's use of the term "wacko birds" became an internet sensation rather quickly as he was asked right after who he was referring to, and he admitted "Rand Paul, Cruz, Amash, whoever." Representative Amash called McCain out rather quickly on Twitter, asking if McCain came up with the phrase at "#DinnerWithBarack."[289]

It is no secret that McCain is not fond of Rand Paul and Ted Cruz's stances on national security issues, with McCain being more of a hawk and Paul and Cruz wanting less government intervention and power. After Senator Paul declared his candidacy to run for President of the United States in April of 2015, McCain stated the following on Fox News: "Put it this way — Senator Paul is the worst possible candidate of the 20 or so that are running on the most important issue which is national security." While Senator McCain absolutely has a right to disagree with the Senator from Kentucky, he could be doing so in a more respectful manner.[290]

Another instance of McCain and Paul in opposition came towards the end of May in the Senate during the debate over the Patriot Act. Senator Paul asked to speak in opposition to something that was being stated, and McCain replied by stating "the senator from Kentucky needs to learn the rules of the Senate…Maybe the senator from Kentucky should know the rules of the Senate." While McCain may be right that Paul is incorrect in not speaking at the proper time, the response could have been phrased in a way more fairly to Senator Paul. This statement by McCain almost seems more like the Senator from Arizona doesn't wish for Senator Paul to speak at all. This is a debatable point, but McCain does not help his cause when he declares Paul's opposition to the Patriot Act a "fundraising exercise." However at the end of the day, Paul won as the Patriot Act expired.[291, 292]

To be fair to McCain, Senator Paul has at times also fought back at McCain, at one point Paul made comments about McCain and Senator Lindsay Graham being too close to President Obama. Paul himself has also been known for being more confrontational. Senator Ted Cruz on the other hand had taken the matter in a different direction, and still attempts to at least publically appear to get along with Senator McCain. However, the two are significantly different on most issues, and many on both sides of the aisle know it.

The truth is, McCain being one of the most decorated veterans of the Republican Party should be leading the way on decorum and honor when it comes to debate. However, he has not done that, and at times has even led the way in attacks against those who disagree with him. If we are to see positive change in politics and make people interested again, we must stop the vicious attacks and the negativity, and bring truth and positivity back into politics. While McCain can absolutely call out those he disagrees with, calling them "wacko birds" certainly isn't the way to do it.

McCain and Immigration

One of the biggest challenges of the 21st Century for the United States of America has been over immigration. This has caused quite a bit of controversy between Governors, Senators, Presidential candidates and even everyday citizens. Since September 11, 2001, several attempts have been made in both the Senate and the House of Representatives to pass "comprehensive" immigration reform. What exactly "comprehensive" has meant has been different from bill to bill and from sponsor to sponsor. If there has been one politician at the center of the majority of these debates it has been John McCain. Of course this makes sense, with McCain being a strong national security and defense hawk, and being a Senator from the border state of Arizona.

However, Senator McCain has actually found himself on a rather surprising side of the immigration debate, the side that has angered his constituents in Arizona, many conservatives across the United States and even members of his own party in Arizona. McCain's stance on immigration is even rumored to be the most significant cause of the new primary challenge to McCain for the 2016 election cycle.

McCain's first significant encounter with immigration reform came in 2005 when McCain worked with Democratic Senator Ted Kennedy to introduce the Secure America and Orderly Immigration Act, also known as the McCain-Kennedy bill. The bill had the goal of incorporating legalization, guest worker programs and border security all into one bill. The bill would never be voted on in the Senate, but would be used as a talking point and a starting point for bills in the next two years.[267]

The next bill, known as the Comprehensive Immigration Reform Act of 2006 was also quite controversial, but had more support in the Senate besides McCain and Kennedy, and actually would pass a Senate vote. The goal of the bill was to again increase border security, allow some long time illegal immigrants to stay in the United States if they had proved themselves to be law abiding citizens and if they paid a fine, and to increase guest worker programs. The number of years considered in the legalization process was five years, three years and less than two years. The bill failed in the House of Representatives.[267]

The final bill for a period of time would be the Comprehensive Immigration Reform Act of 2007, in which the sole sponsor would be Democratic Senator Harry Reid, but McCain would be known to be a part of the "Gang of 12," a term that the Associated Press would use in several articles when discussing those that contributed to the bill. Also noted by the Associated Press in an article in NBC News titled *'Gang of 12' mulls over immigration bill'* was that the bill "would allow 12 million unlawful immigrants to stay in the U.S. legally." This is best known to conservatives and most Americans as "amnesty." The bill would attract a significant amount of opposition within the Senate and across the United States, and would not pass. An article by the New York Times credits the grassroots as being the cause of the collapse of the bill. The article, written by Julia Preston, even noted this in the title, *Grass Roots Roared and Immigration Plan Collapsed.* The article discussed how online conservative organizations like a site called Grassfire.org played key roles in derailing the bill, with Grassfire itself collecting over 700,000 signatures on petitions that opposed the bill. The article discusses how some Senators, including California Democrat Dianne Feinstein, received tens of thousands of phone calls to their office in opposition to the bill. In the end, the bill was not even voted on in the Senate, as Senators could not even get past debate.[273, 294, 295]

The fight over immigration in those previous years did not end up hurting McCain's chances in winning the GOP nomination for President in 2008, which he did with ease. However if anything, the fight over those years should have shown McCain that immigration reform that many considered to be "amnesty" (even if he didn't consider it to be amnesty) is significantly unpopular and would not pass anytime soon. In the 2010's, McCain would show he did not realize this in those previous years.

In 2010 McCain would win re-election handily despite a primary challenger. However, it is in this fifth term where McCain would have the majority of his controversies, including those already discussed regarding the Arab Spring. In 2013 McCain would be at the forefront of another immigration bill, this one was known as the Border Security, Economic Opportunity, and Immigration Modernization Act of 2013. Those working on the bill would again be noted as being a part of a "gang," this time the "Gang of Eight." Those members were McCain, Senator Lindsay Graham(R-South

Carolina), Jeff Flake(R-Arizona), Marco Rubio(R-Florida), Chuck Schumer(D-New York), Bob Menendez(D-New Jersey), Dick Durbin(D-Illinois) and Michael Bennet(D-Colorado). The bill would end up being one of the most contested bills in the Senate for a significant period of time.

For the most part, the members of the Gang of Eight were quite open about the intention of the bill. What surprised most was the work of Florida Senator Marco Rubio, who campaigned on the promise that he would never support amnesty. Rubio would end up being the only Senator in the group who would continuously state that the bill was not amnesty. New York Senator Chuck Schumer, who is slated to be the next leader of the Senate Democrats after Harry Reid retires, was quoted in an article on ABCnews.com titled *Gang of Eight Accelerates Immigration Reform Pace* as stating "The bottom line is a path to citizenship for the 11 million." McCain himself would then be quoted stating "Having a country with 11 million people living in the shadows… is not something we want to teach our kids about." These seem quite contradictory to what Senator Rubio had been stating in his interviews.[295]

In writing for usnews.com, Mike Krikorian, the Executive Director of the Center for Immigration Studies notes that the Gang of Eight bill attempts to introduce a check in/check out system, but that Congress has attempted to implement one six times before, Krikorian states "Is the seventh time supposed to be the charm?" This fits in well with the question posed earlier of why does McCain think an amnesty bill will work now when it didn't earlier?[296, 297, 298]

Again McCain's bill would be defeated, although it did pass in the Senate. The House of Representatives and Speaker John Boehner would refuse to take up the deal, noting its key flaws and how quickly it was passed through the Senate. Many considered the bill to be one that would disrespect the current rule of law and discourage legal immigration, and that was a message that certainly resonated with the people. It was right around this point that people would start to realize that McCain was no longer the strong conservative he had considered himself to be in the past, and that maybe it was time to consider a new alternative.

Economics and Obamacare

When McCain was first elected to the Senate, he promised to be someone who would cut spending and oppose the raising of deficits and debt ceilings. To be fair to McCain, he certainly was in his first few years. However, this has seemed to change in McCain's fifth term, and many are beginning to wonder why. McCain would also start to waiver on his opposition to Obamacare, with his reluctance to stand with conservatives in some of the bolder plans such as defunding the measure (although Majority Leader McConnell would be acting the same way as McCain, so it was not much of a surprise).

McCain would face a lot of criticism in 2013 when he supported the deal to end the fight over defunding Obamacare with the upcoming budget bill. McCain, like McConnell, would state that he was in opposition to the strategy from the start. McCain stated that he warned they would lose in advance by stating "we would not be able to win because we were demanding something that was not achievable." In September of 2013, McCain would even go as far as to call the effort "not rational."[299] The truth is, the goal would have been achievable and rational if Republicans had stood and fought against the measure, but they were not united in doing so. McCain was elected on the promise that he would fight against Obamacare, and he didn't do so this time around when he had the chance. While McCain would support the defund effort at first, he was one of many Republicans who ditched the effort in the end.

At the end of 2013, McCain would go on record stating he would still repeal Obamacare. However, earlier in 2013, McCain had stated he did not believe that Republicans in the Senate could repeal Obamacare. The change was a surprise to many, but they also were not sure if the Senator meant he would continue to work to repeal Obamacare or not in the coming years.[300, 302]

In the end McCain would support the Senate negotiated deal that ended the shutdown and current hopes of defunding Obamacare. McCain would also then go onto support the Ryan-Murray spending increase, something McCain would have opposed before. At the end of 2014, McCain also supported the infamous Cromnibus bill that so many others would be strongly opposed to due to the significant increase in spending and the failure to strip President Obama of the executive amnesty funding. Other votes that McCain have received heavy criticism for include his vote to raise the debt ceiling in 2014, his vote to fund the Department of Homeland Security and President Obama's executive amnesty in 2015, his vote to save the Export-Import Bank (which actually failed), and his vote to continue funding Planned Parenthood after all of the controversies there. All of this would be relevant for 2015 and 2016, as it is arguments conservatives would use to launch a primary challenge to McCain for the 2016 election.

McCain's Challenges

In a move that many believe had been coming for a few years now, the Arizona GOP finally decided to call out John McCain in January of 2014. During a party convention the state GOP passed a resolution to censure McCain by a vote of 1,150-351. The cause of the vote was because many felt that McCain had been too liberal in the past. An article in azcentral.com titled *Arizona GOP censures McCain for 'disastrous'* record discusses the reasons for the move, and what the voters had to say about it.[303]

The resolution itself was quoted as stating: "Only in times of great crisis or betrayal is it necessary to publicly censure our leaders… Today we are faced with both. For too long we have waited, hoping Senator McCain would return to our Party's values on his own. That has not happened." The resolution also contended that McCain was too involved with the immigration reform plans that supported amnesty and that he failed to support the effort to defund Obamacare when he had a significant chance.[303]

The author of the measure, Timothy Schwartz, is quoted in the article as stating that he felt that McCain "has abandoned us." Certainly Schwartz wasn't the only one feeling that way. The article also points out several times that while 351 people voted against the measure, not all of them voted against it in order to support McCain. Some voted against the measure because another alternative was not put forth, others voted against it because they worried about infighting. The point is, the measure passed by a significant margin, and while it does not directly do anything to the Senator, it does hurt his reputation within Arizona. It also shows that his constituents feel he has not been representing them, and that a change may be soon necessary.

Also quite telling is McCain's response to the measure. This is noted in an article by the Washington Post titled *McCain: Censure by state GOP makes me more likely to run.* Just as the article indicates, McCain stated in the article that "If there's such a thing as motivation to more seriously consider it, it's what just happened." McCain then also added "shows that, again, a very extremist element of the party has taken over the party apparatus."[304] McCain is showing that instead of trying to fix the situation and appease to his constituents, he is blaming "extremists" for not agreeing with him. This just shows the absolute ignorance that has grown in the Senator after being in office for so long. However, it is this very same ignorance that has cost some politicians their careers. McCain has made it quite clear he is no fan of the Tea Party or conservatives. However, it is likely not just conservatives who are upset with

McCain, and that is something that he should remember if he wishes to stay in office.

Turning the tables to 2015, McCain has turned the tables on the state Tea Party faction. An article by Politico titled *McCain's big purge* details how McCain has been attempting to unseat local party officers who were against McCain. So far the effort had been somewhat successful for McCain, as one of the ousted activists was Timothy Schwartz, who had been the leader on the resolution to censure McCain earlier in the year. While McCain can keep trying to put his own allies in office to avoid state leaders from fighting against him, McCain cannot stop grassroots activists who will continue to fight, and the everyday people who will see actions like this in the media and even in their own neighborhoods. Overall, there is one thing that McCain can never run from, and that is the voters.[305]

2016 Primary- McCain Gets a Serious Challenger

Since McCain's censure in 2014, conservatives had been looking for someone to challenge John McCain for his Senate seat in the 2016 primary election. The top two choices were Representative Matt Salmon, a member of the House Freedom Caucus, and State Senator Kelli Ward. Representative Salmon declined to challenge McCain, and Senator Ward entered the race in July of 2015 to challenge McCain. In an interview with Breitbart, Ward stated she believed that McCain had moved to the right for each election, and that the people of Arizona were looking for new ideas, adding that McCain did not offer them. In August of 2015, a poll came out by Gravis Marketing that gave Ward a nine point lead over McCain, with Ward polling at 45 percent and McCain polling at 36 percent.

At the very least the new challenger shows a growing frustration within Arizona with McCain. McCain cannot win without the support of his voters, many of which he has alienated in recent years with comments about "extremists." Only time will tell if Ward will be able to oust McCain, but this is certainly a challenge that McCain should be taking very seriously if he is to have any chance of continuing his political career.[306, 307]

Conclusion

Arizona Senator John McCain shows qualities quite similar to that of John Boehner and Mitch McConnell. He has been in Congress for far too long, now going on 33 years and counting, while also seeking a sixth term. If McCain were to serve the entirety of this sixth term, McCain would have spent 40 years in Congress between the House of Representatives and the Senate. We have seen over the years those who spend more time in Congress tend to change their views and become the very thing they campaigned against in the first place.

Numbers provided by Heritage Scorecard and Conservative Review back these assumptions, as McCain had a 75% rating with Heritage in the 2011-2012 session, but has floated around 50% since. Conservative Review has McCain even lower with a lifetime score of 41%. Even analysts discussing the 2008 election contend that McCain didn't win because he did not do enough to encourage conservatives to support his effort. McCain may not have alienated the base at that time, but he certainly hadn't done much to encourage it either. Failure to unite Republican voters has proven to be critical to those running for higher office in recent years, especially in Presidential elections.[308, 309]

McCain is still highly respected and regarded within the Senate by those who have been around close to the time he has. However, it is the younger lawmakers who have concerns with McCain, and who McCain has problems with. This is a trend we have seen with others too including McConnell and Boehner, and it doesn't seem to be changing anytime soon.

McCain has made this list due to his changing views over the years, and his times where he attempts to flip on the issues, swearing one day he is a conservative, but the next willing to call those who always consider themselves conservatives “wacko birds” and “extremists.” McCain doesn’t realize that while he may be addressing lawmakers at that time, he is also referring to millions of Americans who may feel the same way as those lawmakers at that time. McCain has shown in recent years he is not the maverick he once was, and does not have the respect of the people anymore. McCain has shown dishonesty by abandoning those who have put him in office repeatedly. There is a chance that McCain may actually pay for that in the 2016 election. At the end of the day, it is the voters of Arizona who will decide if McCain is worthy of staying in office. In 2008 the United States rejected John McCain as President, and maybe that was a sign of growing discontent with the long time Senator, as it only seemed to go downhill for him from there.

VIII. Conclusion

As shown in the previous parts, each noted candidate brings a unique set of traits and examples to the whole project. They have each individually shown that political dishonesty can be taken in many different ways, and is actually different than regular forms of dishonesty. While politicians are often times also straight up dishonest, lying about their positions on certain issues to be elected, they are often dishonest in other senses, hiding their true views until they are elected, holding closed door meetings to come up with ways to mask their actions, and even taking direct actions contradictory to what their constituents want. One of the worst we saw was the consistent flip flopping over time, where those who have been in power too long have become the very same thing they first stood against.

We The People hold our elected officials in the highest regard in our society. The President of the United States is supposed to represent the country on the world stage, while Senators, Governors and Representatives hold key positions that are similar, representing a given constituency on a large stage. This means that these elected officials are fully responsible to the people. Our system is that of direct election, where we go to the polls to elect the candidates based on their views and behaviors. In other countries such as the United Kingdom citizens instead vote on the party platform. The people of the United States are therefore in a key position to have more of a say over their politicians with our direct election system.

However, this system also assumes that all voting citizens are fully aware of everything going on. This is unrealistic. All of this is the point of this work. The Common Man in society cannot possibly know everything that their elected officials are doing. Whether the officials are trying to hide it or not, it simply isn't possible. There is no way for a farmer in Indiana to know every detail about the President's meeting with the Senate Majority Leader on an upcoming budget deal, and the same is said for any citizen, even the powerful lawyer in New York City with a significant amount of influence and money.

Due to this, the everyday people must rely on the news and the media to find out what they can about the actions of our elected officials. This becomes more complex with the way the media is today. Many people find the media to be biased and negative, and that turns many everyday citizens away. There are still plenty that will pay attention, whether they themselves know the biases or not. However, the key is being able to see through the biases and look at each side of the argument being stated and realize both the big picture and some of the smaller actions at work. Again, this is not something that everyone can do in society today.

The goal of this work has been to portray the view of politics today through the eyes of the Common Man. The small town farmer from Indiana or the big time lawyer from New York City do not have the ability to go to Washington and ask each elected official every single thing that is going on, or even expect to get the full truth even if that happens. Therefore we have little choice but to rely on the media. This work takes the headlines and the news about the big issues, and even some of the smaller ones, puts them all together, and analyzes the impacts. There are some big details that simply cannot be ignored, such as the deals made during government shutdowns or the actions taking by a particular legislator when bills are voted on. In that sense, media bias is still around, but not enough to take away from the truth.

We should also not forget the influence of the modern day Internet either. The majority of research completed for this work was done via the Internet, whether it be searching for articles on candidates and certain issues, or looking through roll call votes for the Senate and the House. Twenty years ago a project like this would not have been possible, even ten years ago it would have been rather difficult. However, the Internet is expanding and growing every single day. The votes cast by every legislator in the Senate and the House is posted online at the very least through Roll Call, and often times is noted in various news articles. Statements one lawmaker makes to another are frequently leaked to the media, and then placed in an article online to be accessed by the constituents of the elected official. It's also far easier to find past speeches, campaign videos and debate coverage on the Internet today. The Common Man can know at any time what exactly each candidate said, what day they said it and where they were when they said it.

Although we praise the Internet we cannot underestimate the power of print as well. Politicians love to write books to get their name out there, especially when preparing for runs for higher offices. Four of our six candidates have written books, Barack Obama, Hillary Clinton, Andrew Cuomo and John McCain. Each of them of course have had ambitions for higher office, or have already attained such. Others such as Majority Leader Mitch McConnell have been highly criticized in literature from those within their own field such as Senator Ted Cruz. Other books have been written with the point of focusing on the actions of one particular candidate, such as many we have seen regarding President Obama and Secretary Clinton in recent years.

Of course we also cannot underestimate the influence of certain interest groups as well. Groups used here such as Heritage Foundation and Conservative Review track the votes of lawmakers. They give an explanation of the bill being voted on, then they state their view of the issue and how they believe it should be voted on, then they mark how the lawmaker voted, whether it was for or against. These groups stay relatively consistent, so when the score of a particular candidate drops, such as we have seen with the Republican candidates, we know that the candidates are changing their views on given issues. Other interest groups may not do the same thing, but still keep an eye on elected officials in order to attempt to keep them true to their campaign promises. If they do not, they turn against them and campaign for their challengers.

Each candidate deserves a final recap of the topics discussed and how they ended up on the list, and then finally final analysis of the topic overall.

President Barack Obama campaigned with a lot of promise for the United States. A significant number of people were excited to elect a man who was young, vibrant and promised a strong amount of change. However, it was the President's divisive attitude that has caused frustrations with him in recent years. The President's most controversial legislation, Obamacare, has been marked with scandal and frustration since day one. Most notably was the idea of "if you like your doctor, you can keep your doctor." Many have found that hasn't been the case. The President has also found his administration wrapped up in several scandals, notably with the IRS and Benghazi, but the President himself denies any knowledge of wrongdoing in the situations. Other frustrations have come from the President's use of executive actions, with many believing he has used more than his predecessors, notably with immigration. People have also been upset with the President's handling of moral issues such as race relations and gun control.

Former Secretary of State Hillary Clinton has come off as a politician with a lot of key experience over the years. However, many believe those experiences have not been something to rave about. Clinton faces a lot of criticism from her time as Secretary of State, especially with the Benghazi attack. The people feel that Secretary Clinton has not been honest with the issue, and the fact that the House of Representatives has had to launch a full investigation into the matter does not help her case. Secretary Clinton is under fire now for her use of a private email server during her time as Secretary of State, which could potentially be a crime, especially if she sent classified material from the server, and it got into the wrong hands due to a lack of security. Clinton also faces criticism for being out of touch with the everyday people.

New York Governor Andrew Cuomo was elected Governor with a message of cleaning up the corruption that has begun to become common with New York and Albany. However, Cuomo has found himself immersed in the corruption scandals. Cuomo set up the Moreland Commission to investigate corruption, but has instead disbanded the commission, stating it was his commission to disband. Cuomo has faced more criticism than even President Obama and Secretary Clinton for being significantly abrasive, stating that conservatives have no place in New York because they are "extremists." Cuomo himself may now be at the center of a corruption scandal.

Speaker of the House John Boehner, the first Republican on the list, now finds himself in an interesting situation. Boehner started his tenure as Speaker with full Republican support, but now leaves with the House Republican caucus in complete shambles. Boehner's career had been mainly positive, with him moving up the latter to become Speaker after a career of being considered a key conservative. It is now the conservatives who have become increasingly frustrated with Boehner, and are helping to push him from office. Boehner has done this to himself by punishing members and failing to stand up to the Democrats on key issues.

Senate Majority Leader Mitch McConnell has found himself in a similar position to Boehner. McConnell considers himself to be a conservative, but does not show it in his voting record or his interactions with other members and Democrats. McConnell was even called out by Texas Senator Ted Cruz for attempting to convince the Republican caucus to fold behind closed doors to make themselves look better. McConnell has also found himself on the wrong side of many votes, voting to increase spending and not to defund Obamacare. McConnell has also shown his absolute disrespect for conservatives by trashing them in elections, notably his Primary challenger in 2014, Matt Bevin. Since Boehner's announcement of resignation, McConnell has become the main member of leadership that conservatives are attempting to force out of office.

Finally, Arizona Senator John McCain exemplifies the exact kind of candidate that has changed his views over the years. McCain came in as a conservative maverick promising to take on high spending and dishonesty. However, McCain has voted for increased spending in recent years, and has become the very politician he came in claiming he would not be. McCain has been censured by the

Arizona GOP, and is attempting to punish them for that action. McCain has also been less and less respectful to those he works with, calling them "wacko birds" and "extremists." McCain's support for amnesty in immigration talks has also earned him the ire of many across the country.

Each of these candidates brings different issues to the table to be discussed, and their own forms of political dishonesty. If there is one thing the Republicans have in common it is that they have been in office for a very long time. Boehner, McConnell and McCain have been in office for combined over 80 years, which is older than the oldest of them. The one thing the Democrats have in common is their divisiveness once in office, and their failure to actually unite people together over various issues.

At the end of the day, every politician has their issues that frustrate the everyday people. However, some issues are more problematic and extreme than others, and require more action and attention. The goal has been to simply relay the information of some of the more controversial figures in American politics. There is no intention to speak ill of any of the candidates, as each of them brings positives to politics as well, and that is why they also carry a significant number of supporters. However, every American deserves to know the truth, and it is our hope that this starts the dialogue of the American people looking into their elected officials. The people deserve to know the truth, and they can make their decisions based on the information available to them.

So the issues have been laid out, and the information has been given. So what can be done? Currently, the only one on the list who is not up for re-election is President Barack Obama. Speaker of the House John Boehner has announced his plans to retire as of October of 2015, but he has not yet left office at the time of this writing. The best way to act is to get informed. If the Common Man is informed of what is going on, they can make an informed decision when voting, and even when calling out their elected officials. The people have every right to call out their elected officials, as they are responsible to the people.

One of the key ways to stop some of the dishonesty in politics today is term limits. We have seen some of these leaders have become more dishonest the more time they have been in office. They have accumulated a mass amount of power over time, and they feel they can actually direct what they do to the people instead of the people directing what they do. There have been several attempts to push for term limits, but these elected officials reject the notion that their time would be limited.

At the end of the day it is up to the Common Man to hold our elected officials responsible. The people deserve to know the truth, and they deserve to question the actions of their elected officials. When a politician is elected to office by the people, they lose not only a great deal of their privacy, but they lose their right to complain against those who are calling them out. They have a right to defend their actions, but at the end of the day the final verdict rests with the people who voted them into office. If our elected officials realized this, there would be far less issues. However, these officials often do not realize this, and it is up to the people to remind them. At the end of the day, everyone should remember to try and stay positive and respectful, the last thing we need is people being more rude and disrespectful to each other these days.

It is our hope that this work has inspired the Common Man to keep an eye on their elected officials and call them out when necessary. We cannot reiterate enough that at the end of the day the power is with the people, and that elected officials are responsible to the people. If these elected officials are doing things unacceptable with the people and things that are politically dishonest, they need to be voted out of office, and a new person who will be more responsible should be elected in their place. As society advances their will likely be even more ways to keep an eye on our elected officials, and even one day call them out even more. It is up to the Common Man to take advantage of this and call out the dishonesty we see in politics today.

God Bless America.

References/Notes

1. "Trust in Government." Gallup.com. Gallup, n.d. Web. 12 Oct. 2015. http://www.gallup.com/poll/5392/trust-government.aspx

2. "“Just like a Bunch of Commies!” Mark Levin SLAMS House GOP over Possible Rule Change to PUNISH Boehner Dissidents." The Right Scoop RSS. The Right Scoop, 22 Sept. 2014. Web. 12 Oct. 2015.http://therightscoop.com/just-like-a-bunch-of-commies-mark-levin-slams-house-gop-over-possible-rule-change-to-punish-boehner-dissidents/

3. Batley, Melanie. "McCain Wages 'All-Out War' to Rid Arizona GOP of Tea Party." Newsmax. Newsmax, 30 Dec. 2014. Web. 12 Oct. 2015. http://www.newsmax.com/newswidget/mccain-re-election-2016-arizona-tea-party/2014/12/30/id/615598/?Dkt_nbr=11550-1&nmx_source=Breitbart&nmx_medium=widget&nmx_content=112&nmx_campaign=widgetphase2

4. Biography. "Barack Obama- Biography." Biography. Biography, n.d. Web. http://www.biography.com/people/barack-obama-12782369#us-senate-career

5. CNN. "2008 Presidential Election." CNN. Cable News Network, Nov. 2008. Web. 12 Oct. 2015. http://www.cnn.com/ELECTION/2008/results/president/

6. "Barack Obama: Campaigns and Elections." Miller Center of Public Affairs, University of Virginia., n.d. Web. 12 Oct. 2015. http://millercenter.org/president/obama/essays/biography/3

7. Newsweek Staff. "Barack Obama: How He Did It." Newsweek. Newsweek, 4 Nov. 2008. Web. 12 Oct. 2015. http://www.newsweek.com/barack-obama-how-he-did-it-85083

8. "Better Coverage, Lower Costs." Barackobama.com. Barack Obama, n.d. Web. 12 Oct. 2015. http://www.barackobama.com/obamacare/

9. Gallup. "Presidential Approval Ratings -- Barack Obama." Gallup.com. Gallup, n.d. Web. 12 Oct. 2015 http://www.gallup.com/poll/116479/barack-obama-presidential-job-approval.aspx

10. Brooks, Jackson. "Obama's Numbers (April 2014 Update)." FactCheckorg. Factcheck.org, 11 Apr. 2014. Web. 12 Oct. 2015. http://www.factcheck.org/2014/04/obamas-numbers-april-2014-update/

11. CNN Library. "Barack Obama Fast Facts - CNN.com." CNN. Cable News Network, 20 Aug. 2015. Web. 12 Oct. 2015. http://www.cnn.com/2012/12/26/us/barack-obama---fast-facts/

12. "Barack Obama Quotes." Barack Obama Quotes. N.p., n.d. Web. 12 Oct. 2015. http://www.notable-quotes.com/o/obama_barack.html

13. Limbaugh, Rush. “The Court Rules: Obamacare is the Largest Tax Increase in the History of the World” Rushlimbaugh.com, June 28, 2012

14. "Nat'l Fed'n of Indep. Bus. v. Sebelius 567 U.S. ___ (2012)." Justia Law. Justia Law, n.d. Web. 12 Oct. 2015. https://supreme.justia.com/cases/federal/us/567/11-393/

15. Liptak, Adam. "Supreme Court Upholds Health Care Law, 5-4, in Victory for Obama." The New York Times. The New York Times, 28 June 2012. Web. 12 Oct. 2015. <http://www.nytimes.com/2012/06/29/us/supreme-court-lets-health-law-largely-stand.html?_r=0>.

16. Crawford, Jan. "Roberts Switched Views to Uphold Health Care Law." CBSNews. CBS Interactive, 2 July 2012. Web. 12 Oct. 2015. <http://www.cbsnews.com/news/roberts-switched-views-to-uphold-health-care-law/>.

17. Amadeo, Kimberly. "What You Really Need to Know About Obamacare." About.com News & Issues. About.com News and Issues, n.d. Web. 12 Oct. 2015. http://useconomy.about.com/od/healthcarereform/f/What-Is-Obama-Care.htm

18. Howerton, Jason. "A Senate Divided: GOP Senator Says Mike Lee’s Plan to Defund Obamacare Is the ‘Dumbest Idea I’ve Ever Heard’." The Blaze. The Blaze, 25 July 2013. Web. 12 Oct. 2015. http://www.theblaze.com/stories/2013/07/25/a-senate-divided-gop-senator-says-mike-lees-plan-to-defund-obamacare-is-the-dumbest-idea-ive-ever-heard/

19. Cruz, Ted. "Senator Ted Cruz's Marathon Speech Against Obamacare." Washington Post. Washington Post, 25 Sept. 2013. Web.

http://www.washingtonpost.com/sf/national/2013/09/25/transcript-sen-ted-cruzs-filibuster-against-obamacare/

20. Lee, Mike, Senator. "Senator Mike Lee: Defund Obamacare." USAToday.com. USA Today, 4 Aug. 2013. Web. http://www.usatoday.com/story/opinion/2013/08/04/defund-obamacare-sen-mike-lee-editorials-debates/2617319/

21. Limbaugh, Rush. "Interview: Senator Mike Lee Explains the Plan to Defund Obamacare - The Rush Limbaugh Show." RSS. Rush Limbaugh, 31 July 2013. Web. 12 Oct. 2015. http://www.rushlimbaugh.com/daily/2013/07/31/interview_senator_mike_lee_explains_the_plan_to_defund_obamacare

22. Obama, Barack. "Remarks by the President on the Affordable Care Act and the Government Shutdown." The White House. The White House, 1 Oct. 2013. Web. 12 Oct. 2015. http://www.whitehouse.gov/the-press-office/2013/10/01/remarks-president-affordable-care-act-and-government-shutdown

23. Kirell, Andrew. "A Brief History of the 2013 Government Shutdown." Mediaite A Brief History of the 2013 Government Shutdown Comments. Mediaite, 17 Oct. 2013. Web. 12 Oct. 2015. http://www.mediaite.com/tv/a-brief-history-of-the-2013-government-shutdown/

24. Yan, Holly. "Government Shutdown: What You Need to Know - CNNPolitics.com." CNN. Cable News Network, 1 Oct. 2013. Web. 12 Oct. 2015. http://www.cnn.com/2013/09/30/politics/government-shutdown-up-to-speed/

25. "Sign Up For ObamaCare: ObamaCare Sign up Deadlines." Obamacare Facts. N.p., n.d. Web. 12 Oct. 2015. http://obamacarefacts.com/obamacare-sign-up.php

26. Bendery, Jennifer. "Kathleen Sebelius Takes Blame For Obamacare Glitches While Being Grilled By Marsha Blackburn." The Huffington Post. TheHuffingtonPost.com, 30 Oct. 2013. Web. 12 Oct. 2015. http://www.huffingtonpost.com/2013/10/30/kathleen-sebelius-marsha-blackburn_n_4177223.html

27. Klein, Philip. "IRS Tells Congress Agency Lost Two Years of Lois Lerner Emails." Washington Examiner. N.p., 13 June 2014. Web. 12 Oct. 2015. http://www.washingtonexaminer.com/irs-tells-congress-agency-lost-two-years-of-lois-lerner-emails/article/2549734

28. Howley, Patrick. "BOMBSHELL MEMO: Jeanne Shaheen Conspired With White House Insider On IRS Targeting Scandal." Dailycaller.com. The Daily Caller, 3 Nov. 2014. Web. 12 Oct. 2015. http://dailycaller.com/2014/11/03/bombshell-memo-jeanne-shaheen-conspired-with-white-house-insider-on-irs-targeting-scandal/

29. Kasperowicz, Pete. "Report Blames Obama White House for Weaponizing the IRS and Turning It Against Conservatives." The Blaze. The Blaze, 22 Dec. 2014. Web. 12 Oct. 2015. http://www.theblaze.com/stories/2014/12/22/report-blames-obama-white-house-for-turning-the-irs-into-a-political-weapon/

30. Ohlemacher, Stephen. "Probe Fails To Link IRS Scandal To White House." Yahoo! News. Yahoo!, 23 Dec. 2014. Web. 12 Oct. 2015. http://news.yahoo.com/issa-probe-fails-white-house-irs-scandal-160604665--finance.html

31. Cox, John Woodrow. "House GOP Leader's Final Report on IRS Targeting Accuses Agency of 'culture of Bias'." Washington Post. The Washington Post, 23 Dec. 2014. Web. 12 Oct. 2015. http://www.washingtonpost.com/blogs/federal-eye/wp/2014/12/23/house-gop-leaders-final-report-on-irs-targeting-accuses-agency-of-culture-of-bias/

32. NPR. "Transcript: President Obama's Full NPR Interview." NPR. NPR, 29 Dec. 2014. Web. 12 Oct. 2015. http://www.npr.org/2014/12/29/372485968/transcript-president-obamas-full-npr-interview

33. U.S. Department of Justice "Meet The Attorney General" justice.gov, October 25, 2015 http://www.justice.gov/ag/meet-attorney-general-0

34. Obama, Barack. "Remarks by the President on Trayvon Martin." The White House. The White House, 19 July 2013. Web. 12 Oct. 2015. http://www.whitehouse.gov/the-press-office/2013/07/19/remarks-president-trayvon-martin

35. Goad, Benjamin. "Holder: Civil Rights Probe into Trayvon Martin Shooting Still Active." TheHill. The Hill, 04 Sept. 2014. Web. 12 Oct. 2015. http://thehill.com/regulation/administration/216705-probe-into-trayvon-shooting-is-active-ag-says

36. Duke, Alan. "Police: Robbers Tell Man, 'This Is for Trayvon Martin' - CNN.com." CNN. Cable News Network, 29 July 2013. Web. 12 Oct. http://www.cnn.com/2013/07/28/us/dc-robbery-hate-crime/index.html?hpt=hp_t2

37. "Victim: Attack Fueled by Zimmerman Verdict." WISN. N.p., 15 July 2013. Web. 12 Oct. 2015.http://www.wisn.com/news/south-east-wisconsin/milwaukee/victim-attack-fueled-by-zimmerman-verdict/20993090?item=0

38. Grinberg, Emanuella. "Ferguson Decision: What Witnesses Told the Grand Jury - CNN.com." CNN. Cable News Network, 26 Nov. 2014. Web. 12 Oct. 2015. http://www.cnn.com/2014/11/25/justice/ferguson-decision-michael-brown-witness-testimony/

39. Jauregui, Andres. "Witnesses Lied Under Oath In Ferguson Grand Jury, Prosecutor Says." The Huffington Post. TheHuffingtonPost.com, 19 Dec. 2014. Web. 12 Oct. 2015. http://www.huffingtonpost.com/2014/12/19/witnesses-lied-ferguson-grand-jury-bob-mcculloch_n_6356804.html

40. "Ferguson, Missouri Grand Jury Decision Announcement." C-SPAN.org. N.p., 24 Nov. 2014. Web. 12 Oct. 2015. http://www.c-span.org/video/?322925-1/ferguson-missouri-grand-jury-decision-announcement

41. State of Missouri v. Darren Wilson "Grand Jury Transcript" August 20, 2014 http://graphics8.nytimes.com/newsgraphics/2014/11/24/ferguson-assets/grand-jury-testimony.pdf

42. Associated Press. "Medical Examiner Says Chokehold by Police Officer Caused Death of NYC Man; Ruled Homicide." Fox News. FOX News Network, 01 Aug. 2014. Web. 12 Oct. 2015. http://www.foxnews.com/us/2014/08/01/medical-examiner-says-chokehold-by-police-officer-caused-death-nyc-man-ruled/

43. Holley, Peter. "Two New York City Police Officers Are Shot and Killed in a Brazen Ambush in Brooklyn." Washington Post. The Washington Post, 20 Dec. 2014. Web. 12 Oct. 2015. http://www.washingtonpost.com/national/two-new-york-city-police-officers-are-shot-and-killed-in-a-brazen-ambush-in-brooklyn/2014/12/20/2a73f7ae-8898-11e4-9534-f79a23c40e6c_story.html

44. Sutton, Joe. "Police Officer Shot and Killed in Florida - CNN.com." CNN. Cable News Network, 21 Dec. 2014. Web. 12 Oct. 2015. http://www.cnn.com/2014/12/21/us/florida-officer-killed/

45. Henderson, Nia-Malika. "President Obama Just Said Something Pretty Significant about Eric Garner and Race."

Washington Post. The Washington Post, 9 Dec. 2014. Web. 12 Oct. 2015http://www.washingtonpost.com/blogs/the-fix/wp/2014/12/09/president-obama-just-said-something-pretty-significant-about-eric-garner-and-race/

46. Benson, Guy. "Guy Benson - Pure Gold: Obama Slams Bush for Expanding Executive Power, Ignoring Congress." Townhall.com. Townhall, 13 Feb. 2014. Web. 12 Oct. 2015. http://townhall.com/tipsheet/guybenson/2014/02/13/pure-gold-obama-slams-bush-for-expanding-executive-power-ignoring-congress-n1794535

47. Somanader, Tonya. ""We Were Strangers Once, Too": The President Announces New Steps on Immigration." The White House. The White House, 20 Nov. 2014. Web. 12 Oct. 2015. http://www.whitehouse.gov/blog/2014/11/20/we-were-strangers-once-too-president-announces-new-steps-immigratio

48. "Obama Vows To Bypass Congress in Fiery State Of The Union." YouTube. YouTube, 29 Jan. 2014. Web. 12 Oct. 2015. https://www.youtube.com/watch?v=53PO8zLnsIo

49. SNL. "Watch How a Bill Does Not Become a Law from Saturday Night Live on NBC.com." NBC. SNL, n.d. Web. 12 Oct. 2015. http://www.nbc.com/saturday-night-live/video/capitol-hill-cold-open/2830152

50. "It's Time to Fix Our Broken Immigration System." The White House. The White House, n.d. Web. 12 Oct. 2015. http://www.whitehouse.gov/issues/immigration/immigration-action#

51. Ehrenfreund, Max. "Your Complete Guide to Obama's Immigration Executive Action." Washington Post. The Washington Post, 20 Nov. 2014. Web. 12 Oct. 2015. http://www.washingtonpost.com/blogs/wonkblog/wp/2014/11/19/your-complete-guide-to-obamas-immigration-order/

52. "Executive Orders." The White House. The White House, n.d. Web. 12 Oct. 2015. http://www.whitehouse.gov/briefing-room/presidential-actions/executive-orders

53. Ashtari, Shadee. "Obama Has Issued Fewer Executive Orders Than Any President In Past 100 Years." The Huffington Post. TheHuffingtonPost.com, 9 Dec. 2014. Web. 12 Oct. 2015. http://www.huffingtonpost.com/2014/11/24/barack-obama-executive-orders-immigration_n_6213800.html

54. Limbaugh, Rush. "Democrats and Drive-Bys Distort Reagan to Validate Obama's Executive Order on Amnesty - The Rush Limbaugh Show." RSS. Rush Limbaugh, 19 Nov. 2014. Web. 12 Oct. 2015. http://www.rushlimbaugh.com/daily/2014/11/19/democrats_and_drive_bys_distort_reagan_to_validate_obama_s_executive_order_on_amnesty

55. "Ronald Reagan Executive Orders - 1987." National Archives and Records Administration. National Archives and Records Administration, n.d. Web. 12 Oct. 2015.http://www.archives.gov/federal-register/executive-orders/1987.html

56. Goldfarb, Zachary Woodrow, and Ed O'Keefe. "Obama Defends Decision to Trade 5 Guantanamo Detainees for Bergdahl." Washington Post. The Washington Post, 3 June 2014. Web. 12 Oct. 2015. http://www.washingtonpost.com/world/national-security/obama-defends-decision-to-trade-5-guantanamo-detainees-for-bergdahl/2014/06/03/759151a8-eb10-11e3-b98c-72cef4a00499_story.html

57. York, Byron. "On Gitmo, Obama vs. Congress." Detroit News. Detroit News, 1 Jan. 2015. Web. 12 Oct. 2015. http://www.detroitnews.com/story/opinion/2014/12/31/york-gitmo-obama-congress/21111751/

58. FoxNews.com. "US Releases 5 More Guantanamo Bay Prisoners, Sends Them to Kazakhstan." Fox News. FOX News Network, 31 Dec. 2014. Web. 12 Oct. 2015. http://www.foxnews.com/politics/2014/12/31/us-releases-5-more-guantanamo-bay-prisoners-sends-them-to-kazakhstan/

59. Korte, Gregory. "Obama Issues 'executive Orders by Another Name'" USA Today. Gannett, 17 Dec. 2014. Web. 12 Oct. 2015. http://www.usatoday.com/story/news/politics/2014/12/16/obama-presidential-memoranda-executive-orders/20191805/

60. Pavlich, Katie. "Katie Pavlich - Federal Judge on Obama's Illegal Immigration Executive Action: It's Unconstitutional." Townhall.com. Townhall, 17 Dec. 2014. Web. 12 Oct. 2015. http://townhall.com/tipsheet/katiepavlich/2014/12/17/federal-judge-on-obamas-illegal-immigration-executive-action-its-unconstitutional-n1933035

61. Kessler, Glenn. "Claims regarding Obama's Use of Executive Orders and Presidential Memoranda." Washington Post. The Washington Post, 31 Dec. 2014. Web. 12 Oct. 2015. http://www.washingtonpost.com/blogs/fact-checker/wp/2014/12/31/claims-regarding-obamas-use-of-executive-orders-and-presidential-memoranda/

62. Howerton, Jason. "Obama Has Been Quietly Issuing 'Executive Orders by Another Name'." The Blaze. The Blaze, 16 Dec. 2014. Web. 12 Oct. 2015.http://www.theblaze.com/stories/2014/12/16/using-stealthy-tactic-obama-is-on-track-to-take-more-high-level-executive-actions-than-any-president-since-harry-truman/

63. "Hillary Clinton." Bio. A&E Television Networks, 2015. Web. 15 Jan. 2015. http://www.biography.com/people/hillary-clinton-9251306#related-video-gallery

64. "About Us." Arkansas Advocates for Children and Families AACF. N.p., n.d. Web. 12 Oct. 2015.http://www.aradvocates.org/about-us/

65. "Hillary Diane Rodham Clinton (1947) - Encyclopedia of Arkansas." Hillary Diane Rodham Clinton (1947) - Encyclopedia of Arkansas. Encyclopedia of Arkansas, n.d. Web. 12 Oct. 2015. http://www.encyclopediaofarkansas.net/encyclopedia/entry-detail.aspx?entryID=2744

66. Galiano, Amanda. "Hillary Rodham Clinton - Her Time As Arkansas' First Lady." About.com Travel. About.com Travel, n.d. Web. 12 Oct. 2015. http://littlerock.about.com/od/politicsandpoliticalorga/p/aahillary.htm

67. "Adoption and Safe Families Act of 1997." Web. Oct. 25. 2015http://www.gpo.gov/fdsys/pkg/BILLS-105hr867enr/pdf/BILLS-105hr867enr.pdf

68. "Overview: The Adoption and Safe Families Act of 1997." PBS. PBS, n.d. Web. 12 Oct. 2015. http://www.pbs.org/wgbh/pages/frontline/shows/fostercare/inside/asfa.html

69. "First Lady Biography: Hillary Clinton." Hillary Clinton Biography. National First Ladies' Library and Historic Site, n.d. Web. 12 Oct. 2015. http://www.firstladies.org/biographies/firstladies.aspx?biography=43

70. Marshall, Josh. "The 1993 Kristol Memo on Defeating Health Care Reform." TalkingPointsMemo.com. Talking Points Memo, 24 Sept. 2013. Web. 12 Oct. 2015. http://talkingpointsmemo.com/edblog/the-1993-kristol-memo-on-defeating-health-care-reform

71. "The Health-Care Plan of 1993 - Boundless Open Textbook." Boundless. Boundless, n.d. Web. 12 Oct. 2015. https://www.boundless.com/u-s-history/textbooks/boundless-u-s-history-textbook/the-challenges-of-globalization-and-the-coming-century-after-1989-31/the-clinton-administration-231/the-health-care-plan-of-1993-1317-9290/

72. Moffit, Robert E., Ph D. "A Guide to the Clinton Health Plan." The Heritage Foundation. The Heritage Foundation, 19 Nov. 1993. Web. 12 Oct. 2015.http://www.heritage.org/Research/Reports/1993/11/A-Guide-to-the-Clinton-Health-Plan

73. Paul Starr, "What Happened to Health Care Reform?" The American Prospect no. 20 (Winter 1995): 20-31.https://www.princeton.edu/~starr/20starr.html

74. Caroli, Betty Boyd. "Hillary Rodham Clinton | United States Senator, First Lady, and Secretary of State." Encyclopedia Britannica Online. Encyclopedia Britannica, n.d. Web. 12 Oct. 2015. http://www.britannica.com/EBchecked/topic/121809/Hillary-Rodham-Clinton

75. O'Shea, Jennifer L. "10 Things You Didn't Know About Hillary Clinton's Senate Career." Usnews.com. US News And World Report, 3 Dec. 2008. Web. 12 Oct. 2015. http://www.usnews.com/news/articles/2008/12/03/10-things-you-didnt-know-about-hillary-clintons-senate-career

76. Washington, Toby Harnden in. "Hillary Clinton's Bosnia Sniper Story Exposed." The Telegraph. Telegraph Media Group, 25 Mar. 2008. Web. 12 Oct. 2015. http://www.telegraph.co.uk/news/worldnews/1582795/Hillary-Clintons-Bosnia-sniper-story-exposed.html

77. Mullins, Melissa. "Attkisson: Brian Williams War Story 'Strangely' Similar to Hillary Clinton on Bosnia." NewsBusters. NewsBusters, 11 Feb. 2015. Web. 12 Oct. 2015.http://newsbusters.org/blogs/melissa-mullins/2015/02/11/attkisson-brian-williams-war-story-strangely-similar-hillary

78. Mason, Jeff. "Hillary Clinton Calls Bosnia Sniper Story a Mistake." Reuters. Thomson Reuters, 25 Mar. 2008. Web. 12 Oct. 2015. http://www.reuters.com/article/2008/03/26/us-usa-politics-clinton-idUSN25408114200803026

79. Saad, Lydia. "Hillary Clinton Favorable Near Her All-Time High." Gallup.com. Gallup, 30 Mar. 2011. Web. 12 Oct. 2015. http://www.gallup.com/poll/146891/hillary-clinton-favorable-near-time-high.aspx#

80. Neuman, Scott. "Clinton: WikiLeaks 'Tear At Fabric' Of Government." NPR. NPR, 29 Nov. 2010. Web. 12 Oct. 2015. http://www.npr.org/2010/11/29/131668950/white-house-aims-to-limit-wikileaks-damage

81. Houissa, Ali. "Arab Spring: A Research & Study Guide * الربيع العربي: Home." Library.cornell.edu. Cornell, 13 July 2015. Web. 12 Oct. 2015. http://guides.library.cornell.edu/c.php?g=31688&p=200747

82. Totten, Michael J. "Year Four: The Arab Spring Proved Everyone Wrong." World Affairs Journal. World Affairs, July-Aug. 2014. Web. 12 Oct. 2015. http://www.worldaffairsjournal.org/article/year-four-arab-spring-proved-everyone-wrong

83. BBC World. "Arab Uprising: Country by Country." BBC News. BBC News, 16 Dec. 2013. Web. 12 Oct. 2015. http://www.bbc.com/news/world-12482311

84. GOP. "Clinton's Hard Choices: Facts Vs. Fiction Volume 4." GOP. GOP, 10 June 2014. Web. 12 Oct. 2015. https://www.gop.com/clintons-hard-choices-facts-vs-fiction-volume-4/

85. Quinn, Andrew. "Clinton Says U.S. Must Embrace Arab Spring despite Dangers." Reuters. Thomson Reuters, 12 Oct. 2012. Web. 12 Oct. 2015. http://www.reuters.com/article/2012/10/12/us-usa-mideast-idUSBRE89B19Z20121012

86. Washington Post Staff. "'Hard Choices': A Chapter-by-chapter Breakdown of Clinton's New Book." Washington Post. The Washington Post, 9 June 2014. Web. 12 Oct. 2015. http://www.washingtonpost.com/blogs/post-politics/wp/2014/06/09/hard-choices-we-read-it/

87. Associated Press. "Hillary Clinton: Obama Administration Divided over 2011 Arab Uprisings." Theguardian.com. The Guardian, 7 June 2014. Web. 12 Oct. 2015. http://www.theguardian.com/world/2014/jun/07/hillary-clinton-obama-administration-split-arab-spring-mubarak

88. Barack Obama. "Remarks by the President on the Situation in Egypt." The White House. The White House, 1 Feb. 2011. Web. 12 Oct. 2015. https://www.whitehouse.gov/the-press-office/2011/02/01/remarks-president-situation-egypt

89. Frizell, Sam. "Hillary Clinton Criticizes Obama on Syria Policy." Time. Time, 10 Aug. 2014. Web. 12 Oct. 2015.http://time.com/3097964/hillary-clinton-syria-isis-the-atlantic/

90. Paul, Rand, Senator. "Dfgdfg." C-SPAN.org. CSPAN, 18 Sept. 2014. Web. 12 Oct. 2015. http://www.c-span.org/video/?c4509034/dfgdfg

91. Scott, Adrianna. "Should The House Have Voted To Arm the Syrian Rebels?" US News. U.S.News & World Report, 18 Sept. 2014. Web. 12 Oct. 2015. http://www.usnews.com/opinion/articles/2014/09/18/should-the-house-have-authorized-obamas-plan-to-arm-syrian-rebels

92. O'Keefe, Ed. "Joe Manchin to Vote against Arming and Training Syrian Rebels." Washington Post. The Washington Post, 17 Sept. 2014. Web. 12 Oct. 2015. http://www.washingtonpost.com/blogs/post-politics/wp/2014/09/17/joe-manchin-to-vote-against-arming-and-training-syrian-rebels/

93. CNN Library. "Benghazi Mission Attack Fast Facts - CNN.com." CNN. Cable News Network, 4 Sept. 2015. Web. 12 Oct. 2015. http://www.cnn.com/2013/09/10/world/benghazi-consulate-attack-fast-facts/

94. Kiely, Eugene. "Benghazi Timeline." FactCheckorg. Fact Check, 26 Oct. 2012. Web. 12 Oct. 2015. http://www.factcheck.org/2012/10/benghazi-timeline/

95. CBS News. "Benghazi Timeline: How the Probe Unfolded." CBSNews. CBS Interactive, 2015. Web. 12 Oct. 2015. http://www.cbsnews.com/news/benghazi-timeline-how-the-probe-unfolded/

96. Pavlich, Katie. "- White House Threatened YouTube Over Bogus Benghazi 'Video'" Townhall.com. Townhall, 23 May 2014. Web. 12 Oct. 2015. http://townhall.com/tipsheet/katiepavlich/2014/05/23/white-house-threatened-youtube-over-bogus-benghazi-video-n1842444

97. United States Cong. Senate 113th Congress 2nd Session Report of the U.S. Senate Select Committee on Intelligence Review of the Terrorist Attacks on U.S. Facilities In Benghazi, Libya,

September 11-12, 2012 together with Additional Views January 14, 2014. Washington Post. Web 16 Oct. 2015. http://apps.washingtonpost.com/g/documents/world/senate-intelligence-committee-report-on-benghazi-attack/748/

98. Clinton, Hillary Rodham. Hard Choices. First Simon & Schuster hardcover edition. Simon & Schuster, 2014.

99. Judicial Watch. "Benghazi Docs Obtained by JW Belie Hillary's No Classified Emails Claim - Judicial Watch." Judicial Watch. Judicial Watch, 12 Mar. 2015. Web. 12 Oct. 2015. http://www.judicialwatch.org/blog/2015/03/benghazi-docs-obtained-by-jw-belie-hillarys-no-classified-emails-claim/

100. Pearson, Michael. "What the Obama Administration Has Said about the Libya Attack - CNNPolitics.com." CNN. Cable News Network, 8 May 2013. Web. 12 Oct. 2015. http://www.cnn.com/2012/10/10/world/libya-attack-statements/

101. "Hillary Clinton Ad - 3 AM White House Ringing Phone." YouTube. YouTube, 15 May 2008. Web. 12 Oct. 2015. https://www.youtube.com/watch?v=7yr7odFUARg

102. Alexovich, Ariel. "Clinton's National Security Ad." The Caucus Clintons National Security Ad Comments. New York Times, 29 Feb. 2008. Web. 12 Oct. 2015. http://thecaucus.blogs.nytimes.com/2008/02/29/clintons-national-security-ad/

103. Sullivan, Sean. "The 8 Memorable Moments From Hillary Clinton's Benghazi Testimony." Washingtonpost.com. Washington Post, 23 Jan. 2013. Web. 12 Oct. 2015. http://www.washingtonpost.com/blogs/the-fix/wp/2013/01/23/four-memorable-moments-from-hillary-clintons-benghazi-testimony-video/

104. Salcedo, Chris "Hillary's server: It's not just about her hiding things from the American people" TheBlaze.com, TheBlaze, 13. April. 2015 Web 28. Oct. 2015. http://www.theblaze.com/blog/2015/04/13/hillarys-server-its-not-just-about-her-hiding-things-from-the-american-people/

105. Leonnig, Carol D., Rosalind S. Helderman, and Tom Hamburger. "FBI Looking into the Security of Hillary Clinton's Private E-mail Setup." Washington Post. The Washington Post, 4 Aug. 2015. Web. 13 Oct. 2015. https://www.washingtonpost.com/politics/fbi-looks-into-security-of-clintons-private-e-mail-setup/2015/08/04/2bdd85ec-3aae-11e5-8e98-115a3cf7d7ae_story.html

106. Hamburger, Tom, and Rosalind S. Helderman. "FBI Probe of Clinton E-mail Expands to Second Data Company." Washington Post. The Washington Post, 7 Oct. 2015. Web. 13 Oct. 2015. https://www.washingtonpost.com/politics/fbi-probe-of-clinton-e-mail-expands-to-second-data-company/2015/10/06/3d94ba46-6c48-11e5-b31c-d80d62b53e28_story.html

107. Klapper, Bradley, and Ken Delanian. "AP EXCLUSIVE: Top Secret Clinton Emails Include Drone Talk." Bigstory.ap.org. AP, 14 Aug. 2015. Web. 13 Oct. 2015. http://bigstory.ap.org/article/b54a250a40e9410baaaca5f9fb58ea94/ap-exclusive-top-secret-clinton-emails-include-drone-talk

108. FoxNews.com. "Gowdy Says New Emails Show Clinton Confidant Naming CIA Source, Pushing Libya Interests." Fox News. FOX News Network, 08 Oct. 2015. Web. 13 Oct. 2015. http://www.foxnews.com/politics/2015/10/08/benghazi-committee-blumenthal-promoted-passed-along-name-cia-source-pushed-for/

109. Fitton, Tom "New Court Action in Hillary Clinton Email Scandal" Breitbart. Brietbart.com 23. March. 2015. Web Oct. 28.

2015. http://www.breitbart.com/big-government/2015/03/23/new-court-action-in-hillary-clinton-email-scandal/

110. Kreutz, Liz "Hillary Clinton Stumbles From 'Dead Broke' to 'Not Truly Well Off" ABC News. ABCNews.com. 23. June. 2014. Web. Oct. 28. 2015
http://abcnews.go.com/blogs/politics/2014/06/hillary-clinton-stumbles-from-dead-broke-to-not-truly-well-off/

111. Biography.com Editors. "Andrew Cuomo Biography." Bio.com. A&E Networks Television, n.d. Web. 12 Oct. 2015. http://www.biography.com/people/andrew-cuomo-21024931#personal-life

112. "Cuomo 2014." Cuomo 2014. Cuomo 2014, n.d. Web. 12 Oct. 2015. http://andrewcuomo.com/about-andrew/

113. "The Official Website of Governor Andrew M. Cuomo." Governor Andrew M. Cuomo. N.p., n.d. Web. 12 Oct. 2015. https://www.governor.ny.gov/about

114. Halbfinger, David, and Michael Powell. "As HUD Chief, Cuomo Earns a Mixed Score." The New York Times. The New York Times, 23 Aug. 2010. Web. 12 Oct. 2015.
http://www.nytimes.com/2010/08/24/nyregion/24hud.html?_r=0

115. DeHaven, Tad. "HUD Scandals." Downsizing the Federal Government. Downsizing The Federal Government, June 2009. Web. 12 Oct. 2015.
http://www.downsizinggovernment.org/hud/scandals#The_Cuomo_Years

116. Lovett, Kenneth. "Cuomo Rebrands Campaign Committee to 'Andrew Cuomo 2018'" NY Daily News. NY Daily News, 3 Apr. 2015. Web. 12 Oct. 2015.

http://www.nydailynews.com/news/politics/cuomo-rebrands-campaign-committee-andrew-cuomo-2018-article-1.2173002

117. Hakim, Danny, and Nicholas Confessore. "Cuomo Opens Campaign for New York Governor." The New York Times. The New York Times, 22 May 2010. Web. 12 Oct. 2015. http://www.nytimes.com/2010/05/23/nyregion/23cuomo.html?_r=0

118. Prokop, Andrew. "The Andrew Cuomo Scandal, Explained." Yahoo! News. Yahoo!, 15 Aug. 2014. Web. 12 Oct. 2015. http://news.yahoo.com/andrew-cuomo-scandal-explained-130002304.html

119. Rothman, Noah. "Why Is Scandal-plagued Andrew Cuomo Not Getting the Christie Treatment in the Press?" Hot Air. Hot Air, 06 Aug. 2014. Web. 12 Oct. 2015. http://hotair.com/archives/2014/08/06/andrew-cuomo-is-in-serious-trouble-and-the-media-doesnt-care/

120. Epstein, Reid J. "N.Y. Legalizes Gay Marriage." POLITICO. Politico, 24 June 2011. Web. 12 Oct. 2015. http://www.politico.com/news/stories/0611/57749.html

121. Vielkind, Jimmy. "Governor to Assembly GOP: Vote for Tax Code Unanimously or Risk Seats." Times Union. Times Union, 8 Dec. 2011. Web. 12 Oct. 2015. http://www.timesunion.com/local/article/Governor-to-Assembly-GOP-Vote-for-tax-code-2391075.php

122. Kaplan, Thomas, and Raymond Hernandez. "Cuomo, in Aid Appeal, Cites Broad Reach of Storm." The New York Times. The New York Times, 26 Nov. 2012. Web. 12 Oct. 2015. http://www.nytimes.com/2012/11/27/nyregion/governor-cuomo-says-hurricane-sandy-was-worse-than-katrina.html?_r=0

123. Odato, James M. "Report Rips State Handling of Superstorm Sandy Response." Times Union. Times Union, 10 Feb. 2014. Web. 12 Oct. 2015.http://www.timesunion.com/local/article/Report-rips-state-handling-of-Superstorm-Sandy-5217760.php

124. "Governor Cuomo Declares State of Emergency in New York in Preparation for Potential Impact of Hurricane Sandy." Governor Andrew M. Cuomo. Governor Andrew M. Cuomo, 28 Sept. 2014. Web. 12 Oct. 2015.https://www.governor.ny.gov/news/governor-cuomo-declares-state-emergency-new-york-preparation-potential-impact-hurricane-sandy

125. Karni, Annie. "Rob Astorino Attacks Gov. Cuomo -- Again -- on Sandy Funds." NY Daily News. NY Daily News, 28 Oct. 2014. Web. 12 Oct. 2015.http://www.nydailynews.com/blogs/dailypolitics/rob-astorino-attacks-gov-cuomo-eve-hurricane-sandy-anniversary-blog-entry-1.1990012

126. Glaser, Howard. "Cuomo Gun Safety Legislation Passes NY State Senate With Bipartisan Support, Assembly Action Today." The Huffington Post. TheHuffingtonPost.com, 17 Mar. 2013. Web. 12 Oct. 2015. http://www.huffingtonpost.com/howard-glaser/cuomo-gun-safety-legislation_b_2476419.html

127. NRA-ILA. "NRA-ILA | Governor Andrew Cuomo Seizes Your Gun Rights Overnight with Secret Deals, Procedural Shortcuts and Midnight Votes in Albany." NRA-ILA. NRA-ILA, 15 Jan. 2013. Web. 12 Oct. 2015. https://www.nraila.org/articles/20130115/new-york-governor-andrew-cuomo-seizes-your-gun-rights-overnight-with-secret-deals-procedural-shortcuts-and-midnight-votes-in-albany

128. Walshe, Shushannah. "New York Passes Toughest Gun-Control Law." ABC News. ABC News Network, 15 Jan. 2013. Web.

12 Oct. 2015. http://abcnews.go.com/Politics/york-state-passes-toughest-gun-control-law-nation/story?id=18224091

129. Weaver, Teri. "NY SAFE Act: New Bi-partisan Effort in Albany to Repeal Parts of the Gun Laws." Syracuse.com. Syracuse.com, 2 Mar. 2015. Web. 12 Oct. 2015. http://www.syracuse.com/politics/index.ssf/2015/03/ny_safe_act_bi-partisan_effort_in_albany_to_repeal_parts_of_the_gun_laws.html

130. Harding, Robert. "Siena Poll: Most New Yorkers Support SAFE Act, but Majority of Upstate Voters Do Not." Auburn Citizen. Auburn Citizen, 26 May 2015. Web. 12 Oct. 2015. http://auburnpub.com/blogs/eye_on_ny/siena-poll-most-new-yorkers-support-safe-act-but-majority/article_b229fa9e-035a-11e5-bb11-a34b139ba3ea.html

131. "Guide To The New York State SAFE Act for Members of the Division of State Police" The Office of Division Counsel, September 2013http://www.nypdcea.org/pdfs/NYSP_Safe_Act_Field_Guide.pdf

132. "NYSAFE Act Gun Reform | Governor Andrew M. Cuomo." NYSAFE Act Gun Reform | Governor Andrew M. Cuomo. Ny.gov, n.d. Web. 12 Oct. 2015. http://programs.governor.ny.gov/nysafeact/gun-reform#quicklinks

133. Cuomo, Andrew, Governor. "Transcript of Governor Andrew M. Cuomo's 2013 State of the State Address." Governor Andrew M. Cuomo. Governor Andrew M. Cuomo, 28 Sept. 2014. Web. 12 Oct. 2015. https://www.governor.ny.gov/news/transcript-governor-andrew-m-cuomos-2013-state-state-address

134. Opelka, Mike. "A Form of Gun Confiscation Has Reportedly Begun in New York State — Here's the Justification Being Used." The Blaze. The Blaze, 9 Apr. 2013. Web. 12 Oct. 2015.

http://www.theblaze.com/stories/2013/04/09/a-form-of-gun-confiscation-has-reportedly-begun-in-new-york-state-heres-the-justification-being-used/

135. Ross, Chuck. "Veteran And Former Cop Sues After Guns Confiscated Because He Sought Treatment For Insomnia." Dailycaller.com. The Daily Caller, 2 Jan. 2015. Web. 12 Oct. 2015. http://dailycaller.com/2015/01/02/veteran-and-former-cop-sues-after-guns-confiscated-because-he-sought-treatment-for-insomnia/

136. Kaplan, Thomas. "U.S. Judge Upholds Most New York Gun Limits." The New York Times. The New York Times, 31 Dec. 2013. Web. 12 Oct. 2015.http://www.nytimes.com/2014/01/01/nyregion/federal-judge-upholds-majority-of-new-york-gun-law.html?_r=0

137. Stepansky, Jospeh, and Thomas Tracy. "Murders in New York City Continue to Rise." NY Daily News. NY Daily News, 6 Apr. 2015. Web. 12 Oct. 2015.http://www.nydailynews.com/new-york/nyc-crime/murders-new-york-city-continue-rise-article-1.2175686

138. Mathias, Christopher. "New York Towns Threaten Secession Over Gov. Cuomo's Ban On Fracking." The Huffington Post. TheHuffingtonPost.com, 20 Feb. 2015. Web. 12 Oct. 2015. http://www.huffingtonpost.com/2015/02/20/new-york-fracking-secession-southern-tier-cuomo_n_6722296.html

139. Gerken, James. "Gov. Andrew Cuomo To Ban Fracking In New York State." The Huffington Post. TheHuffingtonPost.com, 18 Dec. 2014. Web. 12 Oct. 2015.http://www.huffingtonpost.com/2014/12/17/cuomo-fracking-new-york-state_n_6341292.html

140. Clemente, Jude. "Why New York's Fracking Ban For Natural Gas Is Unsustainable." Forbes. Forbes Magazine, 7 June 2015. Web.

12 Oct. 2015.http://www.forbes.com/sites/judeclemente/2015/06/07/why-new-yorks-fracking-ban-for-natural-gas-is-unsustainable/

141. http://www.dangersoffracking.com/

142. Kaplan, Thomas. "Citing Health Risks, Cuomo Bans Fracking in New York State." The New York Times. The New York Times, 17 Dec. 2014. Web. 12 Oct. 2015.http://www.nytimes.com/2014/12/18/nyregion/cuomo-to-ban-fracking-in-new-york-state-citing-health-risks.html?_r=0

143. "A New Opportunityto Grow Your Business." START-UP NY Grow Your Business. Ny.gov, n.d. Web. 12 Oct. 2015.http://startup.ny.gov/

144. Beyer, Scott. "Cuomo's START-UP NY Highlights Failures Of The Empire State Development Corporation." Forbes. Forbes Magazine, 18 Apr. 2015. Web. 12 Oct. 2015. http://www.forbes.com/sites/scottbeyer/2015/04/18/cuomos-start-up-ny-highlights-failures-of-the-empire-state-development-corporation/

145. David, Greg. "Start-Up NY: The Much-touted Jobs Program Created 76 Jobs Last Year." Crainsnewyork.com. Crain's New York, 9 Apr. 2015. Web. 12 Oct. 2015. http://www.crainsnewyork.com/article/20150409/BLOGS01/150409872/start-up-ny-the-much-touted-jobs-program-created-76-jobs-last-year

146. Strauss, Valerie. "Educators Alarmed by Some Questions on N.Y. Common Core Tests." Washington Post. The Washington Post, 19 Apr. 2015. Web. 12 Oct. 2015.http://www.washingtonpost.com/blogs/answer-sheet/wp/2015/04/19/educators-alarmed-by-some-questions-on-n-y-common-core-tests/

147. Bakeman, Jessica. "New Education Commissioner on Common Core and Evaluations." New Education Commissioner on Common Core and Evaluations. Capital New York, 27 May 2015. Web. 12 Oct. 2015. http://www.capitalnewyork.com/article/albany/2015/05/8568841/new-education-commissioner-common-core-and-evaluations

148. Berry, Susan, Dr. "NY Gov. Cuomo Vetoes His Own Common Core Bill." Breitbart News. Breitbart News, 30 Dec. 2014. Web. 12 Oct. 2015. http://www.breitbart.com/big-government/2014/12/30/ny-gov-cuomo-vetoes-his-own-common-core-bill/

149. CBS New York. "NY Teachers' Unions Urge Parents To Opt Children Out Of Common Core Tests." CBS New York. CBS New York, 11 Apr. 2015. Web. 12 Oct. 2015.http://newyork.cbslocal.com/2015/04/11/ny-teachers-unions-urge-parents-to-opt-children-out-of-common-core-tests/

150. Riede, Paul. "Education Commissioner John King to Critical F-M Crowd: Commitment to Common Core 'unwavering'" Syracuse.com. Syracuse.com, 3 Dec. 2013. Web. 12 Oct. 2015. http://www.syracuse.com/news/index.ssf/2013/12/education_commissioner_john_king_to_critical_crowd_commitment_to_common_core_is.html

151. Karlin, Rick. "State Ed Leader John King Jr. Grilled over Common Core." Times Union. Times Union, 23 Jan. 2014. Web. 12 Oct. 2015. http://www.timesunion.com/local/article/State-Ed-leader-John-King-Jr-grilled-over-Common-5170259.php

152. Vielkind, Jimmy. "Poll: Nearly Half of Voters Oppose Common Core." Poll: Nearly Half of Voters Oppose Common Core. Capital New York, 20 Feb. 2015. Web. 12 Oct. 2015. http://www.capitalnewyork.com/article/albany/2015/01/8560444/poll-nearly-half-voters-oppose-common-core

153. Tedisco, Jim “Tedisco Challenges Gov. Cuomo to Take 5th Grade Common Core Tests” Youtube.com, March 31, 2015. Web. 28. Oct. 2015. https://www.youtube.com/watch?v=v2tXbPzXcPQ

154. "New York." State Integrity Investigation. N.p., n.d. Web. 12 Oct. 2015 http://www.stateintegrity.org/new_york

155. New York State “The Moreland Commission To Investigate Public Corruption” Moreland.gov, Web. 28. Oct. 2015. http://publiccorruption.moreland.ny.gov/

156. Craig, Susanne, William K. Rashbaum, and Thomas Kaplan. "Cuomo’s Office Hobbled Ethics Inquiries by Moreland Commission." The New York Times. The New York Times, 22 July 2014. Web. 12 Oct. 2015. http://www.nytimes.com/2014/07/23/nyregion/governor-andrew-cuomo-and-the-short-life-of-the-moreland-commission.html?rref=nyregion

157. Bragg, Chris. "Cuomo on Moreland Tampering: It's My Commission." Latest from Crains New York Business. Crain's New York, 24 Apr. 2014. Web. 12 Oct. 2015. http://www.crainsnewyork.com/article/20140424/BLOGS04/140429924/cuomo-on-moreland-tampering-its-my-commission

158. Craig, Susanne, William K. Rashbaum, and Thomas Kaplan. "The Short Life of an Anticorruption Commission." The New York Times. The New York Times, 22 July 2014. Web. 12 Oct. 2015. http://www.nytimes.com/interactive/2014/07/23/nyregion/timeline-of-the-moreland-commission.html?_r=0

159. Craig, Susanne, Thomas Kaplan, and William K. Rashbaum. "U.S. Attorney Warns Cuomo on Moreland Commission Case." The New York Times. The New York Times, 30 July 2014. Web. 12 Oct. 2015. http://www.nytimes.com/2014/07/31/nyregion/us-attorney-warns-cuomo-on-ethics-case-.html?_r=0

160. Dicker, Fredric U. "Insiders Say Cuomo Is Rattled by Silver Corruption Case." Nypost.com. New York Post, 8 Feb. 2015. Web. 12 Oct. 2015. http://nypost.com/2015/02/08/insiders-say-cuomo-is-rattled-by-silver-corruption-case/

161. Dicker, Fredric U. "Cuomo Increasingly 'paranoid' over Corruption Probe." Nypost.com. New York Post, 8 June 2015. Web. 12 Oct. 2015. http://nypost.com/2015/06/08/cuomo-increasingly-paranoid-over-corruption-probe/

162. Himelfarb, Joel. "Book Depicts Andrew Cuomo as Control-Obsessed 'Bully'" Newsmax. Newsmax, 23 Mar. 2015. Web. 12 Oct. 2015. http://www.newsmax.com/Politics/Andrew-Cuomo-fall-back-candidate-baggage/2015/03/23/id/632044/

163. Barr, Andy. "The GOP's No-compromise Pledge." POLITICO. Politico, 28 Oct. 2010. Web. 12 Oct. 2015. http://www.politico.com/news/stories/1010/44311.html

164. "Biography - John Boehner." John Boehner. N.p., n.d. Web. 12 Oct. 2015. http://boehner.house.gov/about-john/biography/

165. CNN Library. "John Boehner Fast Facts - CNN.com." CNN. Cable News Network, 30 Sept. 2015. Web. 12 Oct. 2015. http://www.cnn.com/2013/02/21/us/john-boehner-fast-facts/

166. "John Boehner." Bio. A&E Television Networks, 2015. Web. 22 July 2015.

167. United States. Congress.107th Congress, 1st Session H.R. 1 No Child Left Behind Act of 2001 (2002 - H.R. 1). GovTrack.us. N.p., n.d. Web. 12 Oct. 2015.https://www.govtrack.us/congress/bills/107/hr1

168. Kasperowicz, Pete. "House Votes 239-186 to Repeal Obamacare – Guess How Many Democrats Joined Republicans." The Blaze. The Blaze, 3 Feb. 2015. Web. 12 Oct. 2015.

http://www.theblaze.com/blog/2015/02/03/house-votes-to-repeal-obamacare-with-no-help-from-dems/

169. Gizzi, John. "WH Claims 56 Attempts to Repeal Obamacare - House Says, 'Try 4'" Newsmax. Newsmax, 05 Feb. 2015. Web. 12 Oct. 2015. http://www.newsmax.com/John-Gizzi/obamacare-repeal-House-republicans/2015/02/05/id/622882/

170. Sullivan, Peter. "Boehner 'proud' of ObamaCare Lawsuit as Court Hearing Nears." TheHill. The Hill, 19 May 2015. Web. 12 Oct. 2015. http://thehill.com/policy/healthcare/242499-boehner-proud-of-obamacare-lawsuit-as-arguments-near

171. Walsh, Deirdre. "Boehner Touts His Lawsuit Challenging Obamacare - CNNPolitics.com." CNN. Cable News Network, 27 May 2015. Web. 12 Oct. 2015. http://www.cnn.com/2015/05/27/politics/obamacare-lawsuit-john-boehner-house-gop/

172. Levine, Sam. "Josh Earnest Slams John Boehner's Criticism Of Obama's Foreign Policy." The Huffington Post. TheHuffingtonPost.com, 29 Mar. 2015. Web. 13 Oct. 2015. http://www.huffingtonpost.com/2015/03/29/john-boehner-obama-foreign-policy_n_6964506.html

173. Torry, Jack. "Speaker John Boehner Challenging President Obama on Foreign Policy." The Columbus Dispatch. The Columbus Dispatch, 1 Feb. 2015. Web. 13 Oct. 2015. http://www.dispatch.com/content/stories/local/2015/01/31/speaker-john-boehner-challenging-president-obama-on-foreign-policy.html

174. Flynn, Mike. "EXCLUSIVE - Nine in Ten Conservative Activists Say Dump Boehner - Breitbart." Breitbart News. Breitbart News, 23 July 2015. Web. 13 Oct. 2015.http://www.breitbart.com/big-

government/2015/07/23/exclusive-nine-in-ten-conservative-activists-say-dump-boehner/

175. "John Boehner." Opensecrets RSS. N.p., n.d. Web. 13 Oct. 2015.
http://www.opensecrets.org/politicians/contrib.php?cycle=2014&cid=N00003675

176. Lipton, Eric. "A G.O.P. Leader Tightly Bound to Lobbyists." The New York Times. The New York Times, 11 Sept. 2010. Web. 13 Oct. 2015.
http://www.nytimes.com/2010/09/12/us/politics/12boehner.html?_r=0

177. Ekins, Emily. "Poll: Americans Oppose Raising the Debt Ceiling Even If U.S. Defaults and Say Government Wastes 60 Cents of Every Tax Dollar." Reason.com. Reason, 12 Sept. 2013. Web. 13 Oct. 2015. http://reason.com/archives/2013/09/12/poll-americans-oppose-raising-the-debt-2

178. "U.S. National Debt Clock : Real Time." U.S. National Debt Clock : Real Time. N.p., n.d. Web. 13 Oct. 2015.
http://www.usdebtclock.org/#

179. Ekins, Emily. "Reason-Rupe September 2013 National Survey." Reason.com. Reason, 10 Sept. 2013. Web. 13 Oct. 2015.
http://reason.com/poll/2013/09/10/reason-rupe-september-2013-national-surv

180. Rogers, Alex. "Boehner Throws in Towel on Debt Ceiling Fight." Time. Time, 11 Feb. 2014. Web. 13 Oct. 2015.http://time.com/6208/debt-ceiling-limit-john-boehner-republicans-clean/

181. "Heritage Action Scorecard." Heritage Action Scorecard. N.p., n.d. Web. 13 Oct. 2015. http://www.heritageactionscorecard.com/members/member/B000589

182. "Conservative Review - Scorecard." Conservative Review - Scorecard. N.p., n.d. Web. 13 Oct. 2015. https://www.conservativereview.com/Members/Scorecard/J/400036#2013

183. CR Staff. "What Is Boehner's Definition of a "Conservative Agenda"?" What Is Boehner's Definition of a "Conservative Agenda"? Conservative Review, 25 June 2015. Web. 13 Oct. 2015. https://www.conservativereview.com/Commentary/2015/06/boehner-definition-of-a-conservative-agenda

184. Blake, Aaron. "Who Voted against Boehner for Speaker and Why?" Washington Post. The Washington Post, 3 Feb. 2013. Web. 13 Oct. 2015.http://www.washingtonpost.com/blogs/the-fix/wp/2013/01/03/who-voted-against-boehner-for-speaker-and-why/

185. Weiner, Rachel. "Amash: Boehner Not 'welcome' in My District." Washington Post. The Washington Post, 12 Dec. 2012. Web. 13 Oct. 2015. http://www.washingtonpost.com/blogs/post-politics/wp/2012/12/12/amash-boehner-not-welcome-in-my-district/

186. http://clerk.house.gov/evs/2013/roll002.xml

187. Lee, Kristen A. "GOP Congressman Says He Fears 'attack' on Family after Opposing Boehner." NY Daily News. NY Daily News, 9 Jan. 2013. Web. 13 Oct. 2015.http://www.nydailynews.com/news/politics/gop-congressman-fears-attack-family-opposing-boehner-article-1.1236281

188. Weisman, Jonathan, and Ashley Parker. "Republicans Back Down, Ending Crisis Over Shutdown and Debt Limit." The New York Times. The New York Times, 16 Oct. 2013. Web. 13 Oct.

2015. http://www.nytimes.com/2013/10/17/us/congress-budget-debate.html?_r=0

189. Newhauser, Daniel, and Sarah Mimms. "Opposition to Omnibus Bill Is Building." National Journal. National Journal, 10 Dec. 2014. Web. 13 Oct. 2015. http://www.nationaljournal.com/congress/democrats-opposition-to-omnibus-bill-is-building-20141210

190. Pyke, Alan. "8 Things To Know About The 'Cromnibus' Budget Deal Congress Just Unveiled." ThinkProgress 8 Things To Know About The Cromnibus Budget Deal Congress Just Unveiled Comments. Think Progress, 10 Dec. 2014. Web. 13 Oct. 2015. http://thinkprogress.org/economy/2014/12/10/3601742/cromnibus-lowlights/

191. Boyle, Matthew. "With Obama's Help, House Passes Boehner's Amnesty-Funding Cromnibus Bill - Breitbart." Breitbart News. Breitbart News, 11 Dec. 2014. Web. 13 Oct. 2015.http://www.breitbart.com/big-government/2014/12/11/obama-passes-boehner-s-amnesty-funding-cromnibus-bill/

192. McAuliff, Michael. "John Boehner Plots A Way Around A Government Shutdown." The Huffington Post. TheHuffingtonPost.com, 2 Dec. 2014. Web. 13 Oct. 2015. http://www.huffingtonpost.com/2014/12/02/john-boehner-immigration-shutdown_n_6254978.html

193. Maloy, Simon. "GOP's "Cromnibus" Ploy: How Boehner Hopes to Appease the Right and Avoid a Shutdown Fiasco." Saloncom RSS. Salon, 2 Dec. 2014. Web. 13 Oct. 2015. http://www.salon.com/2014/12/02/gops_cromnibus_ploy_how_boehner_hopes_to_appease_the_right_and_avoid_a_shutdown_fiasco/

194. United States Congress. 113th Congress 2nd Session "Consolidated and Further Continuing Appropriations Act, 2015"

http://www.gpo.gov/fdsys/pkg/CPRT-113HPRT91668/pdf/CPRT-113HPRT91668.pdf

195. Boyle, Matthew. "Questions About Indiana Republican's Claim Leadership Duped Him Into Supporting Obama-Boehner Cromnibus - Breitbart." Breitbart News. Breitbart News, 12 Dec. 2014. Web. 13 Oct. 2015. http://www.breitbart.com/big-government/2014/12/12/questions-surround-indiana-republican-s-claim-leadership-duped-him-into-securing-obama-boehner-cromnibus-package/

196. Boyle, Matthew. "Rep. Ted Yoho Offers Himself as Alternative to Speaker." Breitbart News. Breitbart News, 03 Jan. 2015. Web. 13 Oct. 2015. http://www.breitbart.com/big-government/2015/01/03/rep-ted-yoho-joins-movement-against-boehner-offers-himself-as-potential-alternative/

197. Gohmert, Louie, Rep. "U.S. Congressman LOUIE GOHMERT: Proudly Serving the First District of Texas." Gohmert Announces Run for Speaker of the House : U.S. Congressman Louie Gohmert. Louie Gohmert, 4 Jan. 2015. Web. 13 Oct. 2015. http://gohmert.house.gov/news/documentsingle.aspx?DocumentID=398171

198. Krietz, Andrew. "Rep. Justin Amash Decides to Vote against Speaker John Boehner for Leadership Spot." Mlive.com. Michigan Live, 6 Jan. 2015. Web. 13 Oct. 2015. http://www.mlive.com/news/grand-rapids/index.ssf/2015/01/rep_justin_amash_decides_to_vo.html

199. May, Caroline. "Conservative Rep: 'I Will Not Vote for John Boehner' - Breitbart." Breitbart News. Breitbart News, 02 Jan. 2015. Web. 13 Oct. 2015. http://www.breitbart.com/big-government/2015/01/02/conservative-rep-i-will-not-vote-for-john-boehner/

200. Congress. 113th Congress. "Election For Speaker" House of Representatives Roll Call Vote January 6 2015http://clerk.house.gov/evs/2015/roll002.xml

201. Sherman, Jake, and John Bresnahan. "Boehner Reelected as Speaker despite Throng of No Votes." POLITICO. Politico, 6 Jan. 2015. Web. 13 Oct. 2015. http://www.politico.com/story/2015/01/john-boehner-house-speaker-vote-113992.html

202. Boyle, Matthew. "Boehner Wins Re-Election With Less Than Majority Of House - Breitbart." Breitbart News. N.p., 06 Jan. 2015. Web. 13 Oct. 2015.http://www.breitbart.com/big-government/2015/01/06/boehner-wins-re-election-with-less-than-majority-of-house/

203. Alberta, Tim, and Daniel Newhauser. "Possible Rules Change Could Punish Boehner Dissidents." National Journal. National Journal, 19 Sept. 2014. Web. 13 Oct. 2015. http://www.nationaljournal.com/congress/possible-rules-change-could-punish-boehner-dissidents-20140919

204. Boyle, Matthew. "Boehner Retaliation Haunts Republicans Who Defended, Voted for Him - Breitbart." Breitbart News. Breitbart News, 09 Jan. 2015. Web. 13 Oct. 2015. http://www.breitbart.com/big-government/2015/01/09/boehner-retaliation-haunts-republicans-who-defended-voted-for-him/

205. Sherman, Jake, and John Bresnahan. "Boehner Takes Revenge." POLITICO. Politico, 7 Jan. 2015. Web. 13 Oct. 2015. http://www.politico.com/story/2015/01/boehner-allies-out-for-revenge-114007.html

206. Allen, Jonathon, and David Weigel. "Bloomberg Politics." Bloomberg.com. Bloomberg, 7 Jan. 2015. Web. 13 Oct. 2015.

http://www.bloomberg.com/politics/articles/2015-01-07/boehner-pays-back-republicans-for-voting-against-him-for-speaker

207. Gehrke, Joel. "John Boehner Is Not a Man to Be Crossed." National Review Online. National Review, 21 June 2015. Web. 13 Oct. 2015. http://www.nationalreview.com/article/420098/john-boehner-not-man-be-crossed-joel-gehrke

208. Quinn, Melissa. "Punished Republican House Rebels Consider Next Move." Newsweek.com. Newsweek, 24 June 2015. Web. 13 Oct. 2015. http://www.newsweek.com/punished-republican-house-rebels-consider-next-move-346239

209. Lucas, Fred. "Boehner Punishing Republicans Who Voted Against Trade - but Guess Who's Pushing Him to Do So." The Blaze. The Blaze, 25 June 2015. Web. 13 Oct. 2015. http://www.theblaze.com/stories/2015/06/25/boehner-punishing-republicans-who-voted-against-trade-but-guess-whos-pushing-him-to-do-so/

210. Boehner, John, Rep. "TPA Stands for Jobs - John Boehner." John Boehner. John Boehner, 03 June 2015. Web. 13 Oct. 2015. http://boehner.house.gov/tpa-stands-for-jobs/

211. Boehner, John, Rep. "BOEHNER COLUMN: TPA Ensures Strong Trade Agreements for Ohio Farmers and Businesses - John Boehner." John Boehner. N.p., 22 May 2015. Web. 13 Oct. 2015. http://boehner.house.gov/boehner-column-tpa-ensures-strong-trade-agreements-for-ohio-farmers-and-businesses/

212. Phillips, Amber. "The Congressional Trade Debate, Explained in 6 Factions." Washington Post. The Washington Post, 12 June 2015. Web. 13 Oct. 2015. http://www.washingtonpost.com/news/the-fix/wp/2015/06/10/heres-what-you-need-to-know-about-the-trade-debate-explained-by-6-house-factions/

213. Disler, Matthew. "House Young Guns Buck Boehner on Trade | RealClearPolitics." House Young Guns Buck Boehner on Trade | RealClearPolitics. Real Clear Politics, 20 June 2015. Web. 13 Oct. 2015. http://www.realclearpolitics.com/articles/2015/06/20/house_young_guns_buck_boehner_on_trade.html

214. Wolf, Connor D. "This Is The Difference Between TPP And TPA (Hint: They Are Not The Same Thing)." Dailycaller.com. The Daily Caller, 23 May 2015. Web. 13 Oct. 2015. http://dailycaller.com/2015/05/23/this-is-the-difference-between-tpp-and-tpa-hint-they-are-not-the-same-thing/

215. Davis, Susan. "House Passes 'fast Track' Trade Bill." USA Today. Gannett, 18 June 2015. Web. 13 Oct. 2015. http://www.usatoday.com/story/news/politics/2015/06/18/house-vote-tpa-standalone/28917811/

216. Miller, S.A. "House Republicans Break 'Pledge to America,' Allow Rushed Legislation." Washington Times. The Washington Times, 22 Dec. 2014. Web. 13 Oct. 2015. http://www.washingtontimes.com/news/2014/dec/22/john-boehner-house-republicans-break-pledge-to-ame/?page=all

217. Meadows, Mark "Resolution Declaring the office of Speaker of the House Vacant" United States House of Representativeshttp://media.breitbart.com/media/2015/07/MEADOWS.pdf

218. Boyle, Matthew. "John Boehner Couldn't Find Votes to Reelect Him Speaker." Breitbart News. Breitbart News, 02 Aug. 2015. Web. 13 Oct. 2015.http://www.breitbart.com/big-government/2015/08/02/exclusive-john-boehner-embarrassed-his-whip-team-couldnt-find-votes-to-reelect-him-speaker-last-week/

219. FRAM, MATTHEW DALY and ALAN. "Boehner Calls Challenge by Republican 'no Big Deal'" Yahoo! News. Yahoo!, 29 July 2015. Web. 13 Oct. 2015. http://news.yahoo.com/conservative-move-against-boehner-sign-discontent-071019497--politics.html

220. Boyle, Matthew. "It's On: Rep. Mark Meadows Makes Move To Unseat John Boehner As Speaker Immediately - Breitbart." Breitbart News. Breitbart News, 28 July 2015. Web. 13 Oct. 2015. http://www.breitbart.com/big-government/2015/07/28/its-on-rep-mark-meadows-makes-move-to-unseat-john-boehner-as-speaker-immediately/

221. Bash, Dana, Manu Raju, Deirdre Walsh, and Jeremy Diamond. "John Boehner Resigning from Congress - CNNPolitics.com." CNN. Cable News Network, 25 Sept. 2015. Web. 13 Oct. 2015. http://www.cnn.com/2015/09/25/politics/john-boehner-resigning-as-speaker/

222. "U.S. Senate Majority Leader Mitch McConnell." U.S. Senate Majority Leader Mitch McConnell. N.p., n.d. Web. 13 Oct. 2015.
http://www.mcconnell.senate.gov/public/index.cfm?p=Biography

223. Martin, Jonathan. "Mitch McConnell Is Headed Down the Stretch." The New York Times. The New York Times, 30 Aug. 2014. Web. 13 Oct.
2015.http://www.nytimes.com/2014/08/31/magazine/mitch-mcconell-kentucky-senate.html?_r=0

224. Parrott-Sheffer, Chelsey. "Mitch McConnell | Biography - United States Senator." Encyclopedia Britannica Online. Encyclopedia Britannica, n.d. Web. 13 Oct. 2015.
http://www.britannica.com/biography/Mitch-McConnell

225. Rogers, David. "McConnell's Foreign Policy Evolution." POLITICO. Politico, 26 Mar. 2014. Web. 13 Oct. 2015.

http://www.politico.com/story/2014/03/mitch-mcconnell-foreign-policy-105031.html

226. Zengerle, Jason. "Get Mitch." POLITICO Magazine. Politico, 8 Nov. 2013. Web. 13 Oct. 2015. http://www.politico.com/magazine/story/2013/11/get-mitch-mcconnell-99376.html#.Vc9eFflViko

227. Shakir, Faiz. "Mitch McConnell: I Want To Be Senate Majority Leader In Order To Make Obama A One-Term President." ThinkProgress. Think Progress, 25 Oct. 2010. Web. 13 Oct. 2015. http://thinkprogress.org/politics/2010/10/25/126242/mcconnell-obama-one-term/

228. United States. Congress. H.R. 3590 (111th): Patient Protection and Affordable Care Act -- Senate Vote #396 -- Dec 24, 2009. GovTrack.us. N.p., n.d. Web. 13 Oct. 2015. https://www.govtrack.us/congress/votes/111-2009/s396

229. United States. Congress. H.R. 3590 (111th): Patient Protection and Affordable Care Act -- House Vote #165 -- Mar 21, 2010. GovTrack.us. N.p., n.d. Web. 13 Oct. 2015. https://www.govtrack.us/congress/votes/111-2010/h165

230. "Heritage Action Scorecard." Heritage Action Scorecard. N.p., n.d. Web. 13 Oct. 2015. http://www.heritageactionscorecard.com/members/member/M000355

231. "Conservative Review - Scorecard." Conservative Review - Scorecard. N.p., n.d. Web. 13 Oct. 2015. https://www.conservativereview.com/Members/Scorecard/m/300072#2012

232. Sherfinski, David. "Mitch McConnell: We'll Make 'every Effort' to Repeal Obamacare - but Its Namesake Is Still in Office."

Washington Times. The Washington Times, 8 Dec. 2014. Web. 13 Oct. 2015. http://www.washingtontimes.com/news/2014/dec/8/mitch-mcconnell-well-make-every-effort-to-repeal-o/

233. Allahpundit. "Mitch McConnell: Ted Cruz's Filibuster Would Shut down the Government and Keep ObamaCare Funded; Update: Cruz to Launch "talking Filibuster" at 2:30." Hot Air. Hot Air, 24 Sept. 2013. Web. 13 Oct. 2015.http://hotair.com/archives/2013/09/24/mitch-mcconnell-ted-cruzs-filibuster-would-shut-down-the-government-and-keep-obamacare-funded/

234. Boyle, Matthew. "Exclusive-Source: McConnell, Cornyn Whipping Votes Against Ted Cruz - Breitbart." Breitbart News. Breitbart News, 23 Sept. 2013. Web. 13 Oct. 2015. http://www.breitbart.com/big-government/2013/09/23/exclusive-mcconnell-cornyn-whipping-votes-against-ted-cruz/

235. Howerton, Jason. "Mitch McConnell Accused of Sneaking in $2 Billion 'Kentucky Kickback' in Budget, Debt Limit Deal – So Is It True?" The Blaze. The Blaze, 16 Oct. 2013. Web. 13 Oct. 2015. http://www.theblaze.com/stories/2013/10/16/mitch-mcconnell-accused-of-sneaking-in-2-billion-kentucky-kickback-in-budget-debt-limit-deal/

236. Raju, Manu. "McConnell Defends Deal, Slams ACA Tactics." POLITICO. Politico, 18 Oct. 2013. Web. 13 Oct. 2015. http://www.politico.com/story/2013/10/mitch-mcconnell-senate-deal-obamacare-government-shutdown-98496.html

237. Cruz, Ted "A Time For Truth" Broadside Books Publishers, 2015

238. Reilly, Mollie. "Mitch McConnell Allies Allegedly Threatened Matt Bevin Over Primary Challenge: Report." The

Huffington Post. TheHuffingtonPost.com, 24 July 2013. Web. 13 Oct. 2015. http://www.huffingtonpost.com/2013/07/23/mitch-mcconnell-matt-bevin_n_3642012.html\

239. Walshe, Shushannah. "Important Week in the Kentucky Senate Race as New Matt Bevin Ad Hits Mitch McConnell." ABC News. ABC News Network, 24 Feb. 2014. Web. 13 Oct. 2015. http://abcnews.go.com/blogs/politics/2014/02/important-week-in-the-kentucky-senate-race-as-new-matt-bevin-ad-hits-mitch-mcconnell/

240. Warren, Michael. "And They're Off: Kentucky Republican Senate Primary Begins with Dueling Ads." And They're Off: Kentucky Republican Senate Primary Begins with Dueling Ads. The Weekly Standard, 24 July 2013. Web. 13 Oct. 2015. http://www.weeklystandard.com/blogs/and-theyre-kentucky-republican-senate-primary-begins-dueling-ads_740908.html

241. Metzler, Rebekah. "Tea Partier Matt Bevin Takes Aim at Kentucky's Mitch McConnell." US News. U.S.News & World Report, 8 Aug. 2013. Web. 13 Oct. 2015. http://www.usnews.com/news/articles/2013/08/08/tea-partier-matt-bevin-takes-aim-at-kentuckys-mitch-mcconnell

242. Walker, Hunter. "Mitch McConnell Is Vowing To 'Crush' The Tea Party Everywhere." Business Insider. Business Insider, Inc, 09 Mar. 2014. Web. 13 Oct. 2015.http://www.businessinsider.com/mitch-mcconnell-crush-conservative-insurgents-2014-3

243. Lachman, Samantha. "Kentucky Republican Primary Heats Up As McConnell, Bevin Campaigns Hurl Insults." The Huffington Post. TheHuffingtonPost.com, 25 Jan. 2014. Web. 13 Oct. 2015. http://www.huffingtonpost.com/2014/01/09/matt-bevin-mitch-mcconnell-_n_4569886.html

244. Youngman, Sam. “Mitch McConnell outlines future opposition to 'Obamacare' if GOP wins Senate majority” Kentucky.com. Kentucky.com, 10 Jan. 2014. Web. 13 Oct. 2015. http://www.kentucky.com/2014/01/10/3027635/mitch-mcconnell-outlines-obamacare.html

245. Cuccinelli, Ken. "Mitch McConnell Surrenders on Obamacare Repeal." Mitch McConnell Surrenders on Obamacare Repeal. Senate Conservatives Fund, 29 Oct. 2014. Web. 13 Oct. 2015. http://www.senateconservatives.com/site/post/2916/mitch-mcconnell-surrenders-on-obamacare-repeal

246. Foley, Elise. "Mitch McConnell Makes Big Promise At CPAC." The Huffington Post. TheHuffingtonPost.com, 6 Mar. 2014. Web. 13 Oct. 2015. <http://www.huffingtonpost.com/2014/03/06/mitch-mcconnell-cpac_n_4911753.html

247. Werner, Erica. "Mitch McConnell Breaks Campaign Promise By Not Holding Friday Votes." PoliticusUSA. PoliticusUSA, 13 Feb. 2015. Web. 13 Oct. 2015.http://www.politicususa.com/2015/02/13/mitch-mcconnell-breaks-campaign-promise-refusing-hold-friday-votes.html

248. Bozell, David. "Mitch McConnell Needs To Do What He Promised And Repeal Obamacare." Dailycaller.com. The Daily Caller, 6 Nov. 2014. Web. 13 Oct. 2015. http://dailycaller.com/2014/11/06/mitch-mcconnell-needs-to-do-what-he-promised-and-repeal-obamacare/

249. "2014 - Kentucky Senate - GOP Primary (May 20) | RealClearPolitics." RealClearPolitics. Real Clear Politics, n.d. Web. 13 Oct. 2015. http://www.realclearpolitics.com/epolls/2014/senate/ky/kentucky_senate_republican_primary-3489.html

250. "2014 - Kentucky Senate - McConnell vs. Grimes | RealClearPolitics." RealClearPolitics. Real Clear Politics, n.d. Web. 13 Oct. 2015. http://www.realclearpolitics.com/epolls/2014/senate/ky/kentucky_senate_mcconnell_vs_grimes-3485.html

251. Lucas, Fred. "Ted Cruz Unloads on Mitch McConnell in Fiery Senate Floor Speech: 'I Cannot Believe He Would Tell a Flat-Out Lie'." The Blaze. The Blaze, 24 July 2015. Web. 13 Oct. 2015. http://www.theblaze.com/stories/2015/07/24/ted-cruz-accuses-mitch-mcconnell-of-lying-and-behaving-like-harry-reid/

252. Raju, Manu. "Cruz Accuses Mitch McConnell of Telling a 'flat-out Lie'" POLITICO. Politico, 24 July 2015. Web. 13 Oct. 2015. http://www.politico.com/story/2015/07/ted-cruz-says-mitch-mcconnell-lies-export-import-bank-120583

253. Killough, Ashley. "Cruz Poised to Make Life Miserable for Mitch McConnell - CNNPolitics.com." CNN. Cable News Network, 4 Nov. 2014. Web. 13 Oct. 2015. http://www.cnn.com/2014/11/03/politics/ted-cruz-harry-reid/

254. LoGiurato, Brett. "Senate Republicans Are Pressing For A Deal To End The Government Shutdown Along With A Debt Ceiling Hike." Business Insider. Business Insider, Inc, 11 Oct. 2013. Web. 13 Oct. 2015. http://www.businessinsider.com/debt-ceiling-government-shutdown-deal-senate-gop-obama-meeting-2013-10

255. LoGiurato, Brett. "WE HAVE A DEAL: SENATE VOTE TO COME SOON ON FISCAL AGREEMENT." Business Insider. Business Insider, Inc, 16 Oct. 2013. Web. 13 Oct. 2015. http://www.businessinsider.com/debt-ceiling-deal-reid-mcconnell-house-vote-boehner-government-shutdown-2013-10

256. CBS/AP. "Senate Approves $1.1 Trillion Spending Bill." CBSNews. CBS Interactive, 13 Dec. 2014. Web. 13 Oct. 2015.

http://www.cbsnews.com/news/senate-clears-way-for-vote-on-1-1-trillion-spending-bill/4

257. Kelly, Erin, and Susan Davis. "McConnell Offers DHS Bill Free of Immigration Measures." USA Today. Gannett, 24 Feb. 2015. Web. 13 Oct. 2015. http://www.usatoday.com/story/news/politics/2015/02/24/homeland-security-funding-immigration-executive-orders/23944801/

258. Everett, Burgess, and Seung Min Kim. "McConnell Offers DHS Fix, but Dems Pause." POLITICO. Politico, 24 Feb. 2015. Web. 13 Oct. 2015. http://www.politico.com/story/2015/02/democrats-homeland-security-funding-mitch-mcconnell-115456

259. "Mitch McConnell Surrenders on Amnesty." Mitch McConnell Surrenders on Amnesty. Senate Conservatives Fund, 26 Feb. 2015. Web. 13 Oct. 2015. http://www.senateconservatives.com/site/post/3063/mitch-mcconnell-surrenders-on-amnesty

260. Poor, Jeff. "McConnell Pressed on TPA: 'Why Not Make the Trade Bill Transparent?' - Breitbart." Breitbart News. Breitbart News, 09 June 2015. Web. 13 Oct. 2015. http://www.breitbart.com/video/2015/06/09/mcconnell-pressed-on-tpa-why-not-make-the-trade-bill-transparent/

261. Boyle, Matthew. "Mitch McConnell Aims To Ram Obamatrade Through Senate With No Amendments, Closed Debate - Breitbart." Breitbart News. Breitbart News, 22 June 2015. Web. 13 Oct. 2015. http://www.breitbart.com/big-government/2015/06/22/mitch-mcconnell-aims-to-ram-obamatrade-through-senate-with-no-amendments-closed-debate/

262. Raju, Manu, and Burgess Everett. "PATRIOT Act Meltdown Strains McConnell-Paul Bond." POLITICO. Politico, 1 June 2015.

Web. 13 Oct. 2015.http://www.politico.com/story/2015/06/patriot-act-meltdown-mitch-mcconnell-rand-paul-bond-118522

263. Nakashima, Ellen. "McConnell Bill Would Extend NSA Surveillance." Washington Post. The Washington Post, 22 Apr. 2015. Web. 13 Oct. 2015. https://www.washingtonpost.com/world/national-security/mcconnell-introduces-bill-to-extend-nsa-surveillance/2015/04/21/fa4b66aa-e89d-11e4-aae1-d642717d8afa_story.html

264. "Congressional Favorability Ratings." - Rasmussen Reports™. Rasmussen, 10 Aug. 2015. Web. 13 Oct. 2015. http://www.rasmussenreports.com/public_content/politics/mood_of_america/congressional_favorability_ratings

265. Nowicki, Dan, and Bill Muller. "McCain Profile: The Keating Five." McCain Profile: The Keating Five. The Arizona Republic, 1 Mar. 2007. Web. 13 Oct. 2015. http://www.azcentral.com/news/election/mccain/articles/2007/03/01/20070301mccainbio-chapter7.html

266. Abramson, Jill, and Alison Mitchell. "Senate Inquiry In Keating Case Tested McCain." The New York Times. The New York Times, 20 Nov. 1999. Web. 13 Oct. 2015.http://www.nytimes.com/1999/11/21/us/senate-inquiry-in-keating-case-tested-mccain.html

267. Biography.com Editors. "John McCain Biography." Bio.com. A&E Networks Television, n.d. Web. 13 Oct. 2015. http://www.biography.com/people/john-mccain-9542249#campaigns-for-president

268. Nowicki, Dan, and Bill Muller. "McCain Profile: McCain Becomes the 'maverick'" McCain Profile: McCain Becomes the 'maverick' The Arizona Republic, 1 Mar. 2007. Web. 13 Oct. 2015.

http://www.azcentral.com/news/election/mccain/articles/2007/03/01/20070301mccainbio-chapter9.html

269. Bernstein, Richard. "Standing Humbly Before a Noble Family Tradition." The New York Times. The New York Times, 30 Sept. 1999. Web. 13 Oct. 2015. http://www.nytimes.com/1999/10/01/books/books-of-the-times-standing-humbly-before-a-noble-family-tradition.html

270. Barrett, Ted. "Senate Bill Would Implement 9/11 Panel Proposals." CNN. Cable News Network, 8 Sept. 2004. Web. 13 Oct. 2015. http://www.cnn.com/2004/ALLPOLITICS/09/07/911.legislation/index.html

271. McCain, John, Senator. "Floor Statements." FLOOR STATEMENT OF SENATOR JOHN McCAIN ON BIPARTISAN CAMPAIGN REFORM ACT OF 2002.http://www.mccain.senate.gov/public/index.cfm/floor-statements?ID=fcade8e9-b6f2-74bb-1333-cd949cc7f628

272. Nowicki, Dan, and Bill Muller. "McCain Profile: The 'maverick' and President Bush." McCain Profile: The 'maverick' and President Bush. The Arizona Republic, 1 Mar. 2007. Web. 13 Oct. 2015. http://www.azcentral.com/news/election/mccain/articles/2007/03/01/20070301mccainbio-chapter11.html

273. Preston, Julia. "Grass Roots Roared and Immigration Plan Collapsed." The New York Times. The New York Times, 09 June 2007. Web. 13 Oct. 2015. http://www.nytimes.com/2007/06/10/washington/10oppose.html?_r=0

274. Nowicki, Dan, and Bill Muller. "McCain Profile: The 'maverick' Runs." McCain Profile: The 'maverick' Runs. The

Arizona Republic, 1 Mar. 2007. Web. 13 Oct. 2015. http://www.azcentral.com/news/election/mccain/articles/2007/03/01/20070301mccainbio-chapter10.html

275. CNN/AP. "McCain Formally Kicks off Campaign - September 27, 1999." McCain Formally Kicks off Campaign - September 27, 1999. Cable News Network, 27 Sept. 1999. Web. 13 Oct. 2015. https://web.archive.org/web/20081026225756/http://www.cnn.com/ALLPOLITICS/stories/1999/09/27/president.2000/mccain/

276. "McCain Launches White House Bid." BBC News. BBC, 25 Apr. 2007. Web. 13 Oct. 2015.http://news.bbc.co.uk/2/hi/americas/6593317.stm

277. "2008 - General Election: McCain vs. Obama | RealClearPolitics." RealClearPolitics. Real Clear Politics, n.d. Web. 13 Oct. 2015. http://www.realclearpolitics.com/epolls/2008/president/us/general_election_mccain_vs_obama-225.html

278. Bash, Dana. "McCain Now Calling for Mubarak to Step down." CNN Political Ticker RSS. CNN, 2 Feb. 2011. Web. 13 Oct. 2015. http://politicalticker.blogs.cnn.com/2011/02/02/mccain-now-calling-for-mubarak-to-step-down/

279. CBS/AP. "McCain: Libyan Rebels Are "my Heroes"" CBSNews. CBS Interactive, 22 Apr. 2011. Web. 13 Oct. 2015. http://www.cbsnews.com/news/mccain-libyan-rebels-are-my-heroes/

280. Basu, Moni, Reza Sayah, and Alan Silverleib Contributed to This Report. "McCain Pushes Heavier U.S. Involvement in Libya." CNN. Cable News Network, 22 Apr. 2011. Web. 13 Oct. 2015. http://www.cnn.com/2011/WORLD/africa/04/22/mccain.libya/

281. Duggan, Andrew. "U.S. Support for Action in Syria Is Low vs. Past Conflicts." Gallup.com. Gallup, 6 Sept. 2013. Web. 13 Oct. 2015. http://www.gallup.com/poll/164282/support-syria-action-lower-past-conflicts.aspx

282. Pecquet, Julian. "Senate Panel Delivers Bipartisan Rebuke to Obama with Vote to Arm Syrian Rebels." TheHill. The Hill, 21 May 2013. Web. 13 Oct. 2015. http://thehill.com/policy/international/301061-senate-panel-delivers-bipartisan-rebuke-to-obama-with-lopsided-vote-to-arm-syrian-rebels

283. AP Foreign. "McCain: Syrian Rebels Need Heavy Weapons." Theguardian.com. The Guardian, 31 May 2013. Web. 13 Oct. 2015. http://www.theguardian.com/world/feedarticle/10818441

284. Easley, Jonathon. "Rep. Gohmert: McCain 'supported Al Qaeda'" TheHill. The Hill, 11 Oct. 2013. Web. 13 Oct. 2015. http://thehill.com/policy/international/328131-gohmert-mccain-supported-al-qaeda

285. Shabad, Rebecca. "Paul: ISIS Emboldened after US Armed Its Allies in Syria." TheHill. The Hill, 22 June 2014. Web. 13 Oct. 2015. http://thehill.com/policy/international/210168-us-has-been-arming-isis-in-syria-sen-paul-claims

286. S.B. "What ISIS, an Al-Qaeda Affiliate in Syria, Really Wants." The Economist. The Economist Newspaper, 20 Jan. 2014. Web. 13 Oct. 2015.http://www.economist.com/blogs/economist-explains/2014/01/economist-explains-12

287. Bowman, Tom, and Alice Fordham. "CIA Is Quietly Ramping Up Aid To Syrian Rebels, Sources Say." NPR. NPR, 23 Apr. 2014. Web. 13 Oct. 2015. http://www.npr.org/sections/parallels/2014/04/23/306233248/cia-is-quietly-ramping-up-aid-to-syrian-rebels-sources-say

288. Lesniewski, Liels. "Senate Votes to Fund Syria Rebels Against ISIS." The World's Greatest Deliberative Body. Roll Call, 18 Sept. 2014. Web. 13 Oct. 2015. http://blogs.rollcall.com/wgdb/senate-passes-bill-funding-syrian-rebels-against-isis-averting-government-shutdown/

289. Weiner, Rachel. "McCain Calls Paul, Cruz, Amash 'wacko Birds'." Washington Post. The Washington Post, 8 Mar. 2013. Web. 13 Oct. 2015. http://www.washingtonpost.com/news/post-politics/wp/2013/03/08/mccain-calls-paul-cruz-amash-wacko-birds/

290. Sherfinski, David. "John McCain: Rand Paul Is the 'worst Possible Candidate' on National Security." Washington Times. The Washington Times, 23 Apr. 2015. Web. 13 Oct. 2015. http://www.washingtontimes.com/news/2015/apr/23/john-mccain-rand-paul-worst-possible-candidate-nat/

291. "John McCain Shuts Down Rand Paul On Senate Procedure." John McCain Shuts Down Rand Paul On Senate Procedure. Real Clear Politics, 31 May 2015. Web. 13 Oct. 2015. http://www.realclearpolitics.com/video/2015/05/31/john_mccain_maybe_the_senator_from_kentucky_should_know_the_rules_of_the_senate.html

292. MacNeal, Caitlin. "McCain: Rand Paul's Opposition To Patriot Act A 'Fundraising Exercise'" TPM. Talking Points Memo, 1 June 2015. Web. 13 Oct. 2015. http://talkingpointsmemo.com/livewire/john-mccain-rand-paul-patriot-act\

293. Nowicki, Dan, and Bill Muller. "McCain Profile: The 'maverick' Goes Establishment." McCain Profile: The 'maverick' Goes Establishment. The Arizona Republic, 1 Mar. 2007. Web. 13 Oct. 2015. http://www.azcentral.com/news/election/mccain/articles/2007/03/01/20070301mccainbio-chapter12.html

294. Associated Press. "'Gang of 12' Mulls over Immigration Bill." Msnbc.com. MSNBC, 25 May 2007. Web. 13 Oct. 2015. http://www.nbcnews.com/id/18842287/#.VhhD_vlViko

295. Deruy, Emily. "Gang of Eight Accelerates Immigration Reform Pace." ABC News. ABC News Network, 30 Jan. 2013. Web. 13 Oct. 2015.
http://abcnews.go.com/ABC_Univision/Politics/gang-accelerates-immigration-reform-pace/story?id=18354593

296. US news. "Should the Senate Pass the Gang of 8's Immigration Bill?" Usnews.com. US News And World Report, 2013. Web. 13 Oct. 2015.http://www.usnews.com/debate-club/should-the-senate-pass-the-gang-of-8s-immigration-bill

297. Krikorian, Mike. "The Complete Phoniness of the Gang of 8's Immigration Bill." Usnews.com. US News And World Report, 17 Apr. 2013. Web. 13 Oct. 2015.http://www.usnews.com/debate-club/should-the-senate-pass-the-gang-of-8s-immigration-bill/the-complete-phoniness-of-the-gang-of-8s-immigration-bill

298. Alvarado, Luis. "The Sausage-Making Is Ugly, But the Effort Is Necessary." Usnews.com. US News And World Report, 17 Apr. 2013. Web. 13 Oct. 2015. http://www.usnews.com/debate-club/should-the-senate-pass-the-gang-of-8s-immigration-bill/the-sausage-making-is-ugly-but-the-effort-is-necessary

299. Arkin, James. "McCain: Defund Effort 'not Rational'" POLITICO. Politico, 9 Sept. 2013. Web. 13 Oct. 2015. http://www.politico.com/story/2013/09/john-mccain-obamacare-097081

300. Weisman, Jonathan. "Senators Restart Talks as Default Looms." The New York Times. The New York Times, 15 Oct. 2013. Web. 13 Oct. 2015.

http://www.nytimes.com/2013/10/16/us/politics/congress-budget-debate.html?hp&_r=1&

301. Barrett, Ted, and Tom Cohen. "Senate Approves Budget, Sends to Obama - CNNPolitics.com." CNN. Cable News Network, 18 Dec. 2013. Web. 13 Oct. 2015. http://www.cnn.com/2013/12/18/politics/senate-budget-deal/

302. Howerton, Jason. "New Call for 'Total Repeal' of Obamacare From Unexpected Senator." The Blaze. The Blaze, 13 Nov. 2013. Web. 13 Oct. 2015.http://www.theblaze.com/stories/2013/11/13/sen-john-mccains-stunning-flip-flop-on-total-repeal-of-obamacare-watch-the-before-and-after/

303. Sanchez, Yvonne Wingett. "Arizona GOP Censures McCain for 'disastrous' Record." Azcentral.com. The Arizona Republic, 25 Jan. 2014. Web. 13 Oct. 2015. http://www.azcentral.com/news/politics/articles/20140125arizona-republican-party-mccain-censure-gop.html

304. Blake, Aaron. "McCain: Censure by State GOP Makes Me More Likely to Run." Washington Post. The Washington Post, 28 Jan. 2014. Web. 13 Oct. 2015. https://www.washingtonpost.com/news/post-politics/wp/2014/01/28/mccain-censure-by-state-gop-makes-me-more-likely-to-run/

305. Isenstadt, Alex. "McCain's Big Purge." POLITICO. Politico, 12 Dec. 2015. Web. 13 Oct. 2015. http://www.politico.com/story/2014/12/john-mccain-arizona-tea-party-113849

306. Moons, Michelle. "State Sen. Kelli Ward Launches 2016 Primary Challenge to Sen. John McCain - Breitbart." Breitbart News. Breitbart News, 14 July 2015. Web. 13 Oct.

2015.http://www.breitbart.com/big-government/2015/07/14/state-sen-kelli-ward-launches-2016-primary-challenge-to-sen-john-mccain/

307. Brekhus, Keith. "Tea Party Insurgent Kelli Ward Leads John McCain In Arizona GOP Senate Race Poll." PoliticusUSA. PoliticusUSA, 22 Aug. 2015. Web. 13 Oct. 2015. http://www.politicususa.com/2015/08/22/tea-party-insurgent-kelli-ward-leads-john-mccain-arizona-gop-senate-race-poll.html

308. Conservative Review, "John McCain" Web. 16. Oct. 2015 https://www.conservativereview.com/Members/Scorecard/j/300071#2015

309. Heritage Action "John McCain" Web. 16. Oct. 2015 http://www.heritageactionscorecard.com/members/member/M000303

www.ingramcontent.com/pod-product-compliance
Lightning Source LLC
Chambersburg PA
CBHW071335280526
45787CB00001B/99

9781519583536